THE DISCIPLES COLLEGES:

A HISTORY

THE DISCIPLES COLLEGES:

A HISTORY

By

D. Duane Cummins

CBP Press
St. Louis, Missouri

CBP Press
Box 179
St. Louis, MO 63166

Library of Congress Cataloging-in-Publication Data

Cummins, D. Duane.
  The Disciples colleges.

  Bibliography: p. 153.
  Includes index.
  1. Disciples of Christ—Education—United States—History.   2. Church colleges—United States—History.
I. Title.
LC568.C86   1987   377'.866   87-12372
ISBN 0-8272-0615-1

Printed in the United States of America

To
the honored memory
of
MARJORIE L. WHITE
a
great champion
of
the faith

CRITIQUES
From the College Presidents

"As educator, historian and churchman, Dr. D. Duane Cummins has written an important and readable 150-year history of the contribution of the institutions of the Christian Church (Disciples of Christ) to American higher education. While a story of the institutions of a particular denomination, the work also has wider significance in chronicling the history of the tension between the development of the intellect and of character which is particular to the Disciples institutions, but also important to all of higher education. Set in the context of the emerging themes of American society it also reports with insight, clarity and eloquence the way in which these institutions have both impacted on and reflected our changing national scene in a way characteristic of our best institutions of higher education. It is thus a book which belongs on many desks and in many libraries."

Dr. George Rainsford
President, Lynchburg, College

"In addition to providing a solid and comprehensive study of Disciples higher education over the past century and a half, Dr. Cummins underscores the need for enriching the cherished tradition of faith and learning in the Christian Church (Disciples of Christ), now and in the years ahead."

Dr. William E. Tucker
Chancellor, Texas Christian University

"Dr. Cummins has the experience and knowledge to write a discerning history and analysis of higher education among the Disciples of Christ. It is a tale of intrigue and guile, foolhardiness and ambition, and commitment and grace. This book will be a standard resource for years to come."

Dr. Joe R. Jones
President, Phillips University

From Education Associations

"This splendid work is much more than a history of the Disciples colleges. This absorbing story is set in the larger context of the overall development of American higher education in the past century and a half. Readers of this volume will be well rewarded . . . a highly interesting and useful history which should serve as a model for others who try their hands at the histories of denominational colleges."

Dr. John W. Chandler
President, Association of American Colleges

"Thorough, interesting, and eminently readable, *The Disciples Colleges: A History* is an important historical record of a significant sector of American private higher education. Clearly infused with both scholarship and love, the book is a distinguished and noteworthy addition to the literature in the field of educational research."

Dr. Allen P. Splete
President, Council of Independent Colleges

"This book is much more than a narrow history of rather special colleges in America. It speaks clearly about a special kind of college in the full context of America's intellectual and education history. I'm sure it will be a valued reference for many years to come . . . it is an impressive accomplishment."

Dr. Ernest L. Boyer
President, Carnegie Foundation
for the Advancement of Teaching

"*The Disciples College: A History* is an objective look at the past, present, and future of Disciples education. In many ways, the history of the Disciples colleges mirrors that of American higher education. There are the individualistic roots; turbulent debates over curriculum, finances, and civil rights; and the shrinking enrollments and calls for reform we see today. Yet the book also chronicles a determined search for religious renewal in America and the wisdom, faith, and hope of those who wrestle with the dilemma of unifying worldly and spiritual truth."

Dr. Gary H. Quehl
President, Council for Advancement
and Support of Education

"A unique and highly readable history of colleges founded by the Disciples of Christ Church that links the curriculum and atmosphere of such small church-related institutions to the recommendations of current national reports urging reform in undergraduate education."

Dr. Robert L. Gale
President, Association of Governing
Boards of Universities and Colleges

From the Disciples Church Leaders

"Education has been a centerpiece for Disciples since the founding of this communion. Church related higher education, with its emphasis on classical heritage, shaped by the rhythms of this developing nation in the mid-nineteenth century, was at the forefront of the life of the Christian Church (Disciples of Christ). D. Duane Cummins has done the church a real service in recounting historical developments and currents in our church related colleges, with insightful projections regarding society, church and the college in the 1980's and beyond. This volume should have wide readership among us, at great profit to our self understanding."

Dr. John O. Humbert
General Minister and President

"This is a vivid and memorable account of higher education in the history of the Christian Church (Disciples of Christ) in the United States and Canada. What it tells about the creation of colleges in the 19th century is available nowhere else. But it is more than that! Dr. Cummins has written an introduction to Disciples intellectual origins and development, an indispensable aspect of the life of a North American religious movement . . . it is both timely and authoritative."

Dr. William J. Nottingham
President, Division of Overseas Ministries

"A great blend of past history and future challenge, it is must reading for every Disciple leader. It will become a classic among Disciples historical books."

Dr. Harold R. Watkins
President, Board of Church Extension

"This is a must book for anyone who wants an in-depth look at what church related higher education really means for our times. It is more than a volume on a history of colleges related to the Christian Church (Disciples of Christ). Dr. Cummins leads the reader in a careful consideration of the critical role church-related higher education occupies in the total spectrum of higher education in today's world."

Dr. James I. Spainhower
President, Lindenwood College

*Grateful and abiding appreciation
is expressed
to the following contributors
whose generous gifts
made possible the publication
of this volume*

KENNETH R. WHITE

AMY SHELTON McNUTT TRUST

RALPH AND HENRY ETTA CHANEY

Table of Contents

Acknowledgments

This book, begun in 1982, has grown out of the thoughtful and timely assistance of many persons. Expressions of appreciation are due to all of these steady and patient supporters. Deep appreciation, abiding gratitude, and profound indebtedness are expressed:

To Kenneth and the late Margorie L. White, Ralph and Henry Etta Chaney, and the trustees of the Amy Shelton McNutt Trust for so generously providing all the necessary funding to underwrite the preparation and publication of this volume.

To Lawrence S. Steinmetz and John M. Imbler, my close and trusted colleagues in ministry, for responsibly and effectively administering the Division of Higher Education during the periods of my absence to write, and for generously and creatively engaging in discussions to help shape thoughts in the manuscript.

To Leslie P. Schroeder, my loyal and valued associate of many years, who graciously assisted in the research, typing, and proofreading of the manuscript.

To Deanna L. Lofton and Patrice Rosner for contributing their competent services as researchers and to Deanna for her final draft prooftyping.

To my colleagues in the General Manifestation of the church for their understanding of my absence from several meetings across the last four months.

To James M. Seale and the staff of the Disciples Historical Society for their unfailing good will and assistance throughout the course of research.

To Ronald E. Osborn and Thomas R. McCormick, fellow authors of companion volumes, for the many cherished and happy hours of discussion shared across the months of conceptualizing and writing the three volume series.

To the colleges and especially their presidents who were always ready to supply information and material in response to my several inquiries.

To the members of my precious family, who through the years have grown accustomed to the demands of writing and who are invariably supportive, encouraging, and generous with the gift of irreplaceable time.

D. Duane Cummins
November 1, 1986

Preface

One hundred fifty years ago this month Bacon College was founded in Georgetown, Kentucky, as the first higher education institution in the Campbell-Stone Religious Movement. Sustaining the life of that little college became the earliest form of congregational outreach among Disciples and from that meager beginning a higher education ministry was launched which eventually brought the founding of 209 known colleges and 205 academies and institutes. More than one million persons have been educated in these Disciples houses of learning and untold millions of dollars have been contributed by Disciples to this enterprise for fifteen decades. Yet, a historical synthesis of this higher education ministry, the oldest and largest form of outreach in the denomination, has never been attempted.

Harry O. Pritchard, president of the Disciples Board of Education from 1919 to 1934, planned hopefully and confidently for a history of the colleges to appear in 1936 as a part of the centennial celebration of Disciples higher education ministry. Scarcity of funds during the early Depression years along with the forced dissolution of the Board of Education assets and Pritchard's own premature death prevented the project from becoming a reality. Publication of the three volume series including *The Disciples Colleges: A History*, *The Education of Ministers for the Coming Age*, and *Campus Ministry in the Coming Age* in 1986 is part of the sesquicentennial celebration of Disciples ministry in higher education and at last fulfills the long cherished dream of Harry Pritchard.

This volume chronicles and analyzes the denomination's historic infatuation with higher education and the evolution of the 209 colleges and 205 academies and institutes related to the Campbell-Stone Religious Movement. The story is told within the socio-cultural-political context of American History, within the context of educational trends and reforms of each historic era, and within the context of the changing nature of the Campbell-Stone Religious Movement across 150 years. Among the themes receiving emphasis in this study are (1) a chronological history of the Disciples involvement in higher education, revealing the rhythms, patterns, and continuities drifting out of the distant past to mold the present; (2) the educational philosophy of Alexander Campbell; (3) the effects of socio-economic sectionalism upon the development of Disciples colleges; (4) the effects of Scots-Irish ethnicity upon the character of the colleges; (5) the effects of theological fission upon the proliferation of colleges; (6) the changing relationship between the church and the colleges, from free and independent institutions, to a period of ecclesiastical control and ownership, to loose affiliation through an association structure, to the present relationship through "covenant" in the 1980's; (7) the Disciples development of education for Blacks, moving from a ministry of evangelism to a ministry of education; (8) the changing nature of

Disciples colleges curriculum, from Bacon to the present, reflecting the character of the times and responding to educational reforms; (9) the educational contributions of Disciples to the stream of American higher education; (10) the sense of social justice infused into the fabric of campus life and into the larger educational mission of each institution; (11) the statistical profile and analysis of institutional enrollments, endowments, graduates, and budgets of the colleges in the twentieth century; and (12) the twentieth century shift from a strategy of founding additional colleges to a strategy of coordinating a ministry with existing ones by creating a unit of the church for that purpose. The work concludes with a challenge to the colleges and to the church to respond through their unique symbiotic relationship to today's compelling need for human community and for a new world of wholeness.

D. Duane Cummins
November 1, 1986

Bacon College: 1836

Bacon College: 1840

Chapter 1

BACON COLLEGE AND THE HERITAGE OF THE CHURCH-RELATED COLLEGE IDEAL

BACON COLLEGE: A PROLOGUE

The friends of unsectarian literature, free discussion and unbiased discipline . . . have set on foot a new school on the broad principles of a general education, without respect to any of the peculiar shibboleths of the age.[1]

Alexander Campbell

It all began on an early November day in 1836. The place was Georgetown, Kentucky, a frontier hamlet fixed on a bend of the North Fork of the Elkhorn River and encircled by the fabled lands of the Bluegrass. Here, on the former hunting grounds of the native Shawnee, amid the semi-literate settlements of Scots-Irish yeomen, in an obscure county-seat town, a few venturesome "Reforming Baptists" (Disciples) launched the movement's first institution of higher learning—Bacon College.

Alexander Campbell, announced to the readers of his journal in January 1837 that "Friends of the reformation in Kentucky were endeavoring to establish a permanent literary institution at Georgetown."[2] That endeavor was conceived by Thornton F. Johnson, an exceptionally popular, talented, and intransigent faculty member at the Baptist-controlled Georgetown College. Johnson, a graduate of West Point, owed his extraordinary popularity to the subjects he taught. Civil engineering and mathematics were in pressing demand by a developing industrial economy and an expanding frontier transportation system, both of which required surveys, turnpikes,

1

railroads, and navigable rivers. His well-organized field trips with students to survey uncharted lands spoke to his effectiveness as a teacher.

His peppery diatribes against Baptists embroiled him in a sectarian feud. Johnson was an active charter member of the Georgetown Christian Church, pastored by Barton W. Stone, a relative by marriage. He served simultaneously as a faculty memeber at the Baptist college where his vigorous support of religious reform was viewed by faculty colleagues as a contaminating plague on the body of Baptist orthodoxy. Deepening rancor led to his outright dismissal from the faculty and prompted his initial thoughts toward founding a literary and scientific academy.[3]

Before Johnson could bring a new institution to life he was invited to return to Georgetown College. Due to the absence of a president, he performed the administrative responsibilities along with his regular teaching chores during the years 1834, 1835, and most of 1836. The school flourished, growing from nine to 104 students. Johnson appears to have kept an enrollment count, carefully distinguishing the "sons of reformers" from the "sons of Baptists." In 1836 the Kentucky Baptist Education Society reclaimed the school and selected a new president, who immediately appointed to the faculty two loyal orthodox Baptists described by Johnson as "men who had exhausted the vocabulary of epithet upon my friends, and who were concentrating their strength at Georgetown, to effect the overthrow of what they called Cambellism."[4] Fueling the Baptist-Disciples enmity, Johnson decided to resign and establish a competitive college in the same community.

Within a matter of days following his November 5 resignation, Johnson purchased a brick building to house the college, temporarily identified his school as the "Collegiate Institute and School of Civil Engineers," assembled a faculty of seven, and issued a promotional description for publication:

Collegiate Institute and School For Civil Engineering
Faculty—Dr. Knight, Professor of Moral and Intellectual Philosophy
S. G. Mullins, Professor of Ancient Languages
C. R. Presriminski, Professor of Modern Languages
M. Saweski, Professor of Drawing and Painting
T. F. Johnson, Professor of Mathematics and Civil Engineering
J. Crenshaw, Principal of the Preparatory Department

-This institution is wholly unconnected with the Baptist College at this place, and will be conducted independently of all extraneous influences.
-The course of instruction will be as full and thorough as in any of the Western Colleges.
-The Professors will be diligently employed throughout the day, for six days in the week, giving instruction to the Students, and will in the main adopt the government and discipline that prevailed in the Georgetown College during the last session.
-A large and spacious house has been procured for the purpose and every attention will be paid to the comfort, as well as the morals and the progress of the pupils.

-A chemical apparatus has been procured, and a philosophical apparatus will be received by the middle of the session.

Expenses—
Tuition for the winter session will be $21.00, payable in advance. Boarding and lodging, $2.00 per week.

November 7, 1836[5]

On Thursday morning, November 10, 1836, at least forty students enrolled at Johnson's new Institute on Clinton Street and the first Disciples institution of higher learning officially "blundered into existence without a charter, without a board of trustees, and even without a name."[6] Shortly the school was given the permanent name of Bacon College in honor of Francis Bacon, the renowned seventeenth century philosopher-statesman.

By December a board of trustees, numbering sixteen persons and representing ten Kentucky counties, had been assembled to manage the business of the school. Its membership was composed of merchants, farmers, clergy, and two educators.[7]

Bacon College, Kentucky

Trustees

Walter Scott, President	J. H. Daviess, Scott
J. T. Johnson, V. Pres. & Sec'y.	T. C. Flournoy, Scott
S. Hatch, Treasurer	G. W. Nuckolls, Chelby
John Curd, Fayette	Geo. W. Williams, Bourbon
Sam'l Nuckolls, Woodford	H. M. Bledsoe, Bourbon
Asa R. Runyon, Mason	Thomas Smith, Lincoln
Henry Johnson, Fayette	James Bowman, Mercer
P. S. Fall, Franklin	James Challen, Fayette

On February 23, 1837, the Kentucky Legislature, despite sharp opposition, granted a charter to Bacon College by votes of nineteen to thirteen in the Senate and sixty-one to thirty in the House.[8] Public opinion was clearly mixed. One citizen of Scott County wrote derisively to an editor that the institution was founded by "the Apostle, a Polander and another whose character is ruined in the estimation of every unprejudiced person," and then added that "the chartering of Bacon College was a singular instance of legislative blindness: as it was in direct opposition to the wishes of those most interested, the citizens of Scott County, in which Georgetown is situated."[9] Disciples opinion was equally sharp. J. Allen Gano, a loyal enthusiast of the Disciples religious reform, expressed pointed displeasure with the idea of founding a college:

"I am unwilling . . . that the birth of [Bacon] . . . be viewed as a part or even an appendage of the reformation for which we plead. The cause of Christ is one thing—the college another—as essentially distinct as the Church of Christ and this republican government."[10]

The college founders responded that even though the majority of citizens of Scott County were opposed, the legislature—which had granted many charters to the Baptists, but "until now, not one to us"—acted for more than Scott County alone.

Soon after the November opening of classes, Walter Scott, a celebrated Disciples evangelist from Carthage, Ohio, accepted appointment as professor of Hebrew literature and first president of the new College. Although he served in the position for only one year, he proved to be an effective fundraiser and promoter. His inaugural address, "United States' System," delivered at Bacon College in February 1837, is a little known contribution to the higher education legacy of the church. It was an ambitious address containing (a) a lengthy summary of Bacon's famous tribute to logic, rationalism, and inductive philosophy, *Novum Organum*, (b) a suggested curriculum design composed of four categories: nature, religion, art, and society, (c) a proposed universal education system, and (d) a proposed national education system which championed the cause of the public school movement. Near the close of his address Scott mentioned briefly the "perfection of human nature," and the matter of character:

> In short, we intend to impart to you knowledge with a direct reference to the formation of your character as men and as citizens of the Republic of the United States.[11]

On the occasion of the first semi-annual commencement, the pride of the founders in the growing success of Bacon College gave flight to their estimation of its quality. The commencement addresses delivered by students were described by Scott and J. T. Johnson as the most eloquent ever heard, addresses that "would have done honor to the Senate Chamber, to Fanniuel [sic] Hall or to the Halls of Cambridge." The students were declared "unsurpassed for talent, orderly deportment and moral rectitude in any college in America." It was further proclaimed that the fame of the College had spread over the continent and for the short time it had existed, "has no parallel in the annals of Literary Institutions."[12]

The Department of Engineering accounted for 90 percent of the student enrollment at Bacon and created the first popular student club, the Newton Philosophical Society. By March of 1837, a company of cadets was organized to furnish "order, discipline and subordination." As the second term commenced in March, the institution promoted itself to the public as a specialized and tightly disciplined school for engineers:

> The School for Civil Engineers connected with Bacon College, is conducted by two Professors, one educated at West Point, and the other at the Polytechnic School of France. The West Point course is adopted throughout, and the two vacations (April and October) are devoted to practical operations in the field. They have a full supply of the best instruments and will set out on Monday next for the spring Campaign—traveling on foot, submitting to all the fatigues

and privations of the camp—schooling the class in the delightful exercise of reducing the principles of science to practice, and preparing them for an enviable career of usefulness.[13]

By the fall of 1837, the future of Bacon College seemed assured. The enrollment had grown to 203 students from twelve states and the District of Columbia; Walter Scott had been succeeded as president by David S. Burnet; five of the seven original faculty members had been replaced; and despite the scientific emphasis of its curriculum and the clashes of sectarian prejudices, the institution received the cautious imprimatur of Alexander Campbell:

> Bacon College Georgetown, Ky., is now a successful operation . . .
> I have been backward hitherto to say much about this Institution, until I could ascertain from a personal interview with its principal managers and conductors, their views and designs, their prospects and means, etc. but especially with reference to the discipline and moral culture under which the youth are to be placed who attend this College; for this, with me, now is above all other sorts of eminence. I give my vote for learning and science and for high attainment in all branches of useful knowledge, but I would not give *morality* for them all; and therefore I have resolved never to speak in favor of any literary institution, from a common school to a university, however superior their literary eminence, that does not first of all, and above all, exercise a sovereign and supreme guardianship over the morals of its students and wards, and endeavor to make good rather than great men. Colleges without this are no blessing to any country.
> I was happy to learn that such is the firm determination of each of the Trustees and Faculty with whom I conversed . . . we can now say, that we hope that all who wish their sons well educated in all that is valuable in literature and science, without hazard to their morals, will send them to [Bacon].[14]

Every turn in this deeply obscure and long forgotten story of the 1836 founding of Bacon College was shaped by the forces of a classical heritage and by the contemporary rhythms of Jacksonian America. Out of the centuries came the voices of Plato, Aristotle, Augustine, Aquinas, Bacon, and a host of others speaking eloquently to the issue of where formal education should direct its energy—toward the mind or toward the soul, toward the human intellect or toward character. Out of the socio-cultural ethos of the 1830's came the voices of Jacksonian Democracy shaping utilitarian institutions, calling for "useful" knowledge, and espousing egalitarian patterns of thought. The Jacksonian order contained an enormous belief in the worth, capacity, and perfectibility of the individual; a lack of confidence in American institutions; a hostility to privilege; a revived Protestant faith characterized by bitter denominational rivalries; an undercurrent of cultural tensions between ethnic groups, social classes, and urban and rural ways of life; a fervor for social reform; and a compulsion for enterprise, competition, and opportunity. Although a few intent Disciples reformers gave institutional birth to Bacon College, this new institution drew its life from the interplay of classical and Jacksonian elements, rather than the church.

CLASSICAL HERITAGE

Grace does not destroy nature; it perfects her.

Thomas Aquinas

Four centuries before the birth of Christ, just outside the walls of Athens, Plato (427-347 B.C.) founded a school near the grove of Academus. Plato's Athenian Academy, which educated persons for political leadership, was guided by the precept that the central question for civilization was how wisdom and virtue could be cultivated in humankind. Plato thought the core of a human being was the soul, consisting of appetite, will, and reason. He believed that in the well-ordered soul reason governed will which in turn governed appetite. Therefore, *shaping the souls* of persons in a total culture through education was the way to bring order to civilization.

Aristotle (384-322 B.C.), too, founded a school in a grove—the grove of Lyceus. His Lyceum, called "the house of the reader," celebrated the primacy of intellect, the rule of reason and logic. Here Aristotle developed a library and zoological garden, a scientific combination making it one of the earliest research centers in Western Civilization. Intellectual contemplation was valued by Aristotle as the supreme human act and the *discipline of the mind* was taught as the way to bring order to civilization.[15]

Across the ages leaders of Western thought have toiled endlessly to fuse the Academy and the Lyceum, to define the relationship between mind and soul, between reason and faith. With each epoch of human history the emphasis within educational systems has shifted alternately between the mind and the soul, between the refinement of moral character and the refinement of intellect.

Augustine (A.D. 354-430), bishop, teacher and conscience of the Western world in his day, wrote at length of the conflict between secularism and Christian faith. Like Plato, he searched for universal good by turning inward. Unlike Plato, he believed that the will held primacy over reason and that human beings often acted against their knowledge. He saw in each individual a struggle between spiritual will and worldly will. When the worldly will was dominant, persons loved themselves and neglected God. When the spiritual will was dominant, persons loved God, not self. Augustine thought of humanity as grouped into two communities, the City of God and the City of Earth. The life of those cities extended from the beginning of time to the end of the world. While they were mixed physically, they were separated spiritually, symbolizing the continuous struggle of will in every human soul. Augustine, therefore, espoused a Christian system of learning, designed to influence the will within the soul of humanity.[16]

By the twelfth century the pattern of Western thought developed a view that "reason supported faith," that rationalism enhanced the tradition of revelation. The church experienced much tension with this view and occasionally forbade the reading of Aristotle or condemned him altogether. Thomas Aquinas (A.D. 1225-1274), a brilliant scholar within the Dominican Monastic order, who wrote at the apogee of Medieval Civilization, envisioned a single body of knowledge, a synthesis of faith and reason. He advanced the notion that God was not separate from humanity, that logic and revelation, philosophy and theology, mind and soul, faith and reason must *coexist*. Aquinas believed that while reason and revelation were clearly separate, they did not present a "double truth" or stand in opposition of each other. There was only one truth. All truth came from a single source and there was an order and harmony in all parts. In one of Aquinas' most quoted phrases, "Grace does not destroy nature; it perfects her," we are able to sense his vision of the unity of knowledge.[17]

In the century that followed, the souls of faith and the minds of philosophy withdrew from each other increasingly into separate worlds. Humanist scholars argued that faith had not yet been comprehended at the time Aristotle was writing and that philosophy and theology were separable. They advocated the education of the whole person, complaining that educational systems had erred in subordinating the arts to the interest of theology. Intellectual balance, they argued, was just as important as moral coherence in the education of the whole person for effective citizenship. The utilitarian humanist ideal of the fourteenth century held that the *good* person was the *useful* person.

Troubled human conditions over the next one hundred years caused the leaders of thought to ponder more deeply the resources of a person's inner life. They had grown skeptical of Aristotelian scholasticism and had also distanced themselves from the institutional church. They celebrated both the contemplative soul and the capacity of reason, seeing them in harmony with God. They believed that to change the moral behavior of persons it was necessary to change their hearts rather than their institutions.

The vacillation continued through the succession of eras. Depending on conditions in each age the responding structures of thought shifted their center of gravity between faith and reason as they adapted to the needs of each emerging society. In like fashion, the educational systems—organized to develop loyalty and authority, to transmit general knowledge and the elements of skill essential to earning a living and fulfilling civic responsibilities—always expressed the prevailing religious and secular values of the dominant classes. The church governed the educational system from the sixth to sixteenth centuries; and the state has become largely responsible for educational systems since the Industrial Revolution.

Neither the church nor the humanists thought it important to educate large numbers of people. It was assumed that most people had no need for any intellectual skills beyond that required for useful work. Higher education, therefore, was restricted to the gentry, the gifted, and the clergy. But with the advent of democracy, industrialization, and urbanization a broader base of educated people was required and the *state* was called upon to invest heavily in the education of its citizenry. Across the last three centuries the interplay of faith and reason in the pursuit of truth has occurred in a utilitarian and secular context.

When Bacon College appeared in 1836, secular society was demanding persons with enough skill to build roads while the church was demanding persons with enough moral depth to build character. Thornton Johnson founded Bacon with the single intention of establishing a specialized school to train engineers, a school that responded to the economic demands of the day rather than the ideals of Disciples reformers. It was not created to function as an adjunct of church. The school's utilitarian curriculum featured the practical experience of field trips to survey land, rather than theological interpretation of Biblical literature or exegises of scripture. Walter Scott's inaugural address focused upon the inductive reasoning of Francis Bacon rather than upon the moral formation of character. By contrast, Alexander Campbell envisioned a college as an outpost of faith. Although he advocated "learning, science and useful knowledge," he held morality and the formation of character in much higher regard. The best he could say for attending Bacon was that it would not be a "hazard to morals." He made no claim that it would strengthen morals.

The ancient tension between faith and reason attended the birth of Bacon College. In response, the college acceded to the demands of an advancing people on the frontier line of settlement. It offered practical skills and scientific reason, and gave its lesser emphasis to the moral capacity of the soul.

COLONIAL HERITAGE

After God had carried us safe to New England and wee had builded our houses, provided necessaries for our livelihood, rear'd convenient places for Gods worship, and settled the Civill Government: one of the next things we longed for, and looked after was to advance Learning and perpetuate it to Posterity; dreading to leave an illiterate Ministry to the Churches, when our present Ministers shall lie in the Dust.:

"New England's First Fruits"
Old South Leaflets, Vol. III, No. 51

Exactly 200 years before the founding of Bacon College, the General Legislature of Massachusetts appropriated a sum of £400 "towards a schoale or colledge." Out of that modest October 1636 allocation emerged Harvard College, the illustrious ancestor of higher learning in America. Nearly two decades earlier, the Virginia Company had ambitiously begun to gather resources for a "university to be planted at Henricus" but an Indian reprisal in 1622 destroyed the Colony and along with it any hope for the early founding of a school in Virginia. Massachusetts Bay, then became the first colony to establish a school and was in fact sixty years ahead of the appearance of the second such institution in the seaboard settlements. Given the rigorous challenge of survival which overlaid the complex process of raising a civilized community out of a pristine wilderness, the success of New England Puritans in establishing a college in so short a while after their 1620 arrival is extraordinary.[18]

Church, college, town, and commonwealth were the four institutional pillars of an interdependent and convenanted social-ecclesiastical order in Colonial New England. It was in fact a theocracy, a religious commonwealth, heavily dependent upon a literate ministry and educated magistrates. The existence of a college was absolutely essential to the life of that society, and its purpose was twofold: (1) to spread religion and (2) to spread enlightenment. Echoing one of Francis Bacon's famous works, the founders of Harvard called for the college "to advance learning," and they called for that advancement so they would not "leave an illiterate ministry to the churches." Few communities ever exhibited more faith in the value of learning and intellect than Massachusetts Bay:

> In its inception New England was not an agricultural community, nor a manufacturing community, nor a trading community: it was a thinking community; an arena and mart for ideas; its characteristic organ being not the hand, nor the heart nor the pocket, but the brain . . . Probably no other community of pioneers ever so honored study, so reverenced the symbols and instruments of learning.[19]

The Puritan educational ideals of a "learned clergy and a lettered people" profoundly effected the educational development of America for two hundred years.[20]

By the eve of the American Revolution the Atlantic Coast Colonies had established nine colleges:

Date	Institution	Sponsoring Body
October 28, 1636	Harvard	Congregational Church
February 8, 1693	William & Mary	Anglican Church
October 16, 1701	Yale	Congregational Church
October 22, 1746	Princeton	Presbyterian Church
October 31, 1754	Columbia (Kings)	Non-Sectarian
June 16, 1755	Pennsylvania	Non-Sectarian
October 24, 1765	Brown	Baptist Church
November 10, 1766	Rutgers (Queens)	Dutch Reformed Church
December 13, 1769	Dartmouth	Congregational Church

Seven of the nine colleges were founded by Protestant church groups and it is fair to say that the Anglican Church was instrumental in founding the other two, although they were conceived on a broader educational base, governed by ecumenical boards, and therefore regarded as non-sectarian. All nine colleges were religious in tone and uniform in placing the emphasis of their classical curriculum upon the formation of character and moral nurture. Called a "nursery of ministers" and a "child of the church," the typical colonial college was a denominational college reflecting the dominant religious character of the era. "Colleges," wrote president Thomas Clap of Yale in 1754, "are Societies of Ministers for training up Persons for the Work of the Ministry."[22]

The Eighteenth Century European Enlightenment ignited the ancient tension between faith and reason. Leaders of Enlightenment thought—Montesquieu, Rousseau, Diderot, Voltaire, Kant, Locke, Newton, among others—analyzed humanity, nature, and institutions in the sharp light of pure reason. Even belief in the existence of God was approached almost solely on rational grounds. Enlightenment thought was characterized by an intense interest in science and nature; a firm belief in the worth and perfectibility of the individual; and the full expectation that humanity would always achieve progress through the continuous refinement of individual ability. The empiricism, deism, naturalism, humanitarianism, and rationalism of the Enlightenment seeped into colonial society and soon began to penetrate the college curriculum.[23]

Colonial response to the Enlightenment came in the form a popular movement in the 1740's known as the "Great Awakening." This new religious enthusiasm, strongest in rural areas and among lower classes, injected a revivalist fervor into Protestant faith. One of its effects was to divide churches into "Old Light" and "New Light" factions, those who were comfortable with religion as it was and those who sought a spirited regeneration of religion to confront Enlightenment reason. In an effort to counter the charge that they were indifferent to education and that their ministers were unlearned, the New Lights decided to establish colleges of their own. The foundings of Princeton, Brown, Rutgers, and Dartmouth were directly rooted in the religious rivalry inspired by the Great Awakening, an effective force in preventing the Enlightenment from immediately displacing the religious function of education. The religious tone of the colleges remained essentially intact and they continued to educate ministers, espouse religious values, and promote the development of morals. But the rising class of secular merchants and the spread of the Enlightenment brought increasing demands for scientific and utilitarian education. Schools founded during post-Revolutionary America reflected a marked trend toward secularization.

Democratic ideals released by the American Revolution spread a liberating influence upon education. The separation of church and state unsettled the stable, controlled, and designed pattern of colonial "state-church" college development. Colleges had represented the wholeness of the established order. But the separation created two groups of colleges: one group founded by competing religious sects, and the other group founded by the states. Nineteen colleges were established between 1782 and 1802, fifteen by denominations and four by the states (the Universities of Georgia, North Carolina, Vermont and Ohio.)[24]

States were prompted to take a more active role in the life of higher education because of the new democratic idealism. "Wisdom and knowledge, as well as virtue, diffused generally among the body of the people, being necessary for the preservation of their rights and liberties," declared the Massachusetts Constitution of 1780, the *government* must provide "the opportunities and advantages of education in various parts of the country, and among the different orders of the people."[25] Education was considered a responsibility of Republican government and the college was viewed as an instrument of state as well as the church. The Revolution infused a sense of nationalism into the colleges and they readily accepted the additional responsibility of preparing persons for citizenship to serve the new nation.

Befriended by France, the Revolution quite naturally introduced a powerful French influence into the American college curriculum. French philosophy, French deism, and the French language became popular discourse. Orthodox religion, directly challenged by the deist and rationalist thought of French philosophies, saw its influence on education begin to lessen. The diminished influence of religion on the character of the college is reflected in a description of late eighteenth century Yale:

> Yale College was in a most ungodly state. The College church was almost extinct. Most of the students were skeptical, and rowdies were plenty. Wine and liquors were kept in many rooms; intemperance, profanity, gambling, and licentiousness were common . . . Most of the class before me were infidel, and called each other Voltarie, Rousseau, etc.[26]

The Enlightenment, the separation of church and state, the growth of a merchant class, and the experience of Revolution combined to give American colleges a more secular tone. Before the Revolution, the Colonial college curriculum was generally a fixed body of knowledge composed of classical languages (Greek, Latin, and Hebrew), the reformed philosophy of Aristotle, theology, logic, and moral nurture. After the Revolution, curriculums, in addition to the basic core of philosophy, theology, and the classics, displayed new components of sciences and languages including astronomy, botany, mathematics, economics, natural history, constitutional government, and the French and English languages. The educational curriculum was shifting its emphasis toward an understanding of humanity as social and biological beings and away from its traditional emphasis upon the formation of character and morals.

Expansion of business, commerce, urbanization, and political interests simultaneously increased the demand for utilitarian education. The steady decline of theological authority over American life in the last half of the eighteenth century and the appearance of theological seminaries, which began to remove the training of ministers from colleges, reduced sectarian influence throughout the college network during the post-Revolutionary years. By the close of the century the realm of reason was clearly in the ascendancy.[27]

RELIGIOUS HERITAGE

We've already started three colleges and have the logs cut for four more.
An Ohio Settler

Nineteenth century America arrived bearing a tension in thought regarding the best way to regulate the conduct of citizenry. One point of view held that religion—fostering morals and values—was the most effective instrument in a well-ordered society to develop acceptable human behavior. The other position, less sure of the efficacy of religion and education, looked to the institutions of government as the only dependable means to control human conduct. Discord between the two points of view was heightened by growth in the number of colleges following the American Revolution. One side began to develop centralized structures of state education subject to the will of the majority, and the other side developed a network of individualized, denominational colleges, fashioned out of local community support and subject to the will of religious minorities.[28] The ancient debate between faith and reason flared once again as America tried to determine if the future of its educational enterprise would be a function of the state or a function of the church. Over the short-term, the little, denominational colleges, empowered by their vision of moral reform of individuals, perpetuated the early Colonial pattern of education which temporarily stalled the growth of state colleges and the rise of reason.

A significant factor contributing to their early dominance was the landmark United States Supreme Court decision, *Dartmouth College v. Woodward*. John Wheelock, president of Dartmouth, and the board of trustees of the college had become locked in a test of institutional control and the trustees asserted their authority by dismissing the president. The dispute evolved into the larger issue of Dartmouth being either a public university subject to the state legislature by charter as Wheelock argued or a private institution subject only to its own board as the trustees believed. In 1817 the Superior Court of New Hampshire sided with Wheelock, proclaiming Dartmouth a public corporation and appointing a board of overseers to replace the trustees. But the trustees appealed the case all the way to the United States Supreme Court where one of their attorneys, an 1801 Dartmouth alumus named Daniel Webster, argued eloquently that "It is the case, not merely of that humble institution, it is the case of every college in the land."[29]

In one of the most important decisions in the history of the Supreme Court, the justices, by a five to one margin, reversed the New Hampshire

Superior Court decision. Dartmouth College was judged to be a private corporation, a product of private philanthropy, subject to its own board of trustees and safeguarded from interference by a state legislature:

> Dartmouth College is an eleemosynary institution, incorporated for the purpose of perpetuating the application of the bounty of the donors to the specified objects of that bounty; that its trustess or governors were orginally named by the founder, and invested with the power of perpetuating themselves; that they are not public officers, nor is it a civil institution, participating in the administration of government; but a charity school, or a seminary of education, incorporated for the preservation of its property, and the perpetual application of that property to the objects of its creation.[30]

The Dartmouth College case is a benchmark in the history of American higher education: (a) it prevented private colleges from being reconstituted by state legislatures into state universities, a restriction which in effect checked the development of state universities until the post-Civil War period; (b) it increased the distance between the colleges and the people who tended to see the schools as institutions of privilege; (c) it clarified the distinction between public and private colleges and cleared the way for their separate development; (d) it unleashed an era of denominational college founding, and (e) it gave classic expression to an American concept of community control.[31]

More important to the early dominance of the church-related college over the state college was the new surge of religious revivalism which spilled across the trans-Appalachian frontier during the first thirty-five years of the nineteenth century and then flowed back into the Eastern towns and cities during its second phase beginning in the 1840's. Called by many names—"The Second Great Awakening," "The Great Revival in the West," "Presbygational Evangelism," "The Soul Rush"—this religious phenomenon brought a simplification and humanization of faith, a religious independence which contrasted sharply with the rigid fatalism of Calvanist theology. The movement, rooted in democratic individualism, birthed a score of new religious sects, ushered in decentralized forms of church organization, and provided the spawning ground for an unprecedented number of sectarian colleges.

The century between the First and Second "Awakenings" was a period of ecclesiastical uncertainly over the nature, purpose, and function of church. The confusion had grown directly out of the separation of church and state which produced "the most profound revolution . . . in the entire history of the church . . . on the administrative side" since the time of Constantine.[32] Church organization had been neatly centralized and tightly woven into the warp and woof of colonial society where it thought of itself as responsible for the quality of that society. But with the separation of church and state, the church was suddenly cut loose and left to struggle with the reordering of its own internal structure of governance and to discover a new societal relationship.

Demands for religious freedom within the church itself, as it experimented with new concepts of order, touched off a second Great Awakening. Among the radical advocates of religious liberty was Barton W. Stone, a founding father of the Disciples, a major American religious spokesman for a reordered church, and a key leader of the celebrated and strategic 1801 revival at Cane Ridge, Kentucky. Stone, angered by an ecclesiastical suspension in 1803, argued for individual freedom *within* the church. He proposed, boldly, that the church should be an association of equal and autonomous individuals and that it reorganize its life along congregational and voluntaristic lines with lay control vested in decentralized structures. In Stone's view there was no need for ecclesiastical authorities, creeds, ceremonies, or distinctions of rank among Christians—a set of ideas which repudiated orthodox church government. The new "Revivalism" was abetted and advanced by Stone's concept of privatized religion and individualized structures of governance.[33]

The church, in its new cellular form, was supposed to regenerate persons rather than serve society. Preserving cultural values or transplanting social institutions were not accepted as responsibilities of the frontier churches. They were sects on their way to being churchs, caring for their own houses first instead of other frontier institutions, and marching to the drumbeat of "individual perfectibility."

Stimulated by the conservative religious revival, the impulse to regenerate and perfect individuals gave rise to several reform societies (American Bible Society, American Sunday School Union, American Home Missionary Society, etc.) that were motivated by a moral rather than a social thrust. The moral reform movements, drawing their force from millennial expectation, tended to be anti-institutional and believed education was the best means to bring reason, conscience, and perfection to the individual. Their individualist posture assumed that reform proceeded from the individual and worked outward through the family, the community, and finally the nation itself. By contrast, institutions and organizational bureaucracy were viewed as barriers to the moral reform of individuals.[34]

Taking their cue from the romantic and perfectionist reform movements of that day, the early nineteenth century frontier sects and churches concentrated at first on the regeneration of individuals rather than institutions. By the 1830's they awakened to the imbalance between their sense of social responsibility and the realities of their position in society. It was also in the 1830's that the sects, in the midst of transforming into denominations, initiated their first concerted effort to make literacy a requirement for ministry. Democratized church structures, privatized religion, and individual perfectibility, all buttressed by the new revivalism, settled easily into denominationalism.

As a rule the frontier Protestant denominations, developing in the great valley beyond the Appalachians during the first half of the nineteenth century, were born out of the life forces of sects. Sects are described as voluntary associations, exclusive in character, individualistic in appeal, separatist in attitude, and always the product of religious revolts of the underclass, the dispossessed, the economically oppressed, those without effective representation in either church or state.[35] Sects are seen as symbols of cultural division between ethnic groups, social classes, urban and rural ways of life. Through the sect the "disinherited classes" are able to fashion a powerful institution for their spiritual expressions and for the dissemination of their economic and social philosophies.

Within the span of a generation sects normally evolve into denominational churchs, which are characterized as natural social groups conforming to the order of social classes, inclusive and national in scope, and reflecting the ethics and morality of the majority. Denominations are also described as responses to the religious needs of geographic sections. The story of American Religion from 1820 to the end of the nineteenth century has often been presented as a history of denominations developing out of sectional conflict:

> . . . constantly recurring strife between East and West has left its mark on religious life in the United States and has been responsible for the divergent development of a number of denominations. . . . the Western frontier . . . produced its own type of economic life and theory, its own kind of political practice and doctrine and created its own typical religious experience and expression. The result was the formation of perculiarly Western denominations . . . indigenous outgrowths of the American environment. The East, upon the other hand, clung fast to the established forms of European religious life and found itself unable to maintain unity with the frontier. Hence there came to pass a division of churches . . . which has its true source in the sectional differences and conflicts of American civilization.[36]

This East-West division was later matched by an even deeper North-South sectional conflict that further subdivided the denominations along economic and cultural class lines.

Disciples formed one of those "peculiarly Western denominations." Native born and a typical representative of Jacksonian and pastoral culture, Disciples developed out of a cluster of rural evangelical sects. Like the Baptists and Methodists, they at first used the methods of revival, emotional fervor, lay preaching, and ordaining their clergymen without requiring theological education. Ethnically, Disciples were predominantly semi-literate, Scots-Irish, frontier farmers. English, Welsh, Germans, a few French, and others were also intermingled with the membership. Some of the urban merchant class in Cincinnati, Pittsburgh, Lexington, and Louisville held membership with the Disciples as well, but the broad base of the movement was a rural, Scots-Irish underclass. Describing the Disciples in 1839, Alexander Campbell observed, "We have a few educated intelligent men, as we have a few rich and powerful; but the majority are poor, ignorant and uneducated." The Disciples represented the lower class prejudices of the frontier and did not develop any significant affinity with the urban East, its people, or its European religions. Nurtured by this socio-ethnic ethos and pastoral heritage, Disciples remained primarily a middle Western, Anglo-Saxon, county-seat town church.[37]

The tincture of Scots-Irish ethnicity has endured as a staple of Disciples heritage, shaping in subtle ways the character of their polity and the nature of their colleges. Theological differences in Colonial and Jacksonian days were often expressions of ethnic separateness and these Anglo-Saxon divisions gave impetus to the founding of new Protestant colleges. Princeton was just as distinctive for its Scottish ancestry as it was for its Presbyterianism. Queens College (Rutgers) was widely known as the *Dutch* College. Lutheran colleges, for example, appealed to the children of German immigrants, and while the immigrants could not conduct a college in German they *could* teach Lutheran theology and morality without opposing the new national spirit. Ethnic groups tended to play down their ethnic distinctiveness and define their differences in religious terms. They de-emphasized their ethnicity and substituted an emphasis upon religion. The nineteenth century Disciples Movement has been described as "the ethnic religious expression of Anglo-Saxon middle America."[38]

Scots-Irish (a hybrid term, the first half biological and cultural, the second geographical), immigrant families from Ulster, began landing at the Delaware River ports of Philadelphia and Newcastle during the early 1700's. Discovering the coastal lands already occupied they made their way across the Appalachians and settled in the country extending from Pennsylvania to the Carolinas and westward into Tennessee and Kentucky. They were energetic religious inventors, intense individualists, inveterate critics of the established order, and given to impetuous group action. The Scots-Irish were the main ethnic component of nearly every major frontier revolt including the Paxton Boys uprising (1763), the North Carolina Regulators revolt (1771), and the Whiskey Rebellion (1794). Their legendary resentment of Easterners—whom they accused of levying unfair taxes, refusing to establish new counties in the west, and refusing reapportionment, thereby allowing Eastern counties to continue holding the balance of power in the legislatures— would contribute heavily to the lack of Disciples interest in developing religious strength in the urban East. Scots-Irish pride in individual judgement, individual initiative, and resistance to all institutional authority would forever leave its stamp upon Disciples polity. Their disdain for privilege and their laboring occupations would lead them to support the ideal of small colleges where children of common folks could study useful, practical curriculum in the context of moral development. Their religious ingenuity would produce a denomination, the Christian Church (Disciples of Christ).[39]

Another significant force behind the early days of college founding was the booster spirit of local communities. Hundreds of little frontier villages thought of themselves as "cities" and in their quest for growth and prosperity they quickly established a newspaper, a church, a hotel and then attempted to make their community the seat of a college. Colleges in the Disciples tradition, like those of most other denominations, were essentially creations of individual denominational leaders and prominent community speculators. It was an odd couple—the preacher and the promoter, the bishop and the booster, the minister and the merchant, the evangelist and the entrepreneur, the servant and the speculator—but the formidable partnership of their visions, their hopes, and their competitive spirit proved remarkably productive.[40]

Early nineteenth century colleges were frequently agents of denominational imperialism, sectarian aggrandizement, community building, and social reform. Between 1800 and 1829 some twenty-four new colleges were founded of which sixteen were sectarian. Yet as late as 1825 the Methodist, Baptist, and Presbyterian splinter groups (which included the Disciples), collectively accounting for more than two-thirds of the church members on the frontier, could not claim one college among them. In 1820 the Baptist convention added to their constitution a provision making education a function of the church and adopted the concept of "Every State its own Baptist College." Within four years the Methodists voted to place a college in every annual conference but did not found their first college until 1830, with the establishment of Randolph-Macon. It was in the decade of the 1830's that the push for colleges among the frontier churches and communities gained full momentum. The contagion of college building between 1830 and 1860 became intensely competitive, producing 133 permanent institutions:[41]

1860 CENSUS: DENOMINATIONAL COLLEGES & CONGREGATIONS

Denomination	Total of Permanent Denominational Colleges	Total Number of Congregations
1. Presbyterian	49	6,379
2. Methodist	34	19,816
3. Baptist	25	12,139
4. Congregational	21	2,230
5. Catholic	14	2,442
6. Episcopal	11	2,129
7. Lutheran	6	2,123
8. DISCIPLES	5	2,066
9. German Reformed	4	676
10. Universalist	4	664
11. Friends	2	725
12. Unitarian	2	263
13. Christian Connection	1	?
14. Dutch Reformed	1	440
15. United Brethren	1	?
Total	180	(42)

It should also be remembered that by 1860 more than seven hundred colleges had died, evidence of the tenuous base of their existence. Success was less frequent than failure.

The period between 1830 and 1860 was a Golden Age for the creation of the small, rural college "with its six to twelve professors, 100 to 300 students, its six arts and sciences and three philosophies along with a mineralogical cabinet and collection of stuffed birds." They are romantically described by some . . .

> For an integrated education, that cultivates manliness and makes gentlemen as well as scholars, one that disciplines the social affections and trains young men to faith in God, consideration for their fellow men, and respect for learning, America has never since had the equal of her little hilltop colleges.[43]

. . . and negatively described by others:

> A principal cause of the excessive multiplication and dwarfish dimensions of Western colleges is no doubt, the diversity of religious denominations among us. Almost every sect will have its college, and generally one at least in each State. Of the score of colleges in Ohio, Kentucky and Tennessee, all are sectarian except two or three; and of course few of them are what they might and should be; and the greater part of them are mere impositions on the public. This is a grievous and growing evil . . . Must every State be divided and subdivided into as many college associations as there are religious sects within its limit? And thus, by their mutual jealousy and distrust, effectually prevent the usefulness and prosperity of any one institution?[44]

Rapid growth of colleges in the West depended heavily upon philanthropy from the East. The economic depression which followed the panic of 1837 brought financial desperation to dozens of small colleges on the Western frontier. Facing ruin and failure, Western colleges abused the benevolence of Eastern funding sources with their incessant demands and uncoordinated appeals. Eastern churches and philanthropists began to suggest that there were too many colleges in the West, that first priority should be given Eastern schools, and that Western colleges were mismanaged and the sources of radicalism. To protect themselves and also the cause of Western colleges, Eastern religious interests cooperated in organizing the Society for the Promotion of Collegiate and Theological Education at the West (SPCTEW) on June 30, 1843. Organized essentially under the auspices of Congregationalists, it was the largest of several, similar private societies, but the first agency with denominational ties to assume any corporate responsibility for church-related coleges. Its purpose was fourfold:

> . . . to unite the appropriate and the best energies of the older and the new States in harmonious cooperation.
> . . . to plant Colleges and Theological Schools when and where they may be most needed.
> . . . to arrest the progress of causes, which threatened not only to weaken, but

even to destroy the benevolent sympathy of the East in the great cause of
Western Education.
. . . to protect the churches of the East against the ill-judged and discordant
appeals of the West (with which we are thronged.)[45]

Denominational boards of education, designed to bring effective institutional
relationships between the churches and the burgeoning networks of colleges,
did not appear until much later (Presbyterian, USA, 1848; United Presbyterian, 1869; Baptists, 1888; Lutheran, 1885; Methodists, 1892; and Disciples,
1894) when denominations had grown better organized and more
bureaucratic.[46]

BACON COLLEGE: AN EPILOGUE

A professor first earned his salary, and then riding a hired horse, would
spend a few weeks in collecting it from subscribers to the college in
different counties.

Bacon College Memory
A. R. Milligan

Bacon College was founded in the crucible of Jacksonian Democracy, a
time of protest against the prevailing order. Like scores of other frontier
colleges founded in that age, Bacon struggled amid the ancient tension
between faith and reason, amid the conceptual tension between Colonial and
Jacksonian views of education, amid the community tension of its booster
trustees as the college moved from town to town, amid denominational
tension between Disciples and Baptists, and amid public tension between
citizens hostile to the idea of a college and those who supported it. Unlike the
majority of other early nineteenth century colleges, Bacon was decidedly
non-sectarian and was not founded for the purpose of supporting a
denomination. It did not have as a primary purpose the education of persons
for ministry, and it did not design its curriculum for the building of morals
and character. Bacon was a college of the community with a specialized
emphasis upon civil engineering to meet the economic needs of a frontier
land. Its denominational tie with the Disciples was a slender one and
certainly not a *raison d' etre*.

Jacksonians were heirs to four distinct educational traditions; (a) the
classical ideal of education designed to produce the scholar-gentleman, (b)
the scientific-utilitarian ideal of education designed to master the physical
world for progress, (c) the ideal of education as a function of church designed
to develop moral, ethical and religious coherence, and (d) the ideal of
education as a function of state designed to train citizens for civic and social
responsibilities. While Jacksonians chose most frequently the model empha-
sizing moral development, Bacon College structured itself around the

scientific-utilitarian ideal. It stressed a practical and secular education rather than the development of moral character.

Like the large majority of other colleges founded during the early nineteenth century Bacon suffered deep financial hardship which led to an early demise. Severe economic depression visited the nation in 1837 and its effect upon the fragile, new life of Bacon College was devastating. The second year of operation saw the enrollment plummet by nearly 50 percent and financial contributions dwindle to a trickle. In 1839, lured by the promise of significant financial support from Mercer county, the college relocated in Harrodsberg, Kentucky. Under the presidency of James Shannon, it struggled through the decade of the 1840's and on into the spring of 1850, when, in order to survive, it reduced its offerings to that of a preparatory school.

In 1858 Bacon college was rechartered as Kentucky University and continued to operate in Harrodsburg under the presidency of Robert Milligan throughout the Civil War. With the vision of creating one great university system, trustee John Bryan Bowman led the institution in designing a three-way merger with Transylvania University and a new land-grant agricultural and mechanical college in Lexington, Kentucky in 1865. The enduring legacy issuing from the life of Bacon College, along with all its dreams and optimisms, are incorporated today in *three* institutions: Lexington Theological Seminary, the University of Kentucky and Transylvania University.

Although it has been said that "Disciples of that period little realized what it took to make a college in money, scholarship and constituency," still they became increasingly attracted to the ideal of the denominational college as a means of perfecting individuals, reforming morals, building their local communities; and enhancing their religious Movement. The denominational colleges would become the earliest form of a loose cooperative mission among Disciples because, "As a community, Disciples were friends of literature and science, believing them to be ministering spirits to religion and morality."[47]

References

1. Alexander Campbell, "Georgetown College," *Millennial Harbinger,* 1837, p. 46.
2. *Ibid.*
3. Dwight E. Stevenson, "The Bacon College Story: 1836-1865," *The College of the Bible Quarterly,* Vol. XXXIX, No. 4, (October 1962), p. 7-14.
4. *The Christian,* Vol. I. (1837), p. 16.
5. *Millenial Harbinger,* 1837, p. 47.
6. Stevenson, p. 7.
7. *The Christian,* Vol. I, No. 1, (1837), p. 23.
8. *Ibid,* p. 20.
9. *The Christian,* Vol. I, No. 6 (1837), p. 132.
10. *Millennial Harbinger,* 1837, p. 284.

11. Walter Scott, "United States' System." *The College of the Bible Quarterly*, Vol. XXII, No. 2. (April 1946), pp. 30. *The Christian*, Vol. I, No. 2. (April 1946), pp. 30.
    Dwight Stevenson, *Walter Scott: Voice of the Golden Oracle.* Christian Board of Publication, 1946, pp. 163-164.
12. *The Christian*, Vol. I, No. 4. (April 1837), p. 90-91.
13. *Ibid.* p. 91-92.
14. Alexander Campbell, "Bacon College." *Millennial Harbinger*, 1837, p. 570-571.
15. Will Durant, *The Story of Philosophy.* Simon & Schuster, 1926, pp. 7-106.
16. Norman F. Canton and Peter L. Klein, *Medieval Thought: Augustine and Aquinas.* Blaisdell Publishers, 1969. p. 14-15.
17. David Knowles, *The Evolution of Medieval Thought.* Alfred Knopf, Inc., 1962, pp. 261-262.
18. Oliver Chitwood, *A History of Colonial America.* Harper & Row, 1961, p. 451.
    Frederick Rudolph, *The American College and University.* Vintage Books, 1962, p. 4.
19. Moses Coit Tyler, *A History of American Literature, 1607-1765.* 1949. p. 85; cited in Richard Hofstadter, *Anti-Intellectualism in American Life.* Vintage Books, 1962, p. 59.
20. Samuel Eliot Morison, *The Intellectual Life of Colonial New England.* Cornell University Press, 1936, 1956, p. 5.
    Samuel Eliot Morison, *The Founding of Harvard College.* Harvard University Press, 1935, p. 45.
21. Donald Tewksbury, *The Founding of American Colleges and Universities Before the Civil War.* Columbia University Press, 1932, p. 32-33.
22. Russel Nye, *The Cultural Life of the New Nation.* Harper & Row, 1960, p. 150.
    Tewksbury, p. 55.
23. Henry May, *The Enlightenment in America.* Oxford University Press, 1976, p. 3-176.
24. Tewksbury, p. 34-35, 62-64.
25. Gordon Wood, *The Creation of the American Republic 1776-1787.* University of North Carolina Press, 1969, p. 426-427.
26. Rudolph, p. 39.
    Tewksbury, p. 60.
27. Richard Hofstadter and Walter Metzer, *The Development of Academic Freedom in the United States.* Columbia University Press, 1955, pp. 120-130.
    Nye, p. 173-190.
28. Wood, p. 428, 570.
29. Leon B. Richardson, *History of Dartmouth College.* 1932, p. 337; cited in Rudolph, pp. 209-210.
30. Henry S. Commanger, *Documents of American History,* 9th Edition. Prentice Hall, 1973, p. 222.
31. Daniel J. Boorstin, *The Americans: The National Experience;* Random House, pp. 161, 312; Rudolph, pp. 208-211.
33. Sidney Mead, "From Coercion to Persuasion: Another Look at the Rise of Religious Liberty and the Emergence of Denominationalism." *Church History*, Volume XXV, No. 4. (December 1956), pp. 317-337.
    Sidney Mead, "American Protestantism During the Revolutionary Epoch." *Church History*, Volume XXII, No. 4. (December 1953), pp. 279-297.
33. Sidney Mead, "From Coercion to Persuasion: Another Look at the Rise of Religious Liberty and the Emergency of Denominationalism." *Church History*, Volume XXV, No. 4. (December 1956), pp. 317-337.
    Ralph Morrow, "The Great Revival, The West, and the Crisis of the Church;" cited in John F. McDermott, *The Frontier Re-Examined.* University of Illinois, 1967, pp. 65-78.
    R. Moore, *Religious Outsiders: The Making of Americans.* Oxford University Press, 1986.
34. John L. Thomas, "Romantic Reform in America, 1815-1865." *American Quarterly*, Volume XVII, No. 4. (Winter 1965), pp. 656-681.
35. H. Richard Neibuhr. *The Social Sources of Denominationalism,* Henry Holt & Company, 1919; Meridan Books, 1962, pp. 17-25.
36. *Ibid.,* pp. 136-137.

37. *Ibid.*, pp. 178-181. Arthur Schlesinger Jr., "The Age of Alexander Campbell;" cited in Perry Gresham, *The Sage of Bethany*. Bethany Press, 1960, p. 34.

Sydney E. Ahlstrom, *A Religious History of the American People*. Yale University Press, 1972, pp. 445-452.

Martin Marty, *Pilgrims in Their Own Land*. Little-Brown & Co., 1984, pp. 196-198.

38. Christopher Jencks & David Riesman, *The Academic Revolution*. Doubleday, 1968, pp. 314-333.

David E. Harrell, *Quest for a Christian America*. Disciples Historical Society, 1966, p. 24.

39. Richard A. Bartlett, *The New Country: A Social History of the American Frontier 1776-1890*. Oxford University Press, 1974, pp. 131-142.

40. Boorstin, pp. 151-161.

Winfred E. Garrison, *Religion Follows the Frontier: A History of the Disciples of Christ*. Harper & Brothers, 1931, p. 255.

D. Duane Cummins, "The Preacher and the Promoter." *Discipliana*, Vol. 4, No. 1. (Spring 1984), pp. 3-7, 14.

41. Tewksbury, pp. 66-79.

Nye, p. 178.

42. Tewksbury, pp. 69-90.

43. Samual Morison, Henry Comanger, and William Leuchtenburg, *The Growth of the American Republic*. Oxford University Press, 1969, pp. 462-463.

44. Comments of Philip Lindsley, President of University of Nashville, 1834, cited in Boorstin, p. 155.

45. Tewksbury, p. 11.

46. John S. Yoder, "An Analysis of Denominational Boards in Church-Related Higher Education." Unpublished Ph.D. Dissertation, University of Denver, 1974, pp. 112-122.

47. Alexander Campbell, *Millennial Harbinger*, 1845, p. 240.

Chapter **2**

DISCIPLES COLLEGES IN THE EARLY NINETEENTH CENTURY

DISCIPLES EDUCATIONAL INITIATIVES BEFORE 1840

In our country there are Catholic Colleges, Baptist colleges, Presbyterian colleges, Methodist colleges, etc., and shall there not be a Christian College? . . . Shall not we who earnestly contend for the necessity of mental illumination in order to the practice of Christianity, be the friends and abettors of learning? We certainly shall be, that none may have occasion to accuse us of being opposed either to the general diffusion of knowledge, or to the highest attainments in it.

Guerdon Gates
J. T. Jones
(MH, 1886)

It was early March along the waters of Buffalo Creek. A small group of local youth—Baptists and Presbyterians, male and female, still endowed with the high spirit of adolescence—gathered in the Bethany farm home of Alexander Campbell. The little band of indocile scholars constituted the first entering class of "Buffalo Seminary" (a preparatory or common school), the earliest educational institution of any kind rooted in the life of the Stone-Campbell Movement.[1]

With the ideal of developing a cadre of advocates for the Restoration, Alexander Campbell established Buffalo Seminary in 1818 and handcrafted its curriculum to prepare students for ministry. The design included daily instruction in scriptures from Genesis to Revelation, study in the French and Hebrew languages, mathematics, science, English grammar, and literature. The faculty, composed of Alexander Campbell, Thomas Campbell, and Jane Campbell, offered a paternalistic tutelage which included corporal punish-

23

ment and the insistence that students participate in both morning and evening devotions, bracketing their academic study in order to receive spiritual as well as intellectual nurture. All students roomed and ate in Campbell's home, paying a boarding fee of $1.50 per week and a tuition assessment of $5.00 per quarter.[2]

Initial response was promising and by summer Alexander Campbell was building an extension on his home to accommodate the seminary and its anticipated growth. But his enthusiasm for the seminary began to wane, due partially to the intractability of the students, whom he thought intellectually marginal and who disappointed him because so few entered ministry as a profession, and due partially to his discovery that debating and publishing served the Restoration Movement more effectively in its early years than teaching. Theoretical inquiry was temporarily subordinated to more practical objectives, and the school was closed in 1823.[3]

A sectarian institution that prepared persons for ministry was conceptually unacceptable to Alexander Campbell. While the planting of theological seminaries flourished during the 1820's, he shut down his own school and publicly inveighed against the others. His resistance grew out of his disdain for a hireling clergy resting upon the "Alms of the munificent devotees of the church."[4] In Campbell's view the seminary produced persons who were narrow, indoctrinated, sectarian, steeped in denominational polity, totally lacking a vision of wholeness, intellectual breadth and spiritual depth. They were prepared only as consecrated functionaries, as yokes on the shoulders of the laity.

Between 1820 and 1870 each major denomination enjoined the race to evangelize a burgeoning population and establish its own network of schools to train ministers. As the decades passed, student bodies became more denominational rather than diverse, and curriculums were styled to serve the political and historic traditions of denominations.[5]

Disciples, to the contrary, guided by the strong volunteer flavor of the Restoration Movement and Campbell's intransigent view of theological seminaries, placed their educational emphasis upon the *laity* rather than a hireling clergy. Throughout the same years that seminaries were taking root across the land, Disciples were founding scores of colleges, institutes, and academies to prepare a leadership of the laity.[6]

Education, fostered through teaching and writing, was not a terrain reserved exclusively for Alexander Campbell. It was the natural turf for all "friends of literature and science," "friends and abettors of learning," and its contours were familiar to each of the four principle founders of the Stone-Campbell Movement. They were all modern, activist, contemporary men, exceedingly well educated for their time and, in response to the national burst of educational energy during the early nineteenth century, all four became teachers and writers—laureates of the Restoration.

One year after Campbell opened Buffalo Seminary, Barton W. Stone, a graduate of David Caldwell's Guilford Academy, became principal of Rittenhouse Academy in Georgetown, Kentucky.[7] For several years prior to that 1819 appointment, Stone taught English grammar, Latin, and Greek at a high school in Lexington, Kentucky; and back before the turn of the century, he had been professor of languages at Hope Hall Academy. From the 1820's until his death in 1844, Stone regularly published the *Christian Messenger*, a religious journal which circulated widely throughout the Stone-Campbell network of congregations.

While Stone was teaching at Rittenhouse in 1819 and the Campbells were teaching at Buffalo Seminary, Walter Scott, newly immigrated fresh from the University of Edinburgh, began teaching Greek and Latin at George Forrester's Academy in Pittsburgh.[8] Scott would later found a Female Institute in Covington, Kentucky, become a trustee of Miami University of Ohio, and serve as president of Bacon College. He was a frequent contributor to *The Christian Baptist* and also publisher of his own religious journal, *The Evangelist*, which served the Restoration Movement.

Thomas Campbell, a graduate of Glasgow University and the Divinity Hall at Whitburn, was instinctively an educator. While still in Scotland he opened a school in Rich Hill, where he and his son, Alexander, taught. Following his immigration to the United States, Thomas Campbell opened a school in Cambridge, Ohio in 1813, founded a school in Pittsburgh in 1815, and later taught at an Academy in Burlington, Kentucky, before joining his son in the 1818 venture at Buffalo Seminary.[9] He gave scores of public lectures and was a prolific contributor to both *The Christian Baptist* and *The Millennial Harbinger*.

Stone, Scott and Thomas Campbell became teachers early in their careers simply as a means of earning a living. But the surging spirit of American nationalism and the developing Stone-Campbell Restoration called for the education of new generations of leaders, and that call drew motives decidedly more altruistic from all four founders. In time Alexander Campbell, through his voluminous writings, became a zealous advocate of education as a way to perfect individuals, to improve the social and economic mobility of the church laity, to develop competent leadership for a young America and a young religious Movement.

Fourteen educational institutions are known to have been founded by Disciples ministers prior to 1840. Eleven of those were established during the 1830's, the decade in which the entire American educational enterprise began its unprecedented expansion. Not one of the fourteen institutions survived beyond the Civil War. Only two of the institutions were colleges. The others were academies, institutes, or seminaries, all forerunners of the modern primary, middle, and high schools. Financed on a modest scale, they regularly solicited congregations as well as individual members for contributions, and only subsequently called for church endorsement. Members responded because they believed in the education of their children and wanted that education to occur in a Christian environment.

EDUCATIONAL INSTITUTIONS FOUNDED BY DISCIPLES: 1813 - 1839

Date Founded	Date Closed	Institution	Location	Founder
1813	1815	Cambridge Academy	Cambridge, OH	Thomas Campbell
1815	1818	Campbell's Academy	Pittsburgh, PA	Thomas Campbell
1818	1823	Buffalo Seminary	Bethany, VA	Alexander Campbell
1831	1863	Popular Hill Academy	Popular Hill, KY	Philip S. Fall
1833	1853	Greenville Institute	Harrodsburg, KY	S. G. Mullins
1833	1833	Christian College	New Albany, IN	John Cook Bennet
1835	-	Wayne County Seminary	Centerville, IN	Samuel K. Hoshour
1835	-	Female Inductive Academy	Franklin, KY	
1836	1865	Bacon College	Georgetown, KY	Thorton F. Johnson
1837	1850	Highland Literary Institute	Mt. Sterling, KY	H. B. Todd
1837	-	Lincoln Academy	Troy, MO	James Jeans
1837	-	Flat Rock Academy	Bourbon, KY	Thorton F. Johnson
1838	1842	Female Collegiate Institute	Georgetown, KY	
1838	1839	Hawk Creek Academy	Montgomery Co., IN	Mr./Ms. James Fannin
1839	1846	Cambridge Seminary	Cambridge City, IN	Samuel K. Hoshour

10

These institutions were privately organized, owned, and maintained by influential personalities within the Restoration Movement. Individual founders were not agents of any ecclesiastical authority; but the Restoration congregations often played a significant role in supporting and sustaining the institutions which were always regarded as part of the Movement. Answering the call for leadership, these early schools responded with more than a proportionate share. Wayne County Seminary, for example during its short history under the leadership of Samuel Klinefelter Hoshour, counted among its students future governors and generals—Oliver P. Morton, Lew Wallace and Ambrose Burnside.[11] Teachers, lawyers, doctors, and ministers educated in Disciples rural boarding schools could be numbered by the score.

Disciples schools were also pioneers in extending education to females and in developing of co-educational institutions. Popular Hill Academy for females, founded by P. S. Fall in 1831, was one of the earliest female schools in the nation, preceding by five years the founding of Mt. Holyoke Female Seminary for girls in Massachusetts, generally considered a landmark in the history of education for women.

Establishing an instituion of learning for females or a co-educational institution during the years before the Civil War required some daring. Prior to the Civil War fewer than a half dozen colleges were co-educational. Virtually every institution founded by Disciples was either co-educational or female. Perhaps in no other area did Disciples so clearly mark themselves as children of the egalitarian West or prophets for the disinherited. This form of mission, emanating from the church, represented an indispensable and distinctive contribution to political freedom and higher education in the United States. It demonstrates that the mission of Disciples church-related colleges was infused with social purpose in addition to commitment to learning and inquiry. Thomas Woodsy's study of women's education in America reveals that the overwhelming majority of all women's colleges founded in the United States were established by churches.

Walter Scott sent his daughter, Emily, to Popular Hill and later wrote P. S. Fall that "young ladies educated by you excel all others." Highland Literary Institute, a Disciples co-educational institution with 160 students, was founded at Mt. Sterling, Kentucky, in 1837, just four years after Oberlin became the first college in the nation to declare itself co-educational. Popular Hill and Highland were parts of the continually expanding Kentucky network of academies and colleges, which inspired Walter Scott to observe in his journal that Disciples have "more and better insitutions of learning in their patronage than any other body of people in the state."[12]

One of those Kentucky institutions of learning, of course, was Bacon College, established in 1836, the only successful *college* founded by Disciples leaders before 1840. The founding of Disciples colleges in this early period was often envisioned and sometimes attempted, but nearly always Alexander Campbell, who judged such efforts to be premature, advised postponement.

John Cook Bennet, after unsuccessful attempts at founding a college in Ohio and Virginia, wrote Alexander Campbell in March of 1833, announcing enthusiastically that he had secured a charter for Christian College to be located in New Albany, Indiana. Enclosing copies of the charter and bylaws and assuming he had been operating with Campbell's encouragement, Bennet requested mention of the new college in *The Millenial Harbinger*.[13] Campbell's published response was not at all what Bennet had expected:

Yours of March 1st now lies before me. The intelligence it communicates was to me wholly unexpected. I heard nothing of this project until it was consummated . . . . Whether such an institution could be erected, is, with me at least, very problematical; . . .

Your project, so far as it fascilitates literary improvement, deserves well of the state. But the Christian church can never be made debtors to an institution which has never conferred on it any benefit. It would, upon the whole, have been more respectful to the judgment and wishes of the brethren to have consulted them on the propriety of such a scheme . . . . But now that it is founded without such an expression of their will, it will remain for them to signify how far they can give it the countenance of their names and their funds. This is a question which neither you nor I ought to wish to decide for them.[14]

In the next issue of *The Millennial Harbinger*, Campbell included a brief statement on the back page: "We are glad to learn that some of the by-laws of the Christian College are about to be amended, and that it will be a purely literary institution. This will explain our not publishing them at this time. As a literary institution, liberal and antisectarian, we will it all success."[15] One year later *The Millennial Harbinger* carried a small notice under the bold type label, CAUTION, in which it was implied that Dr. Bennet had been gambling away the money he received from selling diplomas for Christian College. Campbell added his own cryptic postscript, "From such, Paul says, turn away."[16] There is no record that Christian College ever opened.

Interest in founding a Disciples college, however, continued to grow. Within three years of the abortive effort to establish a Christian College, Guerdon Gates and J. T. Jones wrote a long and impassioned letter urging Disciples to establish colleges. The Gates-Jones letter asserted that founding a college was a religious reponsibility and that Disciples had ample resources to accomplish the task:

> The religion which we advocate, and desire to practice, recommends itself by its purity to the consciences of all men, not upon the ground of enthusiasm and mysticism, but upon the principles of reason and philosophy. Therefore, for the future propagation and reception of this religion, we should endeavor to prepare the way by the establishment of colleges, high schools, and primary schools, as the state of the community and the circumstances of the case may render expedient; as well as by guarding the immediate interests of the church, and attending to her proper discipline. Have we not reason to believe, that in time to come, the church will prosper and flourish, proportionably at least, to the general diffusion of knowledge? Whilst all the parties and sects are doing what they can by means of literary institutions to promote their individual interests; is it not reasonable that we should establish a college somewhere in the great valley of the West—not, however, that we may use it as a engine under the control of a sect for the propagation and defence of its peculiarities; but that we may make it emphatically a *literary* institution for the purpose of educating youths in the knowledge of true science? Considering ourselves as a body, have we not men amply qualified to conduct such an institution, who would be willing to serve God and benefit mankind in this way? And can we not procure funds sufficient to establish a college on a permanent basis? And have we not chldren enough to fill it. . . . If we desire extensively, and for a long time even after our decease to be useful to mankind, it is evident that we should be *up and doing*.[17]

Gates and Jones, proclaiming Disciples "friends and abettors of learning," recommended the establishment of a college at some suitable point within the valley of the Mississippi and called on each congregation to send delegates to a meeting in Louisville, Kentucky for the purpose of planning the development of such an institution.

> . . . every church feeling an interest in so great and so laudable an enterprize, . . . send one delegate, or more, to a meeting to be held in the city of Louisville,

Kentucky on Wednesday, the 28th day of September next . . . . Let [the delegates] select a location, adopt measures for raising funds, and digest some plan or model for the government of the institution; and in general let them attend to all that may be necessary for carrying into complete effect the objects of the meeting.[18]

Alexander Campbell viewed the matter as a "grave question," requiring "grave consideration." To the central question, "Can Disciples have Literary institutions?" and to the immediate proposal of a meeting in Louisville, Campbell responded:

. . . when this question is laid before the brethren, perhaps there may not be the same unanimity—the same deep sense of the necessity—the same clear perception of the utility of such an institution; and, therefore, it appears to me expedient that the matter be calmly, and dispassionately, and profoundly considered; and, therefore, I fear (and I give it as my opinioin) that the time mentioned in the preceding letter is too immediate for the intelligent action of the great community to which the matter is submitted. Two or three months, however, may be added without any real detriment; and it is much better to have the matter well examined before any expression of our views be required.[19]

There is no record that the meeting in Louisville took place.

By August, Campbell was beginning to ease toward the position of the Disciples founding a college. He argued that there was not any reason against Christians being patrons of literature, schools, or colleges, but he thought there was a less expensive way to be a patron than founding a school.

. . . we once suggested an idea of this sort—that, as for our putting ourselves to the trouble and expense of getting up one or more colleges simply for the sake of having the exclusive control of them, it did not appear worthy of any great effort; inasmuch as we should, as the cause we plead flourished, obtain a proportionate share of all the scholars and graduates of the different schools in the country . . . we have in several schools an influence equal, or nearly equal, to our numbers in proportion to some other societies who have been at much more expense than we.[20]

Campbell expressed his satisfaction in the election of James Shannon to the presidency of the University of Louisiana and urged all Disciples in the Southwest to send their children to that institution. To do so, he counseled, was more economical than trying to support new Disciples institutions. In response to the growing number of Disciples who were pressing for the establishment of male and female academies, seminaries, and colleges, Campbell asked, "would it be in accordance with our own principles, would it be right with sacred scripture, to attempt to set up and sustain such an institution?" He conceded that if a school under Christian supervision could be managed without making it a school for preachers and without any features of a theological school, then it could exist. But, he queried, is such a school possible, expedient, or practicable?

By the fall of 1836, the issue was no longer Campbell's to decide. Bacon College, suddenly and without warning, appeared in the Disciples milieu carrying the support of Barton Stone and Walter Scott. Campbell, who had given more thought to the concept of education than anyone else in the Movement, was left with little alternative but to render his support and proceed with the planning of his own college.

ALEXANDER CAMPBELL'S PHILOSOPHY OF EDUCATION

Education, properly defined, is the full development of man to himself, in his whole physical, intellectual and moral constitution, with a proper reference to his whole destiny in the Universe of God.[21]

Alexander Campbell

Chief architect of the higher education philosophy for Disciples in the 19th century was Alexander Campbell. He gained a reputation as a conservative educational reformer during the 1830's, while a member of Cincinnati's Literary and College of Professional Teachers.[22] For thirty years Campbell crowded the pages of his *Millennial Harbinger* with essays, addresses, and lectures on education developed out of his millenial conviction of its humanitarian importance. "Next to Christianity itself," he wrote, "stands education."[23]

Campbell was a thorough student of the best thought of his time, steeping himself in the vitality of eighteenth century Enlightenment ideas. He drew his concepts of economics from Adam Smith, his doctrine of humanity and trust in reason from the French Enlightenment, his political philosophy from John Locke, his pragmatic notions of science from Sir Isaac Newton, and his commitment to intellectual freedom from John Milton. His educational philosophy was developed through study of the writings of Lord Francis Bacon, from the Swiss educator De Fellenberg, from Thomas Smith Grimke and other members of Cincinnati's College of Teachers, and from John Locke's treatise entitled *Thoughts on Education*.[24]

An active participant in the political and religious reforms of the American nation, Campbell, in the 1830's turned a significant share of his attention to education:

. . . the systems of education call for a reformation as radical and extensive as the popular systems of government and religion. In most of our common schools years are squandered in learning little else than an irrational way of 'reading, writing, and cyphering,' with some of the technicalities of grammar and geography. A mere smattering in words, without the knowledge of any thing in nature, society, or religion, is the reward of the literary toils of our children in our common schools. . . .

Those sent to college are very often placed in circumstances not much more advantageous for the formation of useful character. A few years are devoted to the dead languages and mythology of Pagan nations, frequently to the great moral detriment of the student, and seldom much to his literary and intellectual advantage in the acquisition of real knowldege. A peep into 'the sciences,' the hasty perusal of a few authors, rather read than studied, obtain for him his axademic honors; and then he enters the theatre of life without a thorough knowledge of any one art or science, with a large stock of words rather than ideas, and with the knowledge of names rather than of things. His memory had been cultivated much more than his judgement.[25]

Reform of the educational system, he believed, had to begin in the colleges where teachers were educated for the academies and institutes. Far too much emphasis, in Campbell's opinion, was being given to classical literature and to the political and social philosophy of Greece and Rome. Colleges, in his view, had ignored the advancements in human knowledge and had become enslaved to Grecian and Roman models of thought which Campbell believed were failures as authoritative guides for the politics, philosophy, and morals of the new age. Campbell devoted an entire essay to a criticism of the influence of Aristotle and endorsed Thomas Grimke's proposal that educational study should seek a better balance between classical and modern knowledge by giving more attention to the three hundred years of development in the arts and sciences since 1500.[26]

His own experience as a teacher at Buffalo Seminary led Campbell to the conclusion that the educational system not only had the wrong curriculum emphasis but was offering the wrong subjects at the wrong levels:

I have doubted, seriously doubted, for at least fifteen years, whether the present mode of training the human mind in common schools . . . was not almost antipodes to reason, and sailing against the wind and tide of human nature. It is worse than wrong end foremost. We begin in metaphysics, and end in physics. The natural sciences, in the present course, are for young men, the last years of their academic, and the unnatural sciences (pardon the antithesis) are for infants and children! The infant schools, now in experiment, are approximating very much towards reason, towards the philosophy of human nature . . . . I made something like an experiment of this sort when superintending a classical school, in which mathematics, and what are called the natural sciences, were taught, some seven or eight years ago. It was sufficient to convince me that more than half the time spent in the collegiate way was lost, and less than half the acquisitions were made during the whole course, which might, under a rational system, be obtained at the age of from sixteen to eighteen.[27]

From his natural impulse toward moral reform and his abiding belief in the perfectibility of the individual, Campbell was compelled by the possibilities of regenerating the educational order. Consequently, between 1830 and his death, the broad subject of education and the specific work of Bethany College received as much of his thought and energy as any other subject, including church organization.

The first feature of Campbellian educational philosophy was *Wholeness of Person*, the development and proper training of all human powers: physical, intellectual, and moral. He espoused the Lockean concept that the total human being—body, mind and spirit—should be developed through learning. Like Locke, he conceived of this threefold nature in functional or operative terms:

> It is to be hoped that the present century . . . will add to its reknown the glory of substituting phychological fact for hypothesis, and of discarding from our schools and colleges the imaginative conjectures and metaphysical theories of ages more speculative and romantic than the present. Then we are disposed to imagine it will be universally conceded that the excellence of education will consist of three things—in teaching and training man to think, to feel and to act . . .[28]

Campbell never wavered from his view of educating the wholeness of each individual and in one of the last writings he published on education he advanced the theme just as forcefully as he had thirty years before:

> The analysis and synthesis of man and his relations to the past, the present and the future of his being and well being, is the grand essential theme of all physical, intellectual, moral and religious education. These four words . . . ought to be printed with indelible ink on the most enduring parchment, deeply engraven on pillared marble or table brass.[29]

The second, and clearly the predominant feature of Campbell's educational philosophy was the *Moral Formation of Character*. He was held by the conviction that moral excellence was the chief end of education, that the spirit was the radiating center of the whole human system. The moral nature of persons, he argued, is superior to their intellectual and physical nature because it is in the moral nature of persons that the virtues of benevolence, justice, compassion, and generosity are developed and that human excellence is achieved. Without a moral nature, asserted Campbell, human beings are unfit for society. "Oxygen is not more essential to combustion," he wrote, "or respiration to human life than morality to the well-being of society."[30]

Campbell complained bitterly that moral development was almost wholly neglected in the schools, that teachers directed their instruction to the head with very little attention to the heart, that greater value was placed on genius than on benevolence, and that intellect was admired more than moral worth. He argued that education in moral culture should precede intellectual culture, and that it should be the most important branch of a student's early education. "The present infant school institutions," he urged, should "have appended to their literary and scientific character a moral regimen, which would for the first years be rather their principal than their secondary concern."[31] The theme of moral excellence appeared repeatedly in Campbell's writings and invariably referred to what he believed to be the most important characteristic of an educated person. "The formation of moral character, the culture of the heart," wrote Campbell, "is the supreme end of education or rather is education itself. With me education and the formation of moral character are identical expressions."[32]

The third feature of Campbell's educational philosophy was *Biblical Studies*. He considered the Bible the great moral engine of civilization, the noblest of all classics, a book that spoke to the conscience, heart, and soul of humanity. Convinced that the study of the Bible was essential to a comprehensive literary education and the safeguarding of ethics, Campbell offered that a college without the Bible "is not in accordance with the wants of society, with the genius of human nature, with the interest of the state, with the progress of civilization, with the advancement of the church . . . , or with the happiness of man."[33] "A school without the Bible," he added later, "is like a universe without a center and without a sun."[34] Lamenting that the Bible, as a textbook, was excluded from most colleges because of sectarian fears, Campbell suggested how it ought to be used:

> . . . I do not mean the Bible on the shelf, in the college library, or locked up, like an amulet, in a trunk, to ward off spectres, or diseases, or hobgoblins; but to be read, lectured upon, taught in all its facts, events, precepts, laws, ordinances, promises . . . .
> We do not mean that the Bible is to be taught or read theologically, as in the schools of divinity . . . It is to be read and studied historically, and with religious reference. Its whole moral power, and its whole spiritual power, are concentrated in its facts, precepts and promises; and not in those speculative theories called orthodoxy . . . . These belong to denominations, and not to Christians.[35]

In the founding of his own Bethany College, Campbell took special care to honor the Bible among the college classics by including a Department of Sacred History and Biblical Literature as a component of the academic design. The department was not created to displace any part of the normal classical curriculum, but to enhance it.[36]

The fourth feature of his philosophy was *Non-Sectarianism*. "Sectarianism with me," said Campbell, "is neither religion nor morality."[37] In Perry Gresham's phrase, Campbell viewed sectarian education as a "contradiction in terms." It was Campbell's opinion that "A college, in our country and society, should be free from every sectarian influence and tendency,"[38] and that "one of the greatest blemishes in the character, and one of the greatest defects in the system, of most of our literary institutions, is that they are religiously sectarian."[39] Early in his career, Campbell had defended Transylvania University against Presbyterian charges of infidelity, countering that "synods have always aimed at the sovereignty of colleges as subservient to their design; consequently whenever they lose their sway in any seminary, infidelity begins to raise its odious brow."[40] Campbell spoke often of divesting colleges of their sectarian character and he always did so "with reference solely to the public good."[41]

The fifth feature of his educational philosophy was the *Perfectibility of Individuals.* Like all moral reformers of his era, Campbell drew force from millennial expectations and believed solidly in the formative nature of human character. He was fond of quoting three lines of verse:

> Education makes the Man.
> As the twig is bent, the tree's inclined.
> Art and Science humanize mankind,
> soften the rude, can calm the boisterous mind.

They appear repeatedly in his addresses and essays expressing his belief in the transcendant importance of education to the individual.[42] Consonant with the thrust of moral reform in Jacksonian America, Campbell adhered to the premise that social reform was achieved through the perfection of individuals. "Develope individuals," he wrote, "and you develope society; cultivate the minds and enlarge the powers of the citizens, and you promote the glory and increase the influence of the Republic."[43] He saw the college, therefore, as an instrument of social control, an indispensable institution in the romantic crusade to regenerate the social order. He saw schools as essential to every community because they provided avenues of economic and social mobility for individuals, thereby reducing crime, ignorance, and poverty in the society. "One of the most exhilarating and promising signs of a better era in human destiny," he wrote, "is the increased and increasing interest displayed on education."[44]

It is important to add that Campbell affirmed the dignity of all persons and their ability to learn, irrespective of rank, sex, or condition. Education, as a means of reform, was for the "full and entire development of humanity, not in a few favored and gifted sons of the Republic, but throughout the broad bosom of society—in the palace and in the hut."[45] In his advocacy of inclusiveness, Campbell was a step ahead of his time in promoting education for women:

> . . . till within a few years, the opinion was very general, that any sort of education was sufficient for girls. They were not expected to figure, nor shine, or to hold office in society; and, therefore, if they could read, write, and cypher a little, they were fully accomplished for all the duties and business of their station in life. This idea is . . . not yet fully discarded, though it be full time it were universally repudiated. For my part, I may be thought an enthusiast . . . on the other side; but, be this as it may, I will hazard the declaration, that if the question rested on my vote, whether, as a general rule, the female sex, or the male sex, ought to be better educated . . . I would say, The ladies should have it. And if any one asks me, Why? I would answer, Because posterity always depends for its mental and moral character incomparably more upon the mothers than upon the fathers of the existing generation. But I go for equality.[46]

The sixth feature of his philosophy was *Lifelong Learning*. Campbell believed learning began in infancy and spanned the totality of a lifetime. "Man is never out of his pupilage," wrote Campbell:

> The best school does little more than present us with the necessary means of acquiring and communicating knowledge. They are always children . . . . who regard a parchment in their pocket . . . as full proof of scholarship, and themselves as learned . . . To be learned, and wise, and good, and useful members of society, we must be always learning;[47]

His original plan for Bethany, therefore, included an elementary school, high school, and college, all of which he saw primarily as developing the art of inquiry. "Every student," advised an aged Campbell, "that has attained . . . graduation . . . is merely licensed to become his own teacher and pupil . . . Let me say kindly and emphatically . . . that you owe to God, to Society, to your Alma Mater, and to yourselves to continue to be students."[48]

These Campbellian strains echo throughout fifteen decades of Disciples higher education history as a kind of background score: *Wholeness of Person, Moral Formation of Character, Biblical Studies, Non-Sectarianism, Perfectibility of Individuals, Lifelong Learning*. Armed with this philosophy which anticipated many of the educational reforms of Horace Mann and was twenty-five years ahead of other major college reformers, nineteenth century Diciples clergy became zealous in the creation of new institutions of learning. They believed, as Campbell, that education "enlarges, invigorates, beautifies, adorns the soul and spirit of man."[49]

DISCIPLES COLLEGE: THE 1840'S

> We should be glad to see a flourishing University in every State in the Union, sustained by our Christian brotherhood. But, according to my political economy, we cannot now have a model one for an age to come, because we are lavishing our means on too many experiments, or unmatured projects. But we must pay the price of wisdom in the school of folly, and leave our children to wish . . . that their fathers had been more wise."[50]
>
> Alexander Campbell, 1854

Any enterprising member of the Disciples movement was at liberty to found a college because, "the supreme independency which controlled in the organization of churches controlled also in the organization of colleges."[51] One hundred fifteen educational institutions were founded at random by individual Disciples across the two and one-half decades between 1840 and 1866, the year of Alexander Campbell's death.

Of that number, eighty-three constituted an unco-ordinated, localized, and disparate network of private high schools variously called academies, institutes, or seminaries. Life for most was of short duration. As predecessors of the public high school, they represented an ephemeral and transitional stage in American education. No charters, no catalogues, and few records remain to testify that they existed; but their contributions to the literacy of the Movement and of the society are incalculable. The academies, institutes, and seminaries made their contributions over a short historical range, became obsolete, and were soon crowded out of existence by the rapidly expanding public school system. The strongest among them made a gradual transition to two or four year colleges.

Thirty-two of the one hundred fifteen institutions were colleges, rooted in the settled ways of simple, pastoral communities where they attempted to insulate themselves from what they thought to be the evils of urban America. Disciples colleges sprouted all over the Western landscape where the proliferation of industry, railroads, canals, roads, mining, and agriculture was creating a heavy demand for technicians and managers—and for a new scheme of educational preparation. In spite of their rural isolation, Disciples colleges were continually faced with the dilemma of whether their primary obligation was to serve the community or to serve learning. The typical Disciples school attempted to serve both, on its own terms and in the context of building moral character. Charles Darwin and other seminal thinkers brought a new level of maturity to the natural and physical sciences during this period, influencing profoundly the curriculum design of the Disciples colleges. Simultaneously, the expanding industrial economy changed the relationship between college and community: but Disciples colleges generally balanced their curriculum between traditional learning and the practical skills demanded by the rising middle class of manufacturers, merchants, and mechanics. This was not always to the taste of the predominantly rural, lower-middle class majority of the reformation membership, a segment never well represented on the rolls of Disciples colleges.

Most Disciples colleges of that era were founded by entrepreneurial Disciples ministers or professional Disciples educators and mirrored the educational model offered at Bethany College by Alexander Campbell. They were among the earliest schools to pioneer the concept of co-educational and female education in their states, sections, and in the nation at large. Curriculum was determined by the colleges with emphasis placed upon Biblical literacy, classical languages and literature, moral character, and natural sciences. Their graduates were attracted in heaviest proportion to public service—education and ministry, with law a close third.

A 66 percent mortality rate among Disciples colleges, although superior to the 80 percent mortality rate in other denominations, attests to the lack of astute financial management, the lack of any Movement-wide coordination regarding the number of colleges to be established or where they should be founded, and the lack of viable enrollments. Small and declining enrollments resulted from high cost, sectional competition, and the eventual call to Civil

War, but mostly from the fact that the colleges were not meeting the needs of the community. Increasing each year for twelve years prior to 1838 the ratio of students in college total population had grown to one of every 1,294. By 1869 the ratio had declined to one in every 1,927[52] Enrollment at Disciples colleges during the period from 1840 to the end of the Civil War typically declined at least one-third from the average initial enrollment of 100 to 150 students. Concurrently, the movement was quadrupling in size to more than 200,000 members.

At least seven Disciples colleges began operating during the 1840's, of which four did not survive beyond the Civil War. Burritt College, chartered in 1848 and named for a blacksmith of local legend, was secluded high in the Tennessee Cumberlands, amid the liquor stills of Van Buren county. William Davis Carnes, a highly regarded minister, professor and lumber-grist entrepreneur, gave successful leadership to the religious oriented institution at Spencer, from 1849 until 1857. During the 1856-57 term Carnes expelled several habitual drinkers from among the student body, an action viewed by local citizens as impugning the integrity of the main industry of the county. Carnes' home was torched, prompting him to resign. The school experienced an immediate decline and suspended operations in 1860, near the outbreak of Civil War.[53] The influence of the local community clearly prevailed during the early period of Burritt College history.

A widely known Tennessee Disciples leader, Tolbert Fanning, with the help of Bowling Embry, secured a charter for Franklin College, located on Fanning's "Elm Crag" farm near Nashville. It opened in January 1845 with the support of Tennessee Disciples. By July it had enrolled 150 students into a unique adaptation of Fellenburg's work-study concept. The regimen at Franklin began at 5:00 A.M. daily with chapel, proceeded throughout the day with alternating periods of classwork and labor (farming, carpentry, blacksmithing, tailoring, etc.), then concluded with an enforced study period from 6:30 to 9:30 each evening. By contributing their labor, lower middle-class students who could not afford tuition were supposed to pay their way with the produce of their work. The farming operation and trade shops did not prove profitable and the board of trustees refused to seek endowment funds. Those factors combined with declining enrollment led to the suspension of operations in 1861. It reopened briefly in 1865, but was permanently closed that year when a fire destroyed the campus.[54]

Out of the 1840's emerged the earliest institution of higher education founded by Disciples which survived the Civil War, the nineteenth century, and remains soundly operational today as it nears the celebration of its sesquicentennial anniversary. Bethany College, chartered March 2, 1840 and recognized as the "mother of our colleges", is the oldest surviving institution of higher learning in the Movement with a continuous relationship dating from its founding to the present.

EDUCATIONAL INSTITUTIONS FOUNDED BY DISCIPLES 1840-1849[55]

Year of Founding	Name	Location
1840	Georgetown Female Institute	Georgetown, Kentucky
	Hygiea Female Autheneum	Mt. Healthy, Ohio
	IRVING COLLEGE	Warren County, Tennessee
	Lafayette Seminary	Lexington, Kentucky
1841	*BETHANY COLLEGE	Bethany, Virginia
	Female Inductive Institute	Winchester, Kentucky
1842	Inductive Institute	Paris, Kentucky
	Newtonia Female Institute	Whitesville, Mississippi
1843	Berea Academy	Marshall County, Tennessee
	NEWTON COLLEGE	Woodville, Mississippi
1844	Laboring School	Gallatin, Tennessee
	Laural Hill Female Institute	• • • , Tennessee
	Mt. Vernon Female Seminary	Mt. Vernon, Ohio
	Pleasant Hill Seminary	Washington County, Pennsylvania
	South Kentucky Institute for Young Ladies	Hopekinsville, Kentucky
1845	Farmington Academy	Rush County, Indiana
	FRANKLIN COLLEGE	Nashville, Tennessee
	Greenhill Seminary	Lexington, Kentucky
	Ozark Institute	Mt. Comfort, Arkansas
1847	Hampton Male & Female Academy	Hampton, Virginia
	Harpeth Male Academy	Franklin, Tennessee
	Western Military Institute	Georgetown, Kentucky
1848	*CAMDEN POINT FEMALE SEMINARY (WILLIAM WOODS COLLEGE)	Camden, Missouri
	Classical & Mental School for Boys	Maysville, Kentucky
	*WALNUT GROVE ACADEMY (EUREKA COLLEGE)	Eureka, Illinois
	Fairview Academy	Fairview, Indiana
	Fayette Female Academy	Lexington, Kentucky
	Highland Academy	Jackson County, Missouri
1849	Black Rock Female Academy	Buffalo, New York
	BURRITT COLLEGE	Spencer, Tennessee
	Irvine Valley Academy	Buchanan County, Missouri
	*KENTUCKY FEMALE ORPHAN SCHOOL (MIDWAY COLLEGE)	Midway, Kentucky

Functioning and related to the Christian Church (Disciples of Christ) in 1986.

In October 1839, Alexander Campbell announced a comprehensive design for a new institution of learning under the title, "Plan of a Literary, Moral, and Religious School; or the Union of four Institutions in one—The combination of the Family, the Primary School, the College, and the Church in one great system of Education."[56] The *Family*, similar to a modern elementary school, was a home for boys under fourteen years of age. The Primary *School*, was organized as a college preparatory institution, with emphasis upon moral development. The third component was the *College*, a liberal arts institution with a primary focus upon the Bible as a textbook for daily, non-sectarian instruction. The college was the only part of the educational scheme that Campbell actually developed. The *Church*, to which the other three parts were related without being under its control, was the principal source of influence.[57]

Campbell insisted that "the location for the cluster of institutions must be entirely rural, in the country, detached from all external society."[58] For Campbell, to whom education was a character building process, the city was not a proper location for a college. He therefore chose his own Bethany farm, isolated in the heavily timbered hills, on a narrow slice of Northwest Virginia along Buffalo Creek. Campbell's rationale for selecting such a remote location stemmed from his belief that a rural location was "more favorable to health, morals, and study than a village or city location."[59]

Sensitive to the new trends of the time, Campbell attempted to be inclusive with the purpose of Bethany in order to broaden the appeal of the college to as many constituents as possible:

> Primary Schools, an Academy of Arts and Sciences for those who do not take the liberal or College course, but who desire a scientific education adapted to Agriculture, Commerce, or the Mechanical Professions, form a part of this Insitution, as well as a Normal School for the preparation of literary and scientific Teachers.[60]

The college opened in November 1841, under a board of eighteen predominantly local Disciples trustees with a charter that was careful to guard against sectarianism by prohibiting the establishment of a professorship in theology. The cost per year was $250, including board, lodging, washing, and tuition. Alexander Campbell was named president and his seventy-eight year-old father, Thomas Campbell, was elected chair of the board of trustees.

It is said that the curriculum of a college serves as a barometer by which the cultural pressures of any given era can be measured. College curriculums of the 1840's conveyed the concept of a fixed body of knowledge, rather than a concept of knowledge as a progressive field of inquiry. The accepted purpose of education in those years, as affirmed in the famed Yale report of 1828, was to expand the power of the mind and store knowledge inside it, discipline the mind through drill, memorization, and recitation, and adorn the mind with studies of classical literature and languages. Mercantile, mechanical, and agricultural skills as well as Romance languages, it was thought, should be acquired somewhere other than a college. To the ambitious, self-reliant, and democratic frontier developers in hard pursuit of economic and social independence, the old course of study seemed useless. Aristotle was of little value in their daily toil. They advocated a practical concept of knowledge and desired a plan of learning characterized by "usefulness" rather than "adornment."[61]

Campbell outlined a curriculum for Bethany under a charter that responded to the new trends as well as to traditional learning, declaring the purpose of the college to be "instruction of youth in the various branches of science and literature, the useful arts, agriculture, and the learned and foreign languages."[62] The teaching faculty and their subjects were named as follows:

Professor		Subjects
Alexander Campbell	—	Sacred Hisotry, Mental Philosophy, Political Economy, Evidences of Christianity
Andrew F. Ross	—	Ancient Languages, Ancient History
Charles Stuart	—	Mathematics
Robert Richardson	—	Physical Sciences (Chemistry, Geology, Physics, Astronomy, Zoology)
W. K. Pendleton	—	Natural Sciences (Botany, Physiology) Natural Philosophy
Vacant	—	English Literature, Grammar, Logic [63]

More than half the curriculum was devoted to the sciences, underlining Campbell's promise that sciences would form a part of the instruction for those "who desire a scientific education adapted to Agriculture, Commerce or Mechanical professions."[64] By the mid-1840's, Bethany had added Charles Louis Loos as an adjunct professor of modern languages, bringing a further modification to the older, more traditional concept of curriculum. But the most unique feature of the new college was the Department of Sacred History and Biblical Literature. True to his own philosophy, Campbell installed the Bible as the center piece of the total course of study, personally presenting daily lectures on scripture to the entire student body, all toward the supreme end of the formation of moral character in useful persons.

From its very beginning Bethany called for and received the support of the Disciples reformation congregations. When he first announced his plan for the school in 1839, Campbell was forthright in stating that "I have now laid the main principles of the [school] before the [Disciples] community. We shall first want many thousands of dollars, and next many hundreds of students."[65]

The church responded with both students and money. A majority of students came from areas where Campbell traveled and where his influence was strongest. In the first session of the college, one-fourth of the students were from states north of the Mason-Dixon line, three-fourths from south of the line. Woolery's analysis of Bethany enrollment from 1841 to 1861 reveals a student population averaging approximately one hundred persons per year, decidedly Southern, middle-class, and Disciples.

State	Number		Country	Number
Virginia	597		Canada	10
Kentucky	571		Ireland	9
Missouri	210		Mexico	4
Ohio	165		England	3
Pennsylvania	129		Germany	3
Tennesee	96		Scotland	2
Illinois	91			
Louisiana	84			
Mississippi	69			
Iowa	37			
Alabama	35			
South Carolina	29			
Georgia	25			
Texas	24			
North Carolina	21			66

Disciples congregations also responded with their dollars. Lists of individual donors to Bethany appeared throughout the pages of the *Millennial Harbinger* and the first instance of cooperative funding within the Movement on a national scale for higher education occurred in the 1850's when Campbell introduced the idea of a multi-year, $100,000 campaign to endow five chairs at the college, giving each chair the name of a state which would be responsible for raising $20,000 with the help of an "agent" assigned to that state by the college. By 1864, with the nation deep in its third year of Civil War, Campbell published a report from the July audit of the college which contained an account of the progress on the $100,000 campaign to endow the Bethany chairs begun ten years before:

Kentucky Chair	$15,580.16
Missouri Chair	11,752.16
Illinois Chair	10,227.13
Georgia (Tubman) Chair	16,541.16
Virginia Chair	10,206.60
Other Southern States	7,750.71
Total Endowment	$72,057.92
Donations to replace the destroyed college building	44,889.15
Other Donations	1,210.55
Grant Total	$118,157.62

This form of cooperative funding of a higher education mission was a major breakthrough and an important achievement in the life of the Movement. It was accomplished without any sectarian claim or control over the design and function of the college.

Bethany contributed significantly to the leadership of both the Restoration Movement and to the educational vitality of the Mississippi Valley. Among its graduates during the first thirteen years, reported Campbell, "We can enumerate some six presidents of incorporated colleges, some 30 professors in respectable colleges, besides Grammar schools supplied with efficient teachers. And better still, some seventy preachers doing good service . . ."[68] In the years just ahead it would produce among its graduates a speaker of the House of Representatives, a justice of the United States Supreme Court, a governor of New York, and a member of the United States Senate.[69] It is a legacy of leadership in public service well beyond its size as a college and common to the experience of each Disciples institution.

Kentucky Female Orphan School, chartered at Midway, Kentucky, in 1846, also survived the Civil War and continues to exist today as Midway College, presently a two-year institution. The guiding spirit behind its creation was Dr. Lewis L. Pinkerton, physician, Disciples evangelist, and educator, who saw a serious need in that day for an institution of learning to serve the orphaned, poor female—not an orphanage, but a school. Pinkerton's humanitarian proposition, four years in the making, was presented to the Reformation Movement as part of the gospel mandate to "help the poor and the orphan," and it received an enthusiastic response from Kentucky Disciples congregations as well as Alexander Campbell:

> [Kentucky Female Orphan School] seems to be as practicable as it is humane and Christian, and would seem to merit the kind of consideration of the philanthropic and wealthy portion of the Christian community.[70]

With nine trustees and fourteen students, the school opened October 3, 1849, its land ($1,100) and new building ($3,300) essentially debt free. A permanent endowment fund for the college was established immediately and within a year had exceeded $11,000. The school clearly struck a responsive chord with Disciples who enabled the institution to survive repeated fires, economic depressions, and Civil War.[71]

Walnut Grove Academy was another survivor of the 1840's. Through the creative leadership of Ben Major, active Disciples layman and strong supporter of Alexander Campbell, a school was organized along Walnut Creek in Central Illinois during the years 1848-49. Asa S. Fisher, a graduate of Bethany College, was employed as teacher to fulfill the purpose of the school, affirmed by an 1851 Illinois convention of Disciples congregations as "an institution of learning where the young people of both sexes might receive the advantages of a liberal education under the care and influence of Christian teachers, entirely free from all sectarian prejudices." The Academy was incorporated into a college by state charter February 9, 1855 and opened on the following September 10 as Eureka College with an essentially Illinois student enrollment, of 82 women and 131 men. The integrated curriculum design included sacred literature and moral philosophy, ancient languages and literature, natural and physical sciences, rhetoric and logic, and mathematics. Across the decades, graduates form this Disciples college have included twenty-seven college presidents, scores of teachers, ministers and church leaders, and a President of the United States, Ronald Reagan.[72]

Camden Point Female Seminary, founded at Camden Point (Platte County), Missouri in 1848, continues today as William Woods College, a Disciples female college of high quality in Fulton, Missouri. The original female seminary was founded by William Kincaid with support of the local Disciples pastor, A. L. Perrin. A Bethany graduate, Hugh B. Todd, described by Alexander Campbell as "accomplished and energetic . . . and favorably known to me," was named the first principal of the school, which Campbell praised as "embracing all that is literary, moral and ornamental in such institutions."[73] Campbell visited the school on December 27, 1852 and was moved to publish a strong endorsement, stating that:

> . . . in the size, neatness, and good taste of its buildings, and in its apartments, furniture, and general comfort, as well as in the beauty of its environs, [Camden Point Female Seminary] rivals in comfort and convenience similar institutions in the vicinities of New York, Philadelphia or Boston. What a contrast with the Indian wigwams on the other side of the river . . . Within this spacious building daily convene some hundred and forty young ladies, who, for personal beauty, neatness and taste, are seldom equaled . . . in any seminary east or west.[74]

Moses Lard served as the second principal (1857-1859) of the Camden Point school, which was acquired by the Christian Church of Missouri in 1870. Fire destroyed the building in 1889 and Missouri Disciples became embroiled in a dispute over the question of rebuilding, consolidating, or relocating the institution. The disagreement led to the building of two schools: one at Camden Point which survived until 1930; and a second school called the Female Orphan School of the Christian Church of Missouri located in Fulton. The Fulton school soon encountered severe financial difficulties; but at the October 16, 1900 meeting of its board of trustees, Dr. William Stone Woods contributed a gift large enough to retire the debt. The school was appropriately renamed William Woods College.[75]

DISCIPLES COLLEGES: 1850-1866

> "We are building ten where we should have built one. One great University, with a single well-endowed college in each state where we number 50,000, is sufficient. Up to this writing not the semblance of a necessity has existed among us for more than one college. Had we only one, and had that one all the money which from first to last has been spent on colleges, and the control of all the young men we are now sending to eight or ten unbuilt, half-built, and imperfectly endowed institutions, the results would be far better. With us a cherished principle is—but few institutions of learning, and these of the highest order."
>
> Lard's Quarterly
> January 1865, p. 252

The 1850's was a time rife with discussion regarding the purpose and quality of higher learning in the United States. In the opening year of the decade, a widely influential report on higher education was prepared by Francis Wayland, president of Brown University. Entitled "Report to the Corporation of Brown University on the changes in the system of Collegiate Education," it criticized the superficiality of the old college, claiming that its curriculum was too broad and that its concept of community needs was too narrow. The result, charged Wayland, was the production of graduates who were not expert in anything. "All of our colleges teach Greek and Latin," he wrote, "but where are our classical scholars?" He then added:

> The single academy at Westpoint, graduates annually a smaller number than many of our colleges, has done more towards the construction of railroads than all our one hundred twenty colleges united.[76]

Wayland proposed a program of reform that would intensify and expand the curriculum, allowing room for a range of new sciences and providing courses useful to merchants and farmers as well as the professional scholar. The report noted that the nation had 120 colleges, forty-two theological seminaries and forty-seven law schools, but:

> not a single institution designed to furnish the agriculturist, the manufacturer, the mechanic, or the profession to which his life is to be devoted . . .[77]

Wayland argued that college enrollments were declining because "we do not furnish the education desired by the people." He called for modification of the fixed four-year course of study by developing a system of electives and by adding courses in applied science, teaching, and agriculture. His plan of reform, containing the same themes as Alexander Campbell's philosophy developed more than a decade earlier, forecast the modern university system and the land grant colleges of the post-Civil War period; but in the 1850's he succeeded only in stirring controversy and was unable to modify to any significant degree the rigidity of the old system. The response of the president of the University of South Carolina was typical of majority reaction:

> While others are veering to the popular pressure . . . let it be our aim to make scholars and not sappers of miners—apothecaries—doctors or farmers.[78]

Despite delays, created by the financial panic of 1857, more colleges were founded in the United States during the 1850's than any other decade in American history. What was true of the nation was also true of Disciples, who, in that same decade, established twenty colleges and forty-six academies. Only five of the twenty colleges would survive to the present age.

EDUCATIONAL INSTITUTIONS FOUNDED BY DISCIPLES 1850-1859

Year of Founding	Name	Location
1850	*HIRAM COLLEGE	Hiram, Ohio
	McMINNIVILLE COLLEGE	McMinniville, Oregon
	Mt. Enterprise Academy	Rusk County, Texas
	Philomathic Institute	Jessamine County, Kentucky
	Prospect Hill Seminary	Mt. Sterling, Kentucky
	Sulpher Well Academy	Henry County, Tennessee
	Union Academy	Tucker's Cross Roads, Tennessee
	Woodburn Male Academy	Frankfort, Kentucky
	Woodland Seminary	Maysville, Kentucky
1851	Bedford Christian Institute	Bedford, Ohio
	*CHRISTIAN COLLEGE (COLUMBIA)	Columbia, Missouri
	EUREKA COLLEGE	Richland, Mississippi
	Irvine Grove Academy	DeKalb, Missouri
	McCLEAN COLLEGE	Hopkinsville, Kentucky
	Marion Female Seminary	Marion, Alabama
	Platte City Male Academy	Platte City, Missouri
1852	ARKANSAS COLLEGE	Fayetteville, Arkansas
	Baconian Institute	Midway, Kentucky
	FEMALE COLLEGE	Maysville, Kentucky
	McNeeley Normal School	Hopedale, Ohio
	Northeast Academy	Canton, Missouri
	Palmyra Female Seminary	Palmyra, Missouri
1853	ABINGDON COLLEGE	Abindon, Illinois
	*CHRISTIAN UNIVERSITY (CULVER-STOCKTON)	Canton, Missouri
	Somerset Collegiate Institute	Somerset, Pennsylvania
	Two Bayou Academy	• • • , Arkansas
1854	BEREAN COLLEGE	Jacksonville, Illinois
	Christian Female Institute	Covington, Kentucky
	Clay Seminary	Liberty, Missouri
	Hookerton Female Institute	Hookerton, North Carolina
	Hope Institute	Nashville, Tennessee
	Hopkinsville Female Academy	Hopkinsville, Kentucky
	*NORTHWESTERN CHRISTIAN UNIVERSITY (BUTLER)	Indianapolis, Indiana
1855	Bellville Academy	Bellville, Indiana
	Bethel Institute	Bethel, Oregon
	CHRISTIAN COLLEGE	Monmouth, Oregon
	DeSoto Institute	Canton, Missouri
	*EUREKA COLLEGE	Eureka, Illinois
	Paris Female Seminary	Paris, Missouri
	Pleasant Hill Academy	Lane County, Oregon
	St. Joseph Female Academy	St. Joseph, Missouri
	Savannah Collegiate Institute	Savannah, Missouri

*Functioning and related to the Christian Church (Disciples of Christ) in 1986.

1856	Baton Rouge Academy	Baton Rouge, Louisiana
	DAUGHTER'S COLLEGE	Harrodsburg, Kentucky
	HIGHLAND HOME COLLEGE	Highland Home, Kentucky
	KENTUCKY FEMALE COLLEGE	Shelbyville, Kentucky
	Lawrence High School	Bedford, Indiana
	Madison Institute for Young Ladies	Richmond, Kentucky
	Major Seminary	Bloomington, Illinois
	Salem Seminary	Salem, Iowa
	Walkerton Male & Female Academy	Walkerton, North Carolina
1857	Christian Academy	Hustonville, Kentucky
	EMINENCE COLLEGE	Eminence, Kentucky
	Gaylord Institute	Platte City, Missouri
	Hugart School	Wilson, North Carolina
	Muse Academy	McKinney, Texas
	Summerville Institute	Chalson, Mississippi
1858	Audrain Christian Seminary	Mexico, Missouri
	Richmond Female Institute	Richmond, Kentucky
1859	Bloomington Female Academy	Bloomington, Illinois
	CARLTON COLLEGE	Springfield, Missouri
	CHRISTIAN COLLEGE	Burkesville, Kentucky
	Fayetteville Female Academy	Little Rock, Arkansas
	LAWRENCE UNIVERSITY	Lawrence, Kansas
	Rock Spring Academy	• • • , Missouri
	Woodford Female College	Versailles, Kentucky

Compiled from State histories and from the 1964 Claude Spencer list.

Disciples in Ohio, influenced by the success of Bethany College, the unprecedented growth of their movement in the Western Reserve, the long distance to Bethany located on the slavery side of the Ohio River, and a disenchantment with Alexander Campbell over the issue of slavery, were drawn to the idea of founding their own educational institution. On June 12, 1849, a group of Ohio Disciples, mostly farmers, and led by the guiding hand of Amos Sutton Hayden, met near Russell, Ohio where the idea of founding a school was formally congealed. By October it was decided to "establish a school of high grade, but not to clothe it at first with collegiate powers."[79]

Seven towns competed for the new school. Delegates from thirty-one Disciples congregations, meeting in a stormy session at Aurora in November, decided the issue on the thirteenth ballot when Hiram was selected over Russell by a vote of seventeen to ten. Hiram, a small rural village, strung along a country crossroad, was chosen because of its seclusion from large cities and because of its offer of $4,000 cash to help build the school. The following month a board of twelve incorporators adopted the name Western Reserve Eclectic Institute and employed a stonemason to begin construction of $7,500 building in a cornfield on the fifty-six acre farm near Hiram purchased by the board for $1,800.[80]

"Old Eclectic" was guided by the Bethany model. Approved by the Ohio legislature on March 1, 1850, the charter promoted the purpose of the school as "Instruction of youth of both sexes in the various branches of literature and science, especially of moral science, as based on the facts and precepts of the holy scriptures."[81] The curriculum also contained practical utility to attract enterprising interests on the Northeast frontier. When the school opened in November of 1850, it proclaimed that the course of instruction was "designed to embrace whatever is adapted to the developing and training of those under its care for the useful and practical duties of life."[82] While they were pledged to guard against any trace of sectarian character, the Bible was declared the moral basis of the Institute and A. S. Hayden, distinguished Disciples preacher, was named the first principal and assigned the responsibility of presenting daily lectures on sacred history.[83]

Enrollment, predominantly Disciples, totaled 313 from seven states in the 1850-51 term. Students numbered in excess of five hundred in the 1852-53 term, nearly 90 percent of whom were from Ohio and almost no one from Southern states:

WESTERN ECLECTIC INSTITUTE ENROLLMENT: 1852-53

State	Number		Country	Number
Ohio	458		Canada	22
Pennsylvania	19		England	1
New York	10			
Michigan	6			
Illinois	3			
Indiana	3			
Vermont	3			
Wisconsin	1			
Virginia	1			
Maryland	1			
Georgia	1			

[84]

Like students at most church-related colleges, the graduates of "Old Eclectic", (which became Hiram College in 1867), tended toward service professions as attested by alumni occupation records:

OCCUPATIONS OF ALUMNI

	1868-1888	1889-1902
Ministers	10	136
Teachers	30	90
Lawyers	23	28
Businessmen	18	45
Doctors	4	29
Journalists	2	2
Miscellaneous	20	45
	107	375

[85]

The school's most famous graduate was James A. Garfield, later president of the school, a Civil War general, United States congressman and senator, and President of the United States.

A curious footnote on a piece of correspondence dated 1839 gave birth to another Disciples college. The place of issue was Columbia, Missouri, a frontier village of five hundred persons in Boone County. Written to a friend in Kentucky, the intriguing "p.s." contained an element of vision that would ultimately lead to the 1851 founding of what we know today as Columbia College, the first college for women chartered by a state west of the Mississippi River:

> Do you know of any good person well qualified to take charge of a female school—if so, I wish he would come to Columbia . . . a Competent person of the right grit.[86]

The author of the letter was Thomas Miller Allen, one of a talented trio of Disciples destined to be the founding fathers of the school. Allen was a graduate of Transylvania University and a personal friend of both Alexander Campbell and Barton W. Stone, to whom his allegiance was so strong that he gave up a lucrative Kentucky law practice to travel west in 1836 as a minister for the reformation. Allen was equally prominent as a churchman and as a community builder—serving variously as president of the Board of Curators which founded the University of Missouri, trustee of six other schools, member of the State Railroad Commission and the county fair board. He possessed all the necessary attributes for establishing a female college— organizational experience, leadership, wealth, political influence, and two daughters.

The second member of the triumvirate was David Pat Henderson, also a personal friend of both Campbell and Stone, and who also gave up a Kentucky law practice to become co-editor of the *Christian Messenger* with Barton W. Stone in Jacksonville, Illinois.

The third member of the founding trio was the dynamic and impetuous Disciples educator, the Reverend James Shannon. In 1849 the president of the University of Missouri resigned; and in September, Shannon, then in his tenth year as president of Bacon College, was named president of the University of Missouri. Shannon was a graduate of the University of Belfast and had come to America to head the Presbyterian Sunbury Academy. In 1830 he became professor of languages at the University of Georgia, and while there, helped the Baptists found Mercer College, a co-educational institution. He was appointed president of Louisiana State University in 1836. Three years later he became a Disciple when he assumed the presidency of Bacon College in Georgetown, Kentucky.

In 1849 these three aggressive leaders converged their energies in an effort to found a female college. Shortly after his arrival in Missouri in the fall of

1849, Shannon invited two of his former Bacon colleagues, Samuel Hatch and Henry White, to Columbia to assist in formulating a college plan. On Christmas Day, 1850, Allen, Shannon, and Henderson met at Allen's home with a young scholar from Kentucky, John Augustus Williams. Together, the four of them developed a charter for the new institution to be named Christian Female College, with John A. Williams as president. The college was officially chartered by the Missouri Legislature on January 18, 1851. Five of its first six graduates became teachers.[87]

The first charter ever granted by the state of Arkansas to a degree granting institution was issued to Arkansas College, December 14, 1852. Founded by a prominent Arkansas Disciple, Robert Graham, the school carefully emulated the concept of Bethany College following its charter and bylaws, its student rules, its use of the Bible as a textbook, its disallowance of a theological professorship, and even its fourth of July commencement date. Located in Fayetteville, the college received its student population from Arkansas, Missouri, Louisiana, Tennessee, and Indian Territory, and provided them with a curriculum composed of biblical and moral studies, natural science and rhetoric. Like other Disciples schools, Arkansas College produced significant numbers of public servants, primarily teachers, ministers, and lawyers. The coming of Civil War forced the school to close in 1861. It was subsequently occupied by a confederate regiment and burned in 1862.[88]

Two co-educational colleges were opened by Illinois Disciples in the fall of 1854. Abingdon College was established by Patrick H. Murphy and John C. Reynolds, graduates of Bethany and admirers of Campbell. Across its first six years the institution enrolled 1,087 students, 600 males and 487 females. Among its graduates were many church and college leaders including J. H. Garrison and Josephus Hopwood. Discord surrounding its president, J. W. Butler, ultimately caused the school to merge with Eureka College in 1884.[89] Berean College, organized by Jonathan Atkinson in 1854, experienced a similar fate. Chartered to "inculcate the Christian faith and morality of Sacred scripture and for the promotion of arts and sciences," Berean college, like so many others, carboned the model of Bethany. A theological controversy involving President Walter Scott Russell, also a Bethany graduate, led to the closing of the school in 1861.[90]

Another Bethany graduate, Justus M. Barnes, organized a school at Strata, Alabama in the fall of 1856 that would become known as Highland Home College. Patterned after Bethany, Highland Home survived until 1916.[91]

Disciples were equally active in the Far West. W. T. Newby donated fifteen acres of land to found McMinnville College at McMinnville, Oregon, in 1850; but the institution was bankrupt by 1857. It was deeded to the Baptists who converted it to Linfield College. In 1856 Christian University was established at Monmouth, Oregon, and continued to function until 1892, when the trustees were no longer able to finance the operation and it was deeded to the state of Oregon.[92]

Disciples enthusiasm for establishing colleges often outstripped their resources to sustain or their ability to manage. The result was graphically described by Winfred E. Garrison:

> Soon the prairies were scattered with the bones of dead colleges whose very names have been forgotten. It is not suprising that the Disciples of that period little realized what it took to make a college, in money, scholarship, and consitituency. Academic standards were low, secondary schools were almost nonexistent, and teachers were cheap. But education was a magic word, and great sacrifices were made that the church might have its colleges, of whatever grade. The value of their service was incalculable, and even some that could not long survive left a heritage of substantial accomplishment.[93]

Some of the colleges, however, merged their assets and identities with sister schools, which, in effect, preserved their life through the incorporation with other institutions. J. N. Pendegast, minister of the Disciples congregation in Woodland, California, emboldened by the public endorsement of local Disciples, the donation of ten acres of land, and a pledge of $5,000 cash, successfully organized Hesperian College in 1860. Classes began in March 1861, the same month Abraham Lincoln was inaugurated President of the United States. The school functioned for thirty-five years, discontinuing operation in 1897 when its assets were consolidated into Berkley Bible Seminary. When the seminary closed in 1919, the assets were transferred a second time to the newly established California Christian College in southern California. California Christian College soon reidentified itself as Chapman College, the name of its 1919 founding benefactor, and today traces its lineage through Disciples endowment gifts all the way back to Hesperian College.[94]

By the early 1850's some higher education institutions were being created by official action of "cooperations" and state-wide structures within the Disciples reformation movement. Christian University, known today as Culver-Stockton College in Canton, Missouri, was the first college chartered as a co-educational institution west of the Mississippi. Representatives from a cluster of Disciples congregations in Lewis County, Missouri, meeting in Monticello, August 15, 1852, resolved to found an "institution of learning for both male and female . . . to meet the demands and interest of this growing country."[95] They pledged $50,000 toward the construction of a building in Canton and issued an appeal to the citizens of Missouri, Iowa, and Illinois for their cooperation and support. To insure the endorsement of Alexander Campbell, it was further resolved by the Disciples congregation in Canton to unite with other Missouri Disciples in raising $15,000 pledged to Bethany College for the "Missouri Chair." Chartered January 15, 1853, the college commenced operation in September 1855. Principal organizer and promoter of the institution was D. Pat Henderson who had given similar leadership to the establishment of Christian College in Columbia. The curriculum was standard Campellian fare containing natural philosophy and mathematics with the later additions of mental and moral philosophy and ancient languages and literature. James Shannon left the University of Missouri in 1857 to become the first president of Christian University in Canton. Although the college closed briefly during the Civil War, it reopened its doors following the war and continues operations today in relationship with the Disciples. Christian University alumni included legions of ministers and teachers along with sizeable numbers of lawyers, politicians, and corporate executives.[96]

The founding of Northwestern Christian University, chartered January 15, 1850 and opened November 1, 1855, originated by action of the Indiana State Convention of Disciples and sparked a controversy which reflected social and political tensions within the Disciples Movement and within the nation at large. The Little Flat Rock State Convention of Disciples in 1848, noting that Baptists, Presbyterians, and Methodists each had founded a college in Indiana, formally resolved that "it is the duty of the Christian brotherhood in Indiana to proceed to found and endow a college in this state."[97] One year later, the Disciples state convention in Indianapolis adopted a resolution of historic importance, stating that:

A North Western Christian University is founded at Indianapolis as soon as a sufficient amount of funds can be raised to commence it, and that a Committee of seven be appointed by this meeting to take preliminary steps in reference to the founding and endowment of such an institution.[98]

Ovid Butler, influential Indianapolis attorney and prominent Disciples layman of financial means, was named chair of the committee. He became the primary author of the eighteen section charter which articulated the purpose of the University as:

an institution of learning of the highest class for the education of the youth of all parts of the United States, and especially of the States of the Northwest; to establish in said institution departments of liberal and professional education; to educate and prepare suitable teachers for the Christian faith and Christian morality as taught in the sacred Scriptures . . .[99]

The school was to be located near the edge of Indianapolis and it was agreed that $75,000 had to be raised in pledges to purchase the land, construct, and endow the institution before it could open. John O'Kane, a popular Indiana minister, was employed to raise the money.

Butler then wrote to Alexander Campbell, in language that rankled, informing him of the recently secured charter:

The brotherhood of the north-west constitute, as we think, nearly one-half of the whole Christian communion; and yet, Bro. Campbell, there are some, and indeed many of us, who cannot avoid the conviction, that, in religion as in politics, the south claims and receives the principal attention of our leading brethren . . . We know that with you, Bethany College is an object of paramount importance . . . . Influenced, it may be, by its local position . . . you have relied upon the south for its principal support. We think, however, that the north-western brethren are as liberal and enterprising as any other, and that they will . . . favor an institution to be built up amongst them, and sustained by them.[100]

Offended by Butler's letter, Campbell responded with equal directness:

Literature, science and religion are neither northern or southern; neither south-western nor northwestern. . . . I, therefore, cannot see either the wisdom or the utility of giving learning, morality or christianity, either a sectional, political, longitudinal, latitudinal or geographical designation. . . . I, therefore, on this account, regret the indication of such a spirit or policy on the part of our brethren in Indiana. . . . Where is the *South-Western* Christian College or University, that calls forth this geographical and political rival? . . . One good institution, well organized, well furnished with an able cohort of teachers, well patronized by the brethren and the public, is better than ten such as we are likely to have got up and spirited into life by such arguments and efforts, that tend much more to schism, rivalry, and false ambition, than to union, harmony, and successful action. I hope the brethren will hasten leisurely, and hear all the premises and arguments before they act in such a way as to create half-a-dozen of ill-begotten, misshapen, club-footed, imbecile schools, under the name and title of Colleges and Universities.[101]

Within five months Campbell commenced a tour through Indiana, launching a financial campaign to fund the "Indiana Chair" of Ancient Languages at Bethany College. On November 19, 1850, he was invited to Butler's home where he met with Butler and several members of the Northwestern board. It was agreed that John O'Kane would promote both causes — the "Bethany Chair" and Northwestern Christian University—in his fund raising effort with Indiana Disciples. Three years later Campbell bitterly reported in the January 1854 issue of *The Millennial Harbinger* that:

I was indeed sorry to learn from several places in [Illinois] that [John O'Kane] made a new issue, one hitherto unknown amongst us as a Christian people. It was, in brief, that 'Christians living on *free* soil, should not co-operate with Christians living on *slave* soil, in any seminary of learning. That in other words, *political*, rather than *Christian* considerations, should rule and measure Christian co-operation in all seminaries of learning.[102]

The university board responded ambiguously that "this" board did not promise that John O'Kane would promote both the "Indiana Chair" at Bethany and Northwestern Christian University. They also denied that O'Kane had made his presentation on the political merits of slavery but that he simply urged "that its location was in a free state, and that students attending it would not be brought into contact with habits and manners that exist in populations where slavery exists."[103] Unsatisfied with this explanation, Campbell lashed back and the controversy continued throughout the following year, then subsided, but lingered on into the Civil War. There was clear evidence that the 1850 promise to Campbell had indeed been made; with equal clarity, Indiana Disciples did not provide funding for an "Indiana Chair" at Bethany College.

Although it was a small incident, this minor controversy was reflective of larger forces at work within the Movement and the country. As Campbell's reformation grew in number and geography, it encompassed the rivalry of three sections—Northeast, Northwest (linked by the Erie Canal to become one), and South—and their attempts to deal with the great domestic questions of the day. The earlier spirit of nationalism had faded and sectional interests became matters of higher priority than national interests. The North thought of the South as backward, semi-civilized, frozen in the past, and out of harmony with the times; while viewing itself as progressive, cosmopolitan, open to change, and future oriented. The South viewed the North as crude, course, radical, materialistic, a place of hypocritical, and convenient morals, while seeing itself as a place a agrarian virtues, graceful existence, and respect for great traditions. The industrial-capitalistic North and the agricultural-chattle slave-owning South were propelled by dramatically different economic systems, different labor systems, and different social values. A practical-public educational system designed for utility was preferred by the North; while a classical-private education designed for adornment was preferred by the South.

Sensing the affects of sectional rivalry within the Movement, Campbell had earlier addressed the issues of slavery in a series of articles in *The Millennial Harbinger* during 1845.[104] Campbell asserted that he was personally opposed to slavery, but also believed it should be upheld as long as it was the law of the land. The series on slavery created a breach between Campbell and many Northern Disciples who, in retaliation, cut back on their support of Bethany College and joined in supporting the 1849 founding of Western Reserve Eclectic Institute in Hiram, Ohio. The breach was widened when Congress passed the Compromise of 1850 with its infamous Fugitive Slave Law, helping Southern slave owners recapture runaways and deterring Northern sympathizers from aiding and abetting. Campbell supported the measure:

> Some christians are conscientious about giving up a servant to his master. So was not Paul, when he sent the runaway Onesimus home to his master? So was not an angel of God, when he commanded the runaway Hagar to 'go home to her mistress.' . . . allegiance . . . to the laws of the United States, is, by general concession, both political and moral. . . . The law in question, for reclaiming

fugitive servants, is, to any ordinary mind, most obviously and perfectly constitutional, and is so declared by the most learned and able judges.[105]

The seeds of sectional fission spread across the Disciples reformation during the 1840's and 1850's and contributed in a disruptive way to the founding of a few Disciples colleges out of sheer sectional preference, of which Northwestern Christian University was one.

Northwestern Christian University opened on November 1, 1855, announcing six schools of learning: English, mathematics, classics, natural science, intellectual science, and law. It was chartered as a co-educational school and offered the degrees of "Mistress" of Science and "Mistress" of Arts to compliment its "Bachelor" of Science and "Bachelor" of Arts degrees. Horace Mann, then president of Antioch College and greatly admired by Campbell, was offered the presidency of Northwestern. He delivered the 1855 opening address at the university and thoughtfully considered the offer, but ultimately declined. Allen Benton, one of the principle founders, became first president and served until he left in 1866 to help found the University of Nebraska. In 1877 the institution was renamed Butler University, continuing its long relationship with Disciples until 1978, when it requested complete disaffiliation.

During the pre-Civil War years, Disciples founded thirty-three colleges: eight in Kentucky; four each in Tennessee and Illinois; three in Missouri; two each in Mississippi, Oregon, Iowa, and Ohio; and one each in Virginia, Indiana, Arkansas, Alabama, Kansas, and California. Seventeen of these Disciples colleges were founded in Southern states, seven in the old Northwest, and the remainder in the Mid and Far West. Ten of these institutions have survived into our own time and continue in relationship with the Disciples.

Riding the antebellum tide of rural democracy and westward expansion, Disciples enjoyed substantial growth in numbers and structure during the years between 1840 and 1866. Disciples historians call it the "Age of Cooperative Evangelism." Despite being an ill-regarded sect by European denominations, Disciples developed an effective entourage of district "cooperations" for the purpose of evangelizing the rural frontier population into membership, and the Movement increased from 45,000 in 1840 to more than 200,000 in 1860. Across these two decades the cooperative character of the reformation Movement was formed as district "cooperations" began to consolidate into state-wide organizations and ultimately convene in the first national convention of the church in 1849 at Cincinnati, Ohio. This new cooperative thrust was further seaonsed through the united efforts of congregations to establish and sustain colleges as part of a broader mission to society as well as to enhance the Restoration Movement. It was often in a meeting of a remote "district cooperation" that the idea for founding a college

EDUCATIONAL INSTITUTIONS FOUNDED BY DISCIPLES 1860-1866

Year of Founding	Name	Location
1860	ASHLAND COLLEGE	Ashland, Wapello, Iowa
	*HESPERIAN COLLEGE (CHAPMAN)	Woodward, California
	Kinston Female Academy	Kinston, North Carolina
	Madisonville Female Academy	Madisonville, Kentucky
	Mt. Sterling Seminary	Mt. Sterling, Kentucky
	Piedmont Female Academy	Stoney Point, Virginia
	Senatobia Female Institute	DeKalb County, Mississippi
	T. M. LAWRENCE COLLEGE	Alexandria, Tennessee
1861	Paducah Collegiate Institute	Paducah, Kentucky
	OSKALOOSA COLLEGE	Oskoloosa, Iowa
1864	Bethany Collegiate Institute	Bethany, Missouri
1864	Neotrophian Institute	Poestenkill, New York
1865	FRANKLIN COLLEGE	Wilmington, Ohio
	Oakland School	Greenville, Tennessee
1866	Philomath Academy	Jackson County, Tennessee
	SOUTHERN ILLINOIS CHRISTIAN COLLEGE	Carbondale, Illinois

*Functioning and related to the Christian Church (Disciples of Christ) in 1986.
Compiled from State histories and from the 1964 Claude Spencer list.

to serve a growing membership was presented by some enterprising church leader in an appeal for endorsement or support.

The colleges claimed the Movement, and the Movement claimed the colleges. Overwhelmingly, the colleges were founded by influential personalities within the Disciples Movement and only occasionally by ecclesiastical action. Each institution claimed to be non-sectarian, yet all devised charters requiring one-half to two-thirds of their trustees to be members of a Disciples congregation. The bulk of their financial support came from Disciples congregations or individual members with means; and Alexander Campbell's educational philosophy was nearly always the single most important factor shaping the curriculum, character, and purpose of each new institution.

With 100 to 200 students and four to eight faculty members, those colleges were designed to build moral character and to offer a curriculum flavored with the new sciences in order to serve the popular demands of the community as well as preserve the classical traditions of learning. A full decade and more before the fateful year of 1848, when Lucretia Mott and Elizabeth Stanton convened the Seneca gathering that produced the Declaration of Rights for Women and the New York Consitutional Convention voted equal property rights into law, Disciples colleges pioneered in women's education. With few exceptions, these colleges were either female or co-educational. Although the institutional mortality rate was two out of three, the quality and quantity of leadership sent out by these Disciples schools was disproportionate to their small size. The Civil War proved devastating to these schools, siphoning away human and material resources for war and acting as a socio-cultural catalyst to close out the golden era of the traditional college.

Between 1840 and 1866 Disciples colleges appeared on the average of one per year, essentially in response to the need of the Movement to be representative of the economic and social aspirations of its people. The effort produced a solid legacy which Campbell was quick to acknowledge. Yet he perceived a fundamental weakness in the Movement's inability to render comprehensive counsel on the number, location, and support of these institutions:

> I congratulate the whole brotherhood, therefore, that they everywhere harmonize in their views of [education's] importance, and give evidence of their appreciation of it, in the founding of schools of all sorts and for all classes; and that for their age and means, many of them display a becoming liberality. Still . . . we have yet to learn something that we have not learned either by observation or experience . . . there is not State cooperation, no general concentration of mind, of counsel, or of effort, as yet exhibited in these great and most important undertakings.[106]

References

1. Robert Richardson, *Memoirs of Alexander Campbell*. Standard Publishing Company, 1890, Vol. I, pp. 491-496.
   D. Duane Cummins, "From Buffalo to Claremont." *Impact* No. 11. (1983), pp. 5-13.
2. *Ibid.*
3. *Ibid.*
4. *The Christian Baptist.*, Vol. I, No. 5. (December 23, 1823), p. 98.
5. Robert Lynn, "Why the Seminary?" Unpublished manuscript, 1980, p. 20.
6. Ronald E. Osborn, *The Faith We Affirm*. Bethany Press, 1979, p. 18.
7. A. L. Fortune, *The Disciples in Kentucky*. Christian Churches in Kentucky, 1932, p. 57.
   Barton W. Stone, "Autobiography," *Voices from Cane Ridge*. Bethany Press, 1954, p. 57.
   Charles C. Ware, *Barton Warren Stone*. Bethany Press, 1932, pp. 204-205.
8. Dwight E. Stevenson, *Walter Scott: Voice of the Golden Oracle*. Christian Board Publication, 1946, pp. 25-26, 203.
9. Lester G. McAllister, *Thomas Campbell: Man of the Book*. Bethany Press, 1954, pp. 174-175, 181.
10. Claude E. Spencer, Unpublished list compiled in 1964. Disciples Historical Society.
    Alonzo W. Fortune, *The Disciples in Kentucky*. Christian Churches in Kentucky, 1932, pp. 177-185.
    Henry K. Shaw, *Hoosier Disciples*. Christian Churches in Indiana, 1966, pp. 108-111.
    Henry K. Shaw, *Buckeye Disciples*. Christian Board of Publication, 1952, p. 69.
11. Shaw., *Hoosier Disciples.*, p. 109, 169.

12. Article in the *Protestant Unionist*, cited in Alonzo W. Fortune, *The Disciples in Kentucky*. 1932, p. 181.
13. *Millennial Harbinger*, Volume IV, Number IV. (April 1833), p. 189.
14. *Ibid.*, p. 190.
15. *Millennial Harbinger*, Volume IV, Number V. (May 1833), p. 240.
16. *Millennial Harbinger*, Volume V, Number X. (August 1834), p. 384.
17. *Millennial Harbinger*, Volume VII, Number V. (May 1836), p. 198.
18. *Ibid.*, p. 200.
19. *Ibid.*, p. 202.
20. *Ibid.*, p. 377.
21. *Millennial Harbinger*, Vol. VII, No. 4 (March 1850), p. 123.
22. Walter Rush, *The Mind of America 1820-1860*. Columbia University Press, 1975, p. 280.
23. *Millennial Harbinger*, Vol. III, No. 8 (August 1853), p. 439.
24. Perry E. Gresham, *Campbell and the Colleges*. Disciples of Christ Historical Society, 1973, pp. 21-29.
25. *Millennial Harbinger*, Vol. III, No. 8 (August 1832), p. 408-409.
26. *Ibid.*
27. *Millennial Harbinger*, Vol. I, No. 6 (June 1830), p. 252.
28. *Millennial Harbinger*, Vol. XII, No. 9 (December 1836), p. 583.
    Gresham, p. 30.
29. *Millennial Harbinger*, Vol. V, No. 3 (March 1862), p. 112.
30. *Millennial Harbinger*, Vol. VII, No. 9 (December 1836), pp. 580-604.
31. *Ibid.*, p. 602.
32. *Millennial Harbinger*, Vol. IV, No. 4 (April 1840), p. 157.
33. *Millennial Harbinger*, Vol. VII, No. 3 (March 1850), p. 174.
34. *Millennial Harbinger*, Vol. VI, No. 9 (November 1856), p. 649.
35. *Millennial Harbinger*, Vol. V, No. 1 (January 1855), p. 9.
36. *Millennial Harbinger*, Vol. II, No. 1 (January 1845), p. 26.
37. *Millennial Harbinger*, Vol. VII, No. 1 (July 1837), p. 327.
38. *Millennial Harbinger*, Vol. III, No. 7 (July 1860), p. 369.
39. *Millennial Harbinger*, Vol. V, No. 1 (January 1855), p. 10.
40. *Christian Baptist*, Vol. I, No. 5 (December 1823), p. 31.
41. *Millennial Harbinger*, Vol. III, No. 5 (December 1823), p. 31.
42. *Millennial Harbinger*, Appeared in multiple issues. (1842,1855,1859,1860,etc.)
43. *Millennial Harbinger*, Vol. VII, No. 10 (October 1832) p. 447.
44. *Millennial Harbinger*, Vol. VII, No. 9 (December 1836) p. 581.
45. *Millennial Harbinger*, Vol. VII, No. 10 (October 1843) p. 446.
46. *Millennial Harbinger*, Vol. VI, No. 1 (June 1837) p. 257.
47. *Millennial Harbinger*, Vol. VI, No. 1 (June 1837) p. 259.
48. *Millennial Harbinger*, Vol. III, No. 7 (July 1860) p. 391.
49. *Millennial Harbinger*, Vol. VI, No. 9 (November 1856) p. 637.
50. *Millennial Harbinger*, Vol. IV, No. 10 (October 1854) p. 589.
51. William T. Moore, *A Comprehensive History of the Disciples of Christ*. Revell Company, 1909, p. 682.
52. Richard Hofstadter, and D.D. Hardy, *The Development and Scope of Higher Education in the United States*. Columbia University Press, 1952, p. 29.
53. Herman Norton, *Tennessee Christians*. Reed and Co., 1971, pp. 70-73.
54. Norton, pp 68-70.
    Millennial Harbinger, Vol. II, No. 9 (September 1845), p. 420.
    Millennial Harbinger, Vol. III, No. 7 (July 1846), pp. 386-387.
55. Compiled from State histories and from the 1964 Claude Spencer list.
56. *Millennial Harbinger*, Vol. II, No. 10 (October 1839), p. 446.
57. W. K. Woolery, *Bethany years*. Standard Printing Co., 1941, p. 29.
    Wilbur Cramblet, *The Christian Church (Disciples of Christ) in West Virginia*, Bethany Press, 1971, pp. 58-63.
58. *Millennial Harbinger*, Ibid.
59. *Millennial Harbinger*, Vol. V, No. 8 (August 1841), p. 378.

60. *Ibid.*
61. Hofstadter, pp. 10-19.
    Frederick Rudolph, *The American College and University.* Alfred Knopf, 1962, pp. 222-238.
62. *Millennial Harbinger*, Vol. IV, No. 4 (April 1840), p. 176.
63. *Millennial Harbinger*, Vol. V, No. 8 (August 1841), p. 377.
64. *Ibid.*, p. 378.
65. *Millennial Harbinger*, Vol. III, No. 10 (October 1839), p. 451.
66. Woolery, pp. 68-69.
67. *Millennial Harbinger*, Vol. VII, No. 9 (September 1864), p. 411.
68. *Millennial Harbinger*, Vol. I, No. 4 (April 1858), p. 219.
69. Woolery, p. 104.
70. *Millennial Harbinger*, Vol. III, No. 7 (July 1846), p. 419.
71. Harry Giovannoli, *Kentucky Female Orphan School.* 1930, pp. 11-65.
    A.W. Fortune, pp. 232-234.
72. Harold Adams, *History of Eureka College.* M & D Printing Co., 1982, pp. 9-52.
    Nathaniel Haynes, *History of the Disciples of Christ in Illinois.* Standard Publishing Company, 1915, pp. 34-57.
73. *Millennial Harbinger*, Vol. II, No. 9 (September 1852), p. 532.
74. *Millennial Harbinger*, Vol. III, No. 2 (February 1853), p. 72.
75. Griffith A. Hamlin, *In Faith and History: William Woods College.* Bethany Press, 1965, pp. 31-81.
76. Hofstadter, *Ibid.*, pp. 24-25.
77. *Ibid.*, p. 26.
78. Rudolph, *Ibid.*, pp. 238-240.
    Hofstadter, *Ibid.*, 24-26.
79. F.M. Green, *History of Hiram College.* Hubble Printing, 1901, p. 8.
80. *Millennial Harbinger*, Vol. VII, No. 8 (August 1850), p. 476.
81. *Green, Ibid.*, pp. 14-16.
82. *Ibid.*, pp. 52.
83. Henry Shaw, *Buckeye Disciples.* Christian Board of Publication, 1952, pp. 206-208.
    Amos S. Hayden, *Early History of the Disciples in Western Reserve.* Chase and Hall, 1875, pp. 260-266.
84. *Ibid.*, p. 51.
    Mary B. Treudley, *The First Hundred Years of Hiram College.*
85. *Ibid.*, p. 136.
86. Allean L. Hale, *Petticoat Pioneer.* 1956, p. 3; quote from letter of T. M. Allen to John Allen Gano, June 25, 1839.
87. *Ibid.*, pp. 18-33.
88. Lester G. McAllister, *Arkansas Disciples.* Christian Church (Disciples of Christ), in Arkansas 1984, pp. 29-39.
89. Nathaniel S. Haynes, *History of the Disciples of Christ in Illinois.* Standard Publishing Company, 1915, pp. 58-60.
90. *Ibid.*, pp. 60-62.
91. George and Mildred Watson, *History of the Christian Churches in the Alabama Area*, Bethany Press, 1965, p. 114.
92. C. F. Swander, *Making Disciples in Oregon.* Oregon Christian Missionary Society, 1928, pp. 140-143.
93. Windred E. Garrison, *Religion Follows the Frontier: A History of the Disciples of Christ.* Harper and Brothers, 1931, p. 218. Winfred E. Garrison, and Alfred T. DeGroot, *The Disciples of Christ: A History.* Bethany Press, 1948, p. 253.
94. E. B. Ware, *History of Disciples of Christ in California.* 1916, pp. 161-162.
    Clifford A. Cole, *The Christian Churches of California.* Christian Board of Publication, 1959, pp. 67, 74-82.
95. George L. Peters, *Dreams Come True: The Story of Culver-Stockton College.* Bethany Press, 1941, pp. 23-24.
    George L. Peters, *Disciples of Christ in Missouri.* Bethany Press, 1937, pp. 119-123.

96. Peters, *Culver-Stockton*, pp. 126-127.
97. Lee Burns, "The Beginnings of Butler College." *Butler Alumnal Quarterly*, Vol. XV, No. 1 (April 1926), pp. 3-4.
98. Henry D. Shaw, "The Founding of Butler University." *Indiana Magazine*, Vol. LVIII, No. 3 (September 1962), p. 243.
99. Copy of Charter in possession of the Author.
100. *Millennial Harbinger*, Vol. VII, No. 6 (June 1850), p. 330.
101. *Ibid.*, pp. 331-335.
102. *Millennial Harbinger*, Vol. IV, No. 1 (January 1854), p. 42.
103. *Millennial Harbinger*, Vol. IV, No. 8 (August 1854), pp. 465-466.
104. *Millennial Harbinger*, 1845: February, pp. 49-53; March, pp. 145-149; May, pp. 193-196; June, pp. 257-264; July, pp. 306-307; August, pp. 355-358.
105. *Millennial Harbinger*, Vol. I, No. 1 (January 1851), pp. 29-30.
106. *Millennial Harbinger*, Vol. V, No. 9 (September 1855), pp. 578-579.

Bethany College: early 1840's

Bethany College: 1875

Culver-Stockton College: late 1850's

Atlantic Christian College: early 1900's

William Woods College: 1877

Hiram College: early 1850's

Arkansas College: early 1850's

Columbia College: early 1850's

Chapter **3**

DISCIPLES COLLEGES IN THE LATE NINETEENTH AND EARLY TWENTIETH CENTURIES

CHURCH AND SOCIETY DURING THE YEARS OF RECONSTRUCTION

> He is a poor observer of men and things who does not see slowly growing up among us a class of men who can no longer be satisfied with the ancient gospel and the ancient order of things. These men must have changes; and silently they are preparing the mind of the brotherhood to receive changes.
>
> *Lard's Quarterly*
> April 1865

The founders of the Disciples reformation movement were in their graves. Barton Stone died in 1844; Thomas Campbell in 1854; Walter Scott in 1861; and Alexander Campbell in 1866. Still under the rule of its two-fold plea to restore the Ancient Order and to build Christian unity, the Movement entered upon a new forty-year journey marked by dramatic numerical growth, budding denominational consciousness, and deepening internal division of thought.

A choice between options inevitably confronts the second generation of all reforms. The Disciples Movement had to decide if it should crystallize the views of the founders and hold fast to traditions of the old order, or if it should be more flexible and adapt itself to perform ministry in the newly emerging socio-cultural-economic environment of post-Civil War America. Choosing between these two options was compounded by the lingering bitterness of Civil War and the profound paradox of the two-fold plea. The leaders, lacking the personal force of the founders, were not able to consolidate the membership. Part of the Movement veered one direction, part of it went the other way; and they were never reconciled.[1]

Skirmishes within the Disciples restoration were focused on such lesser issues as whether the New Testament forbade or permitted the use of instrumental music in worship, the bureaucratic organization of missionary societies beyond the congregation, or the development of a professional ministry with title and authority. Surface conflicts of this type lasted forty years, but it was the deeper rupture over the Movement's essential purpose, direction, and identity that ultimately severed the relationship between two diverging elements of the Disciples reformation. The *Churches of Christ*, concentrated in the former Confederate states, adhered more rigidly to the guidelines of the founders in their quest to "Restore the Ancient Order." The *Disciples of Christ* (concentrated in the old Northwest, the border states, and the Midwest) were more flexible in their interpretation of the founders' intent, more adaptive to the new age unfolding in the late nineteenth century, and more attuned to that part of The Plea calling for Christian unity.[2]

Between the Civil War and 1906, certain activities contributed to the expansion of thought for the predominantly rural, county-seat town Disciples Movement. Always abundant in editors, Disciples thrived on a score of weekly periodicals, circulating throughout the congregations. Another activity that provided contact with a larger world was a pioneering missionary initiative through the Christian Women's Board of Missions and the Foreign Christian Missionary Society formed in 1874-1875. A third activity was cooperation with other communions. Disciples were charter members of the Federal Council of Churches; and through the creative leadership of Peter Ainslie, established the Council on Christian Union in 1910. And, of course, the movement continued its prolific work in higher education. Across the five decades between 1867 and 1919, Disciples founded an amazing 129 new colleges that can be dated and located, and at least ninety academies, high schools, and institutes. The presence of these institutions engendered a more informed people and contributed to the new sense of denominational consciousness.

Although these kinds of activities were invaluable to late nineteenth century Disciples thought, they were not easily able to overcome the cultural and intellectual limitations of a rural confinement or bridge the chasm between this pre-Civil War religious reform Movement and the new post-Civil War socio-economic developments. The Movement, nurtured by the Jeffersonian ideal of a romantic American pastoralism and guided by a moderate evangelical Protestant consensus, was not adequately prepared to address the new social heterogeneity, to assimilate the growing tide of immigrants, or adjust to the rapidly developing urban-industrial environment.[3]

The post-Civil War era was a time of sweeping economic and social change. Described variously as the "Age of Excess," the "Age of Enterprise," the "Gilded Age," and the "Age of Nationalizing American Life," the years between 1867 and 1919 were marked with an enormous migration of people into the rich interior of the trans-Mississippi West, an exploding industrial growth bringing alternate periods of prosperity and depression that repeatedly convulsed the nation, a huge influx of southern European immigrants who formed a new urban labor force, and early signs of the displacement of agriculture as the socio-economic base of the nation. The post-Civil War generation has been called the first "modern" generation, a generation engrossed in the competitive pursuit of industrial wealth, a generation, it is said, remembered more for its mastery of capital than for its statecraft or its intellectual achievement.

"It is in iron and steel," wrote the novelist William Dean Howells in 1876, "that the national genius most freely speaks." Four years of war, with foundries belching out a record production of arms and munitions, placed a line between the era of agricultural and industrial America and sparked a peacetime binge of mechanization. The construction of 150,000 miles of railroad track during the quarter century following the Civil War created a nation-wide rail network, symbol of the mechanical and industrial genius peculiar to that era and an achievement that revolutionized the socio-economic order of the nation.

The peace and harmony of the old Jeffersonian pastoral ideal of American life had been romanticized many times over in American literature. Washington Irving's description of Sleepy Hollow fairly describes the rural ethos surrounding much of the Movement and its little congregations:

> I mention this peaceful spot with all possible laud; for it is in such little retired ... valleys ... that population, manners, and customs, remain fixed; while the great torrent of migration and improvement, which is making such incessant change in other parts of this restless country, sweeps by them unobserved. They are little nooks of still water which border a rapid stream . . .[4]

This early nineteenth century ideal was a sustaining order of experience for most of America and especially for Disciples and their Restoration Movement. Quite naturally, the appearance and spread of the locomotive with its "fire, smoke, speed, iron, and noise" was seen by many as a wrenching intrusion upon their pastoral world:

> Hark! There is the whistle of the locomotive — the long shriek, harsh, above all other harshness, for the space of a mile cannot mollify it into harmony. It tells a story of busy men, citizens from the hot street, who have come to spend a day in a country village, men of business; in short, of all unquietness; and no wonder that it gives such a startling shriek, since it brings the noisy world into the midst of our slumbrous peace.[5]

Ralph Waldo Emerson heard the whistle of the locomotive as the "voice of civility," the voice of "prophecy;" but Henry David Thoreau listening at Walden Pond heard it "penetrate my woods like the scream of a hawk."[6] The post-war proliferation of the locomotive was the primary symbol of industrial power and utilitarian spirit, the symbol of tension between two distinct systems of value. Technological progress and the pastoral ideal were never fully harmonized within the nation nor within the rural based Disciples Restoration Movement which tended to embrace its pastoral heritage rather than to reach out to the new era of industrial enterprise.

EDUCATIONAL REFORM DURING THE YEARS OF RECONSTRUCTION

The ideal college is Mark Hopkins on one end of a log and a student on the other. (1871)

James A. Garfield
President, Hiram College
President, United States

The Civil War is also a watershed in the history of American higher education, separating the era of the small, sectarian college from the era of the large, secular university. Accompanying post-Civil War industrial expansion was the rise of the university, responding to demands for vocational and specialized education in a capital driven economy, for practical and utilitarian education enhancing social mobility in a democratic society, and for research-oriented education in order to participate in the new advancements of technology and science. Founded by wealthy industrialists rather than clergy, and administered by professional academics instead of ministers, the bevy of new, secular universities included Cornell (1868), Vanderbilt (1875), John Hopkins (1876), Tulane (1884), Stanford (1891), and Chicago (1891). A large number of state universities and land-grant colleges also appeared and, together with the private universities, ushered in the new era of higher education reform.

Government policy, in addition to entrepreneurial wealth, played a significant role in creating the era of the universities. Congressman Justin Smith Morrill of Vermont introduced legislation in 1857 which provided for the appropriation of public land to each state for the establishment of agricultural and industrial colleges. Finally passed as the Morrill Land-Grant College Act in July 1862, it is one of the most important pieces of educational legislation ever enacted. Under the terms of this act, a product of middle-class reformers rather than mechanics or farmers, nearly 13,000,000 acres of public land were given to states to establish "Agricultural and Mechanical Colleges" for the purpose of promoting the "liberal and practical education of the industrial classes."[7] Seventeen states gave the money from the sale of the land to their existing state universities while other states established separate "A & M" colleges, creating a whole new network of institutions. The strongest of these state universities were developed in the Midwest, particularly in those states with heavy concentrations of New England immigrants and their affinity for education.

Another significant element in shaping the age of the university was the 1869 appointment of Charles William Eliot to the presidency of Harvard. Influenced by a rapidly expanding body of scientific knowledge and the urgent demand for vocational specialization, Eliot replaced the prescribed curriculum with an elective system of courses, a model which profoundly modified the nature of college education across the nation. The old colleges had offered a rigidly defined curriculum, a common core of knowledge with an emphasis upon memory and discipline. The new university offered a wide variety of courses on an elective basis with an emphasis upon inquiry and criticism. Introduction of the elective principle sparked a prolonged controversy reflecting divergent opinions about the relationship between higher education and the community. By the turn of the century nearly every college in the nation had adopted the elective concept to some degree. One survey indicated that 40 percent of all colleges had curriculum designs in which 50 percent or more of their courses were elective. The small church-related college, in general, was the last to adapt and the least adaptive.[8]

Accompanying the elective system was an accelerated growth of graduate schools. Virtually unknown in America before the Civil War, graduate departments were added at Yale and Harvard in 1872. By 1876 some twenty-five institutions were offering Ph.D. degrees. The appearance of graduate schools spawned an impressive advance in research techniques, but also a very highly specialized approach to knowledge.

Graduate education, elective courses, the university—concepts growing out of the new post-war socio-economic dynamic—created two distinct educational eras, two contrasting groups of institutions. The small church-related colleges were founded on the premise that education shaped character, rather than scholarship, and that intellectual life was a fundamental part of the character and spiritual dimesion of all human beings. Knowledge, therefore, was not treated by these institutions as simply utilitarian. The old college was a place that spoke for the wholeness of human beings, where teachers were supposed to transmit a common body of knowledge that engendered common learnings, a "community" among college educated persons.

In the new light of post-Civil War developments, the old colleges became objects of severe criticism. They were described as defiant "preserves of denominationalism" with inflexible, dogmatic, and archaic curriculum. They were seen as tradition-centered institutions of the past, limited by petty sectarianism and restricted by provincial reputation.

It was the new university, rather than the old college, that was hailed as the institutional expression of the new age. With at least a state and often a national reputation, its curriculum was designed with a technical, practical, scientific character in response to the vocational demands of the business and technological communities. It quickly and easily accommodated the elective principle, allowing students to concentrate in any one of the variety of specialties. This gave the university campus an avowedly heterogeneous flavor and made it the center of American scholarly research.[9]

But the new university was not without its detractors. Many lamented what they found to be a loss of seriousness about the life of the mind in the practical, acquisitive atmosphere of the new university with its shrinking, common core of courses. The line of distinction between profession and vocation was blurred. It was obviously a secular institution, forfeiting the spiritual tone of the old college by abandoning the senior course in moral philosophy, by eliminating compulsory chapel, by selecting academics rather than ministers to be administrators and board members, and by avoiding relationships with the religious community in general. In its diverse and prodigiously multiplied curricular offerings, designed to produce vocational specialists, the new university failed to speak to the wholeness of the human being.[10]

Among the most profound insights ever recorded on the nature of the university are those of an obscure nineteenth century rector of Catholic University of Ireland, John Henry Newman, in his enduring classic, *Idea of a University*. Originally published in two parts, the first in 1853 under the title "Discourses on University Education," and the second in 1858 entitled "Lectures and Essays on University Subjects," Newman's work was widely read in the late nineteenth century. It spoke insightfully of two kinds of knowledge, two distinct forms of education.

There is, he suggested, useful knowledge and there is liberal knowledge; there are:

> two methods of education; the end of one is to be philosophical, of the other to be mechanical; the one rises toward general ideals; the other is exhausted upon what is particular and external.[11]

Those advocating the mechanical or useful interpretation, wrote Newman:

> . . . insist that education should be confined to some particular and narrow end, and should issue in some definite work, which can be weighted and measured. They argue as if everything, as well as every person, had its price; and that where there has been a great outlay, they have a right to expect a return in kind. This they call making education and instruction 'useful,' and 'utility becomes their watchword' . . . they ask . . . what is the real worth in the market

of the article called 'a liberal education,' on the supposition that it does not teach us definitely how to advance our manufactures, or to improve our lands, or to better our civil economy.[12]

Liberal knowledge or liberal arts or liberal education, contended Newman, was to be understood as the opposite of *servile*, and by "servile work" was meant mechanical employment in which the mind had little or no part. Newman believed that "there is a knowledge worth possessing for what it is, and not merely for what it does."[13] This kind of knowledge Newman described as:

> . . . not a mere extrinsic advantage . . . which we can borrow for the occasion, carry about in our hand, and take into the market; it is an acquired illumination, it is a habit, a personal possession, and an inward endowment. . . . There is a knowledge which is desirable, though nothing come of it, as being of itself a treasure, and a sufficient remuneration of years of labour.[14]

Knowledge that is useful, observed Newman, bears fruit. Knowledge that is liberal tends toward enjoyment. "By fruitful," said Newman, "I mean which yield revenue; by enjoyable, where nothing accrues of consequence beyond the using." Baconian philosophy, he argued, corrupted the humanist tradition with its commitment to science to the individual, and transfered knowledge "from the order of the liberal to the class of the useful."[15]

It was very important in Newman's view to speak of the University as a place of education rather than instruction:

> We are *instructed* . . . in manual exercises, in the fine and useful arts, in trades, and in ways of business; for these are methods, which have little or no effect upon the mind itself, are contained in rules committed to memory, to tradition, or to use, and bear upon an end external to themselves.
>
> But *education* is a higher work; it implies an action upon our mental nature, and the formation of a character; it is something individual and permanent, and is commonly spoken of in connection with religion and virtue. When we speak of the communication of knowledge as being education, we thereby really imply that that knowledge is a state or condition of mind.[16]

The ferment of educational reform between 1867 and 1919 gave rise to the new university and eclipsed the old college of James Garfield's famous description. The new system of higher education blended scientific research with teaching and merged high academic standards with populist social ideals. This was the setting in which Disciples continued to develop their colleges during the late nineteenth and early twentieth centuries. A profoundly new environment had been shaped by the experience of Civil War; and each Disciples college, like the Restoration Movement itself, was faced with the choice of being an instrument of the past or an instrument of the future.

DISCIPLES COLLEGES 1867-1899

No schools for ministerial education should be established apart from
our colleges.

Charles L. Loos
Millenial Harbinger, September, 1865

At war's end, the legacy of Bacon College, lodged at the Disciples-
supported Kentucky University of Harrodsburg, Kentucky, took a fateful
turn. The institution had been occupied by the Union Army to house their
wounded from the Battle of Perryville in 1862, and two years later the
campus burned. In an effort to salvage the school and convert it into a
modern university that was accessible and responsive to a wider community,
John B. Bowman, a prominent Kentucky Disciple, proposed a merger:

> I want to build a *People's Institution*, a great University eventually open and
> accessible to the poorest boy in all the land who may come and receive an
> education practical and suitable for any business or profession in life. . . .
> Hitherto, our colleges and universities have been accessible only to the few.[17]

In 1865, through Bowman's initiative, Kentucky University's (Bacon) cash
endowment of $200,000, her president Robert Milligan, and four of her
faculty were combined with the $59,000 endowment, $125,000 in buildings
and equipment, and two faculty members from Transylvania (then a
preparatory school) and located in Lexington, Kentucky. The consolidation
of these assets was to be supplemented with funds obtained from the sale of
land scrip granted by the federal government through the 1862 Morrill Land-
Grant College Act. With this allocation of land scrip dollars, the Kentucky
Legislature added a third component, a state supported "A & M" College,
thereby creating a three-way merger and retaining the name Kentucky
University. Establishing a large state university on a denominationally-based
campus was a daring experiment, but it was fundamentally flawed in
attempting to combine the support of church and state within a single
institution. Controversy flared for a decade and more around the question of
"Who owned the Institution?" John Bowman, appointed regent of the newly-
formed university, was more interested in developing a university to serve the
people of the state than a school serving only Disciples. John W. McGarvey,
curator of the former Kentucky University (Bacon), outspoken Disciples
pastor in Lexington, and recently appointed to the College of the Bible
faculty in the new university, was more interested in developing a school for
ministers and protecting Disciples' interests. The controversy generated by
the clash of these two strong leaders resulted in bitter charges and counter-
charges, a factional split in the local congregation where both were members,
and the dismissal of both men from the university, although McGarvey was
later reinstated. Unable to bridge the seismic fault in its conceptual design,
Kentucky University in 1878 splintered into three institutions: The College of

Agriculture and Mechanical Arts (renamed the University of Kentucky in 1916); supported by the state; Kentucky University (renamed Transylvania University in 1908), and The College of The Bible (renamed Lexington Theological Seminary in 1965), both supported by the Disciples reformation Movement.[18]

Central to this episode was the appointment of John W. McGarvey in 1865 to the faculty of the College of the Bible at the new Kentucky University, where he immediately set about the task of developing a plan for ministerial education in a "separate college" within the university. His published concept of the school claimed that his own preparation for ministry at Bethany College had been inadequate due to the constriction of a four-year Arts and Science curriculum which did not allow enough time for proper preparation for ministry. He wrote:

> We were familiar with the Pentateuch, but knew little of the gospels, still less of Acts, and almost nothing of the epistles. As for biblical criticism, it was to us a *Terra incognita*.[19]

Adding one or two more years to the regular four-year curriculum, he believed, would make the preparation much too long. The movement needed ministers as soon as possible, and McGarvey's solution was to establish a "separate school" where ministerial students could receive a specialized course of study on the Bible.

McGarvey's plan for ministerial education contained three elements: knowledge of the Bible, moral training, and liberal arts. Although he thought it increased a minister's usefulness, he regarded the liberal arts as the most dispensable of the three because the object of ministerial education was *not* to make "authors or critics or professors."[20]

During the same year, a series of eight articles appeared in various issues of the *Millennial Harbinger* regarding the identical question of establishing "theological schools" or "schools for ministry" to educate Disciples ministers for the new age. The debate was engaged by some of the foremost Disciples of that day. Elder Benjamin Franklin strongly opposed the idea of theological schools, charging that they were totally unnecessary and that the "brotherhood" belonged:

> . . . to the class, no matter whether it be large or small, who have no use for a theological school. In our humble opinion, it would be a fifth wheel. . . . How are we to educate men for the ministry? The answer is, precisely as we educate men, or women, for anything else: in the common schools, the seminaries, colleges and universities.[21]

William K. Pendleton thought that Franklin suffered from the "reformation-prejudice against theological schools" and was therefore opposing "what is daily felt to be a growing want among us. "Let us have a school," Pendleton charged, "for training and qualifying young men in the work of the ministry.":

... the school we want is one for imparting all that a school can impart to fit a preacher for the great practical duties that will devolve upon him as a public minister of the gospel. Theology as a science covers but a part of this preparation. The practical duties of pastoral life, instruction, training, and practice in the composition and delivery of pulpit and congregational ministrations, whether as an evangelist or an elder, together with constant critical study in the Hebrew and Greek Scriptures, with exercises in translation, and such collateral studies in History, etc. as elucidate the Word of God and qualify one for its profitable and practical use in the pulpit ... more can be done in one year in a school specially designed for the purpose, than in half a lifetime in the loose and irregular way proposed by Brother Franklin.[22]

The notion of a theological school was also advocated by Isaac Errett, who wrote that such an institution should be designed to furnish students with knowledge and experience that would "require half a life time to gather up by their own unaided efforts." There were several things, however, that he did *not* want the proposed theological school to do. It was not to teach a *system of theology*. It was not meant to make preaching a *trade* or *profession*. And, it was not intended to produce an exclusive class of *educated ministry*.[23]

Charles L. Loos enjoined the issue on the opposite side with a lengthy three-part article challenging both Pendleton and Errett. Loos asserted firmly "that no school for ministerial education should be established apart from our colleges."[24] To segregate "schools for ministry" from our colleges, he contended, would secularize the colleges:

To separate ministerial education from the colleges, would at once lower the character of these institutions in the very particular in which they ought to stand the highest. ... The establishment of our colleges ... was with special reference to the one end of educating men for the ministry of the Word; and this has ever been the great plea in their behalf before our brethren, and the strongest power in securing their endowment. ... Take away this plea, and the great argument in [their] behalf is no more; there is no sufficient reason for multiplying, at an immense cost, colleges and universities merely to teach the profane arts and sciences ... when this land has already many, and unexceptionable institutions of this kind in it. We have first class institutions in our land where the arts and sciences are taught in a masterly way, and these not of sectarian cast. If the business of colleges is simply to teach literature and science, Greek and Latin, Chemistry and the Philosophies, Logic and Rhetoric, etc. etc., their mission is ended, in our judgement, and the chief ground of their distinctive existence is taken completely away.[25]

Loos argued against the idea of separation on economic grounds, pointing out that the cost to the denomination to multiply the number and kind of institutions was beyond their means and would dissipate their financial support along with their loyalties. It would be far better, suggested Loos, to concentrate the support of the Movement rather than to divide it.[26]

In spite of Loos' arguments, McGarvey established his "separate college" for ministry, the first such institution in Disciples history. But the arguments of Charles Loos proved convincing for the Movement at large, and for the next several decades Disciples were guided by the prevailing view that ministerial education was an integral part of the undergraduate curriculum and should not be consigned to a separate theological school. The majority of Disciples colleges founded between the Civil War and the turn of the century were influenced by this principle, which also became the basic appeal used by the colleges to secure financial support from the Disciples Movement.

During the pre-Civil War years, the number of academies and institutes founded by Disciples far exceeded the number of colleges. As the public school movement began to spread, Disciples gradually shifted their educational emphasis. Between 1867 and 1899, the reformation Movement established seventy-nine colleges and seventy-four academies and institutes. The border states of Kentucky and Missouri accounted for twenty and eighteen colleges respectively, while the south established a total of twenty-five colleges, fifteen of those in Tennessee and eight in Texas. Twelve colleges were founded north of the Mason-Dixon Line, of which eight were in the state of Ohio. The remaining eleven colleges were established in the trans-Missouri West, primarily in California and Oregon.

Of the seventy-four academies and institutes, thirty-seven were founded in the eleven former Confederate states, sixteen in the border states, twelve in the North and nine in the West. Public high schools were exceedingly scarce outside the cities until the 1890's; and the Disciples Movement, with its rural orientation, continued to establish a sizeable number of these institutions, but at a declining rate and predominately in the South were there was no compulsory school attendace law until the 1890's. Impoverished by the war and missing a generation of college age youth who had been consumed in battle, the South was unable to respond to post-war education reforms. Disciples colleges in Southern states held closely to the old college concept and its classical curriculum and were less inclined than colleges in other sections to incorporate the new elective system or other new developments of the period.

With the explosion in number of Disciples colleges during the last third of the nineteenth Century, the loose and unconnected ecclesiastical structure of the Disciples Movement began to exercise a more active role in the government and control of the colleges. This was particularly true in the border states and the West, while Southern states continued to rely upon the initiative of individuals.

It was by formal vote of the Missouri State Convention of Christian Churches in 1869 that the "Female Orphan School of the Christian Churches in Missouri" was established at Camden Point, supplanting the former Camden Point Female Seminary.[27] To support the effort, the convention further agreed to raise $20,000 from the congregations. Another concerted effort to exercise a greater voice in the life of the institutions it was being called upon to support saw the Missouri State Convention of Christian Churches in 1882 add an article to their constitution requiring the Disciples colleges in Missouri to amend their charters so that the State Convention would have the power to approve or reject any trustee being appointed to the college boards. Christian University (Culver-Stockton) and the Female Orphan School complied, but Christian College (Columbia) did not. Two years later, J. H. Garrison, chair of the standing Committee on Schools and

COLLEGES FOUNDED BY DISCIPLES 1867-1879

Year of Founding	Name	Location
1867	Milligan College	Milligan, Tennessee
1868	Alliance College	Alliance, Ohio
	Carlton College	Bonham, Texas
	Tennessee Manual University	Nashville, Tennessee
1869	Bedford Male & Female College	Bedford, Illinois
	Hamilton College	Lexington, Kentucky
	Missouri Christian College	Camden Point, Missouri
	Woodland College	Independence, Missouri
1870	Mars Hill College	Florence, Alabama
1872	Christian College	Santa Rosa, California
	Ghent College	Ghent, Kentucky
	Neophogen College	Gallentin, Tennessee
	Washington College of Sci. & Industry	Irvington, California
1873	Columbia Christian College	Columbia, Kentucky
	Add-Ran Male and Female College (Texas Christian University)	Thorp Spring, Texas
1874	Farmer College	College Hill, Ohio
	Pierce Christian College	College City, California
	St. Paul Commercial College	St. Paul, Minnesota
	Southwestern Christian College	Billings, Missouri
	Waters and Walling College	McMinnville, Tennessee
1875	Bourbon Female College	Paris, Kentucky
	Southern Christian Institute	Edwards, Mississippi
1876	Floral Hill College	Fulton, Missouri
1877	Kentucky Classical & Business College	North Middletown, Kentucky
	Stonewall College	Cross Plains, Tennessee
	Northeastern Kansas Normal College	Pardee, Kansas
	Orange College	Starke, Florida
	Southern Pacific College	Downing, California
1878	College of the Bible	Lexington, Kentucky
	Manchester College	Manchester, Tennessee
1879	Howard College	Kokomo, Indiana

Compiled from State histories and from the 1964 Claude Spencer list.

Education, offered a softer substitute Article which was adopted by the State Convention:

> Those colleges and schools in the state known to be conducted by men associated with our religious movement are requested to make annual reports to this body through the standing Committee on Schools and Education concerning their condition and progress, as a matter of information to the brotherhood.[28]

COLLEGES FOUNDED BY DISCIPLES 1880-1889

Year of Founding	Name	Location
1880	Fayette Normal, Music & Business College	Fayette, Ohio
	Ganard Female College	Lancaster, Kentucky
	Plattsburg College	Plattsburg, Missouri
	Rockport College	Rockport, Missouri
1881	Holden College	Holden, Missouri
	Lampasas College	Lampasas, Texas
1882	Central Ohio Classical & Business College	East Libery, Ohio
	Milligan College	Milligan College, Tennessee
1883	Ash Grove College	Ash Grove, Missouri
	Gordonville Female College	Gordensville, Virginia
	Henry Male & Female College	New Castle, Kentucky
	Home College	Campbellsburg, Kentucky
	Northern Ohio Normal College	Mansfield, Ohio
1884	Fairfield College	Fairfield, Nebraska
	American Normal College	Logan's Port, Indiana
	Christian Bible College	New Castle, Kentucky
	Lafayette College	Higginsville, Missouri
	Salina University	Salina, Kansas
1885	Baird College	Clinton, Missouri
	Freed-Hardeman College	Henderson, Tennessee
1886	Garfield University	Witchita, Kansas
	West Kentucky College	Mayfield, Kentucky
1887	Hale College	Dexter, Missouri
1888	Garfield Normal College & Bus. Institute	Enterprise, Kansas
	Hale's College	Piedmont, Missouri
	National Christian College	Dallas, Texas
1889	Cotner College	Lincoln, Nebraska
	Nevada Christian University	Nevada, Missouri
	Pea Ridge College	Benton County, Arkansas
	Southern Tennessee Normal College	Essary Springs, Tennessee
	Winchester College	Winchester, Kentucky

Compiled from State histories and from the 1964 Claude Spencer list.

During the controversy surrounding Kentucky University in the 1870's, the Christian Churches of Kentucky held a special "Education Convention" in May 1874 to study the matter of church relations with the educational institutions in their state. The conventions appointed a committee to work toward gaining ownership and control of Kentucky University. Failing in this mandate, the committee began to work in conjunction with the Kentucky Christian education society, a loan and grant agency for Disciples ministerial students chartered by the General Assembly in Kentucky in 1856. Together they succeeded in establishing a College of the Bible as an institution independent from Kentucky University.[29]

Other late nineteenth century examples of increasing attempts by Disciples ecclesiastical structures to exert authority over the colleges are abundant. In 1885, G. T. Carpenter published his view that "The Church, through its representative conventions, should hold absolute ownership and control over

COLLEGES FOUNDED BY DISCIPLES 1890-1899

Year of Founding	Name	Location
1890	William Woods College	Fulton, Missouri
	The Orphan School of the C.C. of Missouri	Camden Point, Missouri
	Keuka College	Keuka Park, New York
1891	Corbin Christian College	Corbin, Kentucky
	David Lispcomb College	Nashville, Tennessee
	Northwestern Christian College	Excelisior, Minnesota
1892	Central Christian College	Albany, Missouri
1893	American University	Harriman, Tennessee
	Johnson Bible College	Kimberlin Heights, Tennessee
1894	Carr-Carlton College [Carr-Burdette]	Sherman, Texas
1895	Lockney Christian College	Lockney, Texas
	Southeast Missouri Christian College	DeSoto, Missouri
1896	Southern Illinois Christian	Alma, Illinois
	Bentonville College	Bentonville, Arkansas
	El Neta Christian College	Minco, Indian Territory
	Nazareth University	Corinth, Arkansas
	Owensboro Female College	Owensboro, Kentucky
1897	Bible College of Missouri	Columbia, Missouri
	St. Thomas College	St. Thomas, Ontario
1899	Bellvue College	Colierville, Tennessee
	Kansas Bible College	Harper, Kansas

Compiled from State histories and from the 1964 Claude Spencer list.

these schools."[30] The Nebraska Christian Missionary Society in 1888 established itself as the owner and governing power of Christian University (Cotner College), as well as the Lincoln suburb of Bethany Heights in which it was located. The Articles of Incorporation expressly stated "that all property which may be held by said Board of Trustees shall be held in behalf of the Christian Churches of Nebraska."[31] In 1890, the buildings and grounds of Add-Ran College (Texas Christian University), then in Thorp Springs, Texas, were formally placed under the ownership and control of the Christian Churches in Texas.[32] When Andrew Pierce died in 1871, his three thousand-acre estate was left to the Christian Churches of Colusa County, California, which sold the lots, built a town called College City, and established an educational institution named Pierce Christian College under the ownership and control of the Christian Churches.[33] Compared to the early days of Disciples colleges founding when it was considered altogether sinful for the church structure to interfere with the individual freedom to found a college, these new efforts by state conventions represented a dramatic shift in the Disciples concept of ecclesiastical authority and must be regarded as early signs of a developing denominational consciousness. The movement toward church control of higher education institutions became an established pattern which continued well into the twentieth century. Those institutions which received official endorsement by a state convention enjoyed a much higher rate of survival.

Many of the Disciples schools acquired their campuses through imaginative real estate schemes during the national land speculation boom in the 1880's. Fairfield College (1884) and Christian University (Cotner) (1888), both Nebraska institutions, were initially financed out of the sale of lots from gifts of land received and platted by the church for real estate development. Believing that the land would support the institutions, no cash gifts were sought; and none of the land was held for endowment.[34] Drake University, established in 1881, was fashioned through an interlocking directorate of the University and the University Land Company, which controlled a suburban residential development project in an isolated area encompassing the university on the northwest outskirts of Des Moines.[35] It was through the sale of lots that Northwest Christian College in Mankato, Minnesota, was created in 1884.[36] Garfield University was started in Wichita, Kansas in 1886, on the hope of selling one hundred lots which did not sell. The institution was acquired by the Quakers in 1890 and continued as Friends University. Wildcat real estate ventures were used widely to found Disciples colleges during the 1880's. The majority of the schools born of this method were unable to survive the deflation of land values during the financial panic of 1893 and the depression that followed. The financial panic of 1893 brought the demise of more Disciples colleges than any event in the nineteenth century, other than the Civil War.

Liberal-fundamentalist controversy within the Movement seeped into the life of the colleges. Debate occurred regularly among alumni, church leaders, and trustees on the character of the colleges as either too secularized or too sectarian. Conservative ministers in southern Indiana, disturbed by what they perceived to be a departure from Disciples ideals by other Indiana ministerial leaders, formed their own separate Christian Ministerial Conference of Southern Indiana in 1873. In addition to supporting a separate journal, this association gave its official patronage to Bedford Male and Female College. Bedford was thought to be conducted on strict New Testament principles and claimed as its president J. M. Mathes, who was also president of the Christian Ministerial Conference in Southern Indiana. Because of the theological conflict within the Movement, Bedford College became a direct competitor with Northwestern Christian University (Butler) in the recruitment of Disciples students and in the solicitation of Disciples financial support in Indiana.[37]

Theological disagreement within the movement not only set school against school, but created bitter internal factions on many of the campuses. In 1882, Hiram College had added biblical studies to its curriculum to meet the new expectation of the Movement that Disciples colleges would provide ministers for the congregations by educating them within an undergraduate liberal arts context.[38] Throughout the late 1880's and 1890's, Hiram president, Ely Von Zollars, worked unceasingly to build a strong course of study for Disciples ministers. When he resigned in 1902, a spirited competition developed between two factions of trustees over the appointment of his successor. The younger and newer trustees, attracted to the liberal theology of the "Chicago School" that had become so vital and determined in the 1890's, wanted a liberal thinker to be the new president. The older and more conservative trustees were of a mind that the school needed to be saved from the new theology and prevailed in electing James A. Beattie as the new president. Beattie, who had previously served as president of Bedford Male and Female College in Indiana, resigned after one year and was replaced by C. C. Rowlinson, a nominee of the liberal trustees, who was forced to resign after two years. One faction of trustees was solidly in support of the new liberal theology, the other irrevocably opposed. Hiram survived the controversy; but many Disciples schools, thoroughly dependent upon the Disciples Movement for their financial life, were unable to withstand religious fratricide and were forced to shut down their operations.[39]

The story of college founding in Texas provides a devastating example of the effect of theological division upon resources and loyalties. Colby Hall compiled the following list of institutions established by the Restoration Movement in that state during the late nineteenth and early twentieth centuries with dates encompassing their life-span and with the identity of the theological faction serving as the chief source of support.

TEXAS

Church of Christ Colleges

1. Lockney College   1894-1898
2. Gunter College   1903-1916
3. Southwestern Christian College
   1905-1910
4. Ligleville College   1905-1909
5. ABILENE CHRISTIAN COLLEGE
   1906
6. Sabinal College   1907-1910
7. CleBarro College   1910-1916
8. Thorp Spring Christian College
   1910-1928
9. Littlefield College   1916-1918
10. Texas Christian College   1929-1930

Disciples Colleges

1. Carlton College   1865-1916
2. TEXAS CHRISTIAN UNIVERSITY
   1869
3. Carr-Burdette College   1894-1929
4. Jarvis Institute   1897-1899
5. Randolph College   1899-1902
6. Jarvis College   1900-1904
7. Hereford-Panhandle Christian College
   1902-1915
8. Add-Ran Jarvis College   1904-1909
9. Midland College   1902-1922
10. JARVIS CHRISTIAN COLLEGE
    1913
11. Randolph College   1922-1937

Claimed by Both or Neither

1. Mount Enterprise College   1850-1858
2. Patroon College   1893-1897
3. Burnetta College   1896-1905

The Church of Christ or "conservative" colleges averaged ten years of life while the Disciples or "progressive" colleges averaged twenty-two years. Only three of these institutions exist today: Abilene Christian College, related to the Church of Christ; and Texas Christian University and Jarvis Christian College, in covenant with the Christian Church (Disciples of Christ). Many reasons are cited for the demise of the other twenty-one institutions, but the excessive number of schools spawned out of theological rivalry spread the resources of the Movement much too thin and must be recognized as a major factor contributing to their failure.[41]

Theological differences were no less a problem in Canada where two competing views prevented the establishment of a viable educational institution:

View 1: The development of a religious personality capable of ministering the gospel to average minds through but moderate scholarship, is the end sought. A segregated college is required where our students may be free from the dangers of 'modern knowledge.'

View 2: Lowly based education is insufficient and 'our cause' has always believed in real 'academic' education and must have it. Real critical enlightenment is suitable to enable us to keep abreast of the times.[42]

St. Thomas College was founded in 1897 at St. Thomas, Ontario with John Campbell as president. T. L. Fowler, a Bethany graduate, Greek scholar, pastor, organizer of an earlier Ontario Lectureship Program, was the moving spirit behind the college. It opened in 1897 with forty one students, most of whom were in preparatory courses. The institution changed its name in 1906 to Sinclair College, but then closed in 1909. One other school, Maritime

Bible College, was opened in 1908 at West Gore, Nova Scotia and survived until 1915.[43]

The Cambellian principle of "non-sectarianism" was weakened in the years following the Civil War. The rapid growth of state colleges led many Disciples to fear that state owned insitutions graduated only "infidels" and that they had to insure the safety of their sons and daughters by building and supporting Disciples colleges that inculcated Christian beliefs. The old concept of Disciples colleges serving a broader human purpose than the Movement itself was modified by the general adoption of the idea that the training of ministers should occur in the undergraduate Disciples colleges, and not in separate institutions. The effect was to increase the role of the colleges as servants to the Movement. Controversy over the theological orthodoxy of Disciples college presidents and curriculums suggested that faith was beginning to supercede knowledge. Together, these developments revealed Disciples colleges to be significantly more sectarian during the late nineteenth century than they had been during the early years of founding prior to the Civil War.

In 1869, Bethany College added the Bachelor of Science (B.S.) degree, a signal that it was responding to the socio-economic trends of the new age. Two years later, it also added a Bachelor of Letters (B.L.) degree for ministerial preparation which included studies in Christian doctrine, church history, hermeneutics, homiletics, Greek exegesis, and Hebrew. The expanded scope of the Bethany curriculum is evident in the changing configuration of the degrees awarded by the college during the 1870's:

BETHANY COLLEGE

	1871-1875	1874-1880	
B.A.	38	48	
B.S.	10	43	
B.L.	0	41	[44]

It reflects a common story among Disciples colleges in the late nineteenth century. Most maintained a classical curriculum as the basic component of their course of study, while slowly adding selected science courses and a B.S. degree in response to the practical demands of the burgeoning industrial economy, and also adding ministerial studies in order to meet the expectations and maintain desperately needed support of Disciples congregations.

Even with this modest diversity, the majority of the colleges were not able to survive. The term "college" was used loosely and did not imply standardization. Some were junior colleges; some were the equivalent of high schools; and some were good quality four-year liberal arts colleges. Try though they might, most institutions in the lesser categories did not achieve full college status and were also the institutions with the shortest life span. In 1885, it was reported that the Disciples had "organized 54 colleges and that 13 of these are dead and the others are very sickly."[45] After several failed attempts to establish a college in Alabama, one committee finally reported in exasperation to the state convention:

> Cannot some rich girl marry a consecrated, brainy man and support him from her farm like Mrs. Alexander Campbell did while he builds the college and secures the interest of other men of means to support the faculty?[46]

The reasons for failure covered a wide range including poor management, isolated locations, irrelevant curriculums, competition from the public school and public university movements, a diminishing demand for girls' schools and denominational junior colleges, and an inability of the Disciples Movement through financial resources, demographics, and desire to financially support so many colleges. A wrenching analysis of the typical Disciples college plight was offered by Hiram president, Burris A. Hinsdale, in 1879, after twenty-eight years of enrollment decline at the institution. His painful description spoke for scores of Disciples college presidents:

> When [a school's] average attendance the second seven years is 39 less than the first seven, the third seven 120 less than the second, and the fourth seven 64 less than the third, it is idle to seek to explain the facts by referring them to accidental circumstances; there is at work some persistent and powerful tendency from first to last.
> 1. The unfortunate geographical location of the College.
> 2. Unfortunate economic and social conditions.
> 3. The decay of interest on the part of the public, especially the Disciples churches.
> 4. The enormous development of the common schools.
> 5. The decline of the rural population in the northeastern counties of Ohio.
> 6. The ever-increasing competition of academical and collegiate schools.
> 7. The relative failure of the school to keep up with the times in mechanical equipment.
>
> These forces have acted so powerfully and so constantly that, had it not been for the devotion and sacrifice of a small number of persons, ere this Hiram would have been a thing of the past. The forces that have acted since 1853, persistent as gravitation, will draw Hiram nearer and nearer the earth unless something is done to counteract them. Something must be done or Hiram must die; at most it can do no more than live on in a starved and dwindling condition.
>
> A humble school with a cheap corps of teachers could probably be kept at Hiram for many years; but to think of supporting a College on $3,000 or $4,000 a year is simply farcical. For nine years I have worked with might and main, making reasonable allowances for human infirmity. I have done my best to make good scholars at Hiram; to make good men and women of our pupils; and to give the College standing abroad. I can do no more. I confess I am discouraged. The consiousness that the work is becoming less on my hands, and that I am often blamed as the cause of the decline, weighs on my spirits. I could work on with heart and with hope, if I could see a prospect of future enlargement. But unless I can see larger hope in Hiram than I have seen in the

last few years, then I must begin to lay my plans with reference to some other work.[47]

Unexpectedly, the election of an alumnus, James A. Garfield, to the Presidency of the United States the following year reversed Hiram's fortunes, making the college a "foremost name" in educational circles. Two-thirds of the Disciples colleges, however, in the face of similar circumstances, either closed their doors or merged with another institution.

Two institutions founded during this year, Texas Christian University (T.C.U.) and Drake University, rose above the dreary litany of difficulties to survive into the present age. Both institutions were wisely located in urban communities: Drake from the time of its 1881 incorporation at Des Moines, Iowa; and T.C.U., following moves to Thorp Spring (1873) and Waco (1895), ultimately returned to its initial place of founding in Forth Worth, Texas (1910). Both institutions took seriously the title of "University" and assimilated the new educational reforms of the era. Drake incorporated into its university design schools of medicine, law, business, music, arts, and sciences; while T.C.U., known in its earlier days as Add-Ran College, later organized a similar cluster of diverse schools under a single university structure. Both universities were co-educational and both incoporated the new elective concept into their curricular pattern. Both were situated in the midst of heavy concentrations of Disciples congregations and each university later developed a theological seminary to serve the church membership. In addition, both universities enjoyed the timely and generous patronage of a moderately progressive philanthropist early in their history. Both institutions not only survived the economic and religious vicissitudes of the late 1800's, but flourished. In 1904, just twenty-three years after its founding, Drake University was characterized by denominational leaders as the "youngest and lustiest institution of higher learning" in the Movement and T.C.U. was described in the same year as on its way to becoming "second to none in the brotherhood."[48]

BLACK DISCIPLES AND HIGHER EDUCATION

Nothing appears plainer than that, without education, it will be impossible to elevate the [Black] man to an equal influence in the ranks of a free people. As this is clearly the necessary lever, it is not equally clear that it is the first that should be provided for?

William K. Pendleton
M. H. 1868

Cane Ridge and Brush Run were among the earliest congregations in the Disciples movement and both claimed Black Christians among their members. By 1852 Cane Ridge listed seventy-one Black members, including an Alexander Campbell and Samuel Buckner, both of whom were ordained.

Prior to the Civil War, most Black Christians were members of white congregations, although there is no record of Black board members or elders and only occasionally a deacon.[49]

The first known Black Disciples congregation was organized in 1834 at Midway, Kentucky, and pastored by the ordained Black minister, Alexander Campbell from Cane Ridge. North of the Mason-Dixon Line, the earliest Black Disciples congregation was established at Pickerelltown, Ohio, in 1838. Henry Newson was the ordained Black minister of the Pickerelltown congregation which became an important way-station on the underground railroad. By the Civil War, Black Disciples numbered approximately 7000, of whom 1500 belonged to Black congregations in five states. The other 5500 were members of predominatly white congregations.[50]

Disciples responded initially to the Civil War Emancipation with a spontaneous and erratic evangelical ministry for the salvation of freed Blacks. Lewis L. Pinkerton of Kentucky reminded the conscience of the movement in 1869 that:

> . . . there are two hundred thousand negroes in Kentucky, much needing instruction in everything pertaining to this life and the life to come, and that the Disciples of Christ, many of whom are enjoying the wealth earned by these negroes ought now to labor and pray for their enlightenment and salvation.[51]

A few Northern evangelists, privately financed by Disciples philanthropists such as T. W. Phillips and Ovid Butler, worked zealously in Southern states evangelizing Blacks. Students at Hiram College, emotionally stirred by the campus speeches of Isaac Errett and C. L. Loos, organized a short-lived Freedman's Missionary Society which launched a program of evangelization among freed Blacks in the South. Most Southern Disciples resented what they perceived as Northern interference, a sentiment best expressed by David Lipscomb who counseled Isaac Errett to "attend to the Dutch at Cleveland and leave Southern people to mind their own business.[52]

As the 1870's unfolded, education began to replace evangelization as the chief work of the Movement among Blacks. "I suppose I might baptize one or two or three thousand freemen in a year," wrote Pinkerton, but "it is not baptism that they especially need.":

> I have hope in schools chiefly, and if we could have a normal school in which fifty or more lads or girls could be prepared for teaching, and inspired with reverence for holiness of life, and pride of character, it would do more in a few years than a score of ordinary preachers, brawling about doctrines and ordinances, could accomplish in many.[53]

Disciples state and general conventions passed resolutions throughout the 1870's urging the promotion of education and the establishment of schools for Blacks. These actions served to sharpen the growing polarity between Northern and Southern factions within the Movement.

Peter Lowery of Nashville, one of the most admired and respected Black Disciples leaders in the Movement, obtained a charter on December 10, 1867, to establish Tennessee Manual Labor University. Its charter envisioned the broad purpose of elevating freedmen and promoting "Education, Industry and pure Christianity and providing instruction in Literature and Science, and in Mechanical Arts."[54] In concept the school was solidly endorsed by both *The Millennial Harbinger* and *The Christian Standard:*

> The plan proposes to purchase and put into operation a farm, with mills, etc., for manufacturing agricultural and other useful implements, also cotton and woolen fabrics, that will give employment to one hundred pupils, whereby they may defray the expenses of their education.
>
> Whatever of aid can be elicited in the true direction for the elevation of the [Blacks] by such efforts as this of Bro. Lowry's should be heartily encouraged.[55]

Three hundred acres of land were purchased at Ebenezer near Murfreesboro, temporary buildings were erected, and the institution opened in 1868. Unfortunately, the school was ruined by financial scandal on the part of corrupt development agents and their mishandeling of money raising responsibilities. In spite of an enrollment of 180 students, Tennessee Manual closed in 1870.

Lewis Pinkerton failed in an 1870 attempt to found a school for Blacks in Kentucky, but Winthrop H. Hopson succeeded in organizing the Louisville Bible School in 1873. Under the supervision of Patrick Moss the school was designed to train ministers. Its student enrollment ranged from ten to twenty-five young men, but the lack of adequate financial support forced it to close in 1877.

In 1874, William T. Withers of Mississippi, actively encouraged by James A. Garfield, offered a challenge gift of 160 acres of land near Edwards to establish a school for the training of Black ministers. The following year this offer was accepted by a group of Indianapolis Disciples, including Ovid Butler, who proceeded to draft a charter for an institution to be known as Southern Christian Institute, a capital stock company organized to raise money for a Black junior college, with an emphasis on the preparation of teachers. Early planning by the Southern Christian Institute was conducted by a board of commissioners: eight from the North and eight from the South with only one Southern Black, Levin Wood. After seven years of raising funds in the North to match the Withers challenge, organizing a board of trustees, countering conservative opposition to the project, and compensating for the withdrawal of Withers' pledge of land by purchasing an 800 acre farm near Edwards from T. I. Martin, the school finally opened in October 1882 with thirty students. Enrollment exceeded two hundred the following year, although the first "Disciples" student did not enroll until 1887. Jephthan Hobbs was named president of the school in 1883 and served until 1891.

Students paid for their tuition by working at a rate of 5 cents to 8 cents an hour in the blacksmith shop, dairy or sawmill. Struggling through the 1880's convinced Southern Christian Institute leaders that the institution could only continue if it had regular financial support from the national structure of the church. Ownership of Southern Christian Institute was transferred to the General Christian Missionary Society in 1889, and in spite of all its travail, Southern Christian Institute became the most successful nineteenth century educational ministry of Disciples to freed blacks.[56]

Most attempts to establish schools for Blacks failed before they actually began, or, at best, lasted on the average of two to seven years. A plan to develop National Colored Christian College in Dallas, Texas, was aborted. The Christian Bible College at New Castle, Kentucky, founded through the fund raising efforts of Preston Taylor with extensive organizational participation by Blacks, had a brief life from 1884 to 1891. Some general coordination of Black educational efforts was finally realized with the creation of the Board of Negro Education and Evangelization in 1890, which united education and evangelism in one organization coordinated by one supervisor. This board, under the administration of Charles C. Smith, was headquartered in Louisville, Kentucky where it gave assistance in founding the Louisville Christian Bible School in 1892, which enjoyed a longer life than the majority of Black schools.[57]

BLACK EDUCATIONAL INSTITUTIONS FOUNDED BY THE RESTORATION MOVEMENT

Year	Institution	Location
1868	Tennessee Manual University	Nashville, Tennessee
1873	Louisville Bible School	Louisville, Kentucky
1875	Southern Christian School	Edwards, Mississippi
1882	Clara Schell's School	Washington, D.C.
1884	Christian Bible College	New Castle, Kentucky
1888	National Colored Christian College	Dallas, Texas
1892	Louisville Christian Bible School	Louisville, Kentucky
1900	Goldsboro Christian Institute	Goldsboro, North Carolina
1900	Alabama Christian Institute	Lum, Alabama
1900	Piedmont Christian Institute	Martinsville, Virginia
1913	JARVIS CHRISTIAN COLLEGE	Hawkins, Texas
1920	Nashville Christian Institute	Nashville, Tennessee
1945	College of the Scriptures	Louisville, Kentucky
1945	Winston-Salem Bible College	Winston-Salem, North Carolina
1950	Southwestern Christian College	Terrell, Texas

Javis Christian College is the only Black higher education institution in covenant with the Christian Church (Disciples of Christ) in our own day. It was founded as Jarvis Christian Institute through the encouragement of the Christian Woman's Board of Missions (CWBM) and with a donation of 465 acres of land near Hawkins, Texas, by Mrs. Ida V. Jarvis in 1910. Thomas B. Frost, a graduate of Southern Christian Institute, was appointed by the

CWBM in 1911 to develop the school. With the help of Charles A. Berry Sr., he cleared and fenced the land, built a dormitory-dining hall-classroom building, and designed the course of study by patterning the new institute along the same format as J. B. Lehman's Southern Christian Institute and Booker T. Washington's Tuskegee Institute.[58]

Jarvis Christian Institute opened January 14, 1913, with approximately thirteen students on a rural location near Hawkins, Texas, and was described as offering "opportunity to work, and was also accessible and free from distracting influences." By the fall of 1913, the enrollment doubled; J. N. Ervin was elected as the first president; and plans were made to construct a new dormitory from the timber surrounding the college.

Within six months, the enrollment had reached 148, the faculty sixteen. Jarvis was accredited as a high school in 1924, as a junior college in 1928, and as a full senior college in 1937, although its assets at that time were still controlled by the United Christian Missionary Society.[59]

Disciples accomplishments in educational ministry for Blacks was modest. During the period between 1865 and 1900 the concept of segregation became comfortably accepted by Disciples as seen in the development of independent and separate Black congregations and separate Black schools, owned and controlled by the Movement as "mission" outposts rather than independent educational institutions. By 1876, Black Disciples numbered 20,000 with 168 Black congregations in fifteen states; and in 1900, Black membership among the Disciples stood at 72,000 with 611 Black congregations in twenty-one states.[60] Nearly 60 percent of the Black Disciples were in the area south of the Ohio River and east of the Mississippi River.

DISCIPLES COLLEGES: 1900 - 1919

> The survival of the fittest will ultimately determine which colleges shall live and which shall die.
>
> W. T. Moore, 1909
> *History of the Disciples*

During the first two decades of the new century, fifty-three higher education institutions were founded within the Disciples Movement. Twenty-eight of those were established in the Old South, eleven in Northern states, four in the trans-Missouri West, and the remainder in Kentucky and Missouri. In those same two decades, only nineteen academies appeared, an indication of the declining need for that type of school.

Impelled by the discovery that more Disciples youth were attending state universities than were attending Disciples colleges, the Movement developed new types of educational structures during the 1890's: the religious foundation, the Bible chair, and the affiliated divinity house within a major university. It is considered by many as the Disciples' most constructive and original contribution to education in the United States. The first such institution to be created was the Disciples Divinity House at the University of Chicago in 1894. A companion volume in this series presents the story of the Bible chair and divinity house phenomenon among Disciples and will, therefore, be omitted from this treatment.

COLLEGES FOUNDED BY THE MOVEMENT 1900 - 1909

Year of Founding	Name	Location
1900	ALB Inductive University	Lisbon, Ohio
	Correspondence Literary College	Van, Tennessee
	North Middleton College	North Middletown, Kentucky
1901	Kansas Bible College	Lawrence, Kansas
	Potter Bible College	Bowling Green, Kentucky
1902	Atlantic Christian College	Wilson, North Carolina
	Dexter Christian College	Dexter, Missouri
	Washington Christian College	Washington, D.C.
1903	AlaTannaya College	Bridgeport, Alabama
	Campbell-Hagerman College	Lexington, Kentucky
	Christian College & Business Institute	Lingleville, Texas
	Flemingburg College	Flemingburg, Kentucky
	Gunter Bible College	Gunter, Texas
	Iowa Christian College	Oskaloosa, Iowa
	Virginia Christian College	
	[Lynchburg College]	Lynchburg, Virginia
1904	Austin College	Effingham, Illinois
	Chicago Correspondence Bible College	Chicago, Illinois
	Southwestern Christian College	Denton, Texas
1905	Holman Christian University	Black Mountain, North Carolina
	Western Bible & Literary College	Odessa, Missouri
1906	Abilene Christian College	Abilene, Texas
	Pan Handle Christian College	Hereford, Texas
1907	Clebarro College	Cleburne, Texas
	Cordell Christian College	Cordell, Oklahoma
	Industrial Christian College	Dawson, North Carolina
	Oklahoma Christian College	
	[Phillips University]	Enid, Oklahoma
	Sabinal Christian College	Sabinal, Texas
	Standard Correspondence Bible College	Enid, Oklahoma
1908	Angola Bible College	Angola, Indiana
	California Literary & Bible College	Kings County, California
	Maritime Bible College	West Gore, Nova Scotia
	Pastor's College	Champaign, Illinois
1909	Cofer Bible College	Krum, Texas
	Midland College	Midland, Texas
	Thorp Spring Christian College	Thorp Spring, Texas
	Southern Christian College	West Point, Mississippi

Compiled from State Histories and from the 1964 Claude Spencer list.

The year was 1900. The season was spring. It was commencement day at a small Carolina school where the speaker was Daniel E. Motley, a Johns Hopkins Ph.d., an ordained minister, and the Disciples state evangelist for North Carolina. As he gazed across the sand and pine of the Carolina coastal plain, he spoke with a prophetic flair:

> In a vision that shall be more than a vision, I see yonder in one of our beautiful North Carolina towns, a Christian College with an able Christian faculty.[61]

Following two years of spirited effort, his vision had become reality. In 1902, the Wilson Education Association offered a parcel of property and a gift of $14,000 to the Disciples North Carolina Missionary Society with which to purchase the property; and Atlantic Christian College was born. The doors opened in September with a docket of sixteen fields of study blended into a classical-practical-ministerial curriculum:

Bible	Mathematics
Ancient Languages & Literature	Philosophy
Modern Languages & Literature	Ethics & Logic
English Language & Literature	Political Economy
Natural Sciences	Sociology & History
Expressions & Physical Culture	Music
Business	Fine Arts
Pedagogy	College Preparatory

COLLEGES FOUNDED BY THE MOVEMENT 1910-1919

Year of Founding	Name	Location
1910	College of Missions	Indianapolis, Indiana
1911	Dixie College	Cookesville, Tennessee
	Parker College	Winnebago, Minnesota
1912	Alabama Christian College	Berry, Alabama
	Berry Bible College	Berry, Alabama
	Lamar College	Clarkson, Georgia
	Spokane University	Spokane, Washington
1913	Jarvis Christian College	Hawkins, Texas
	Minnesota Bible College	Minneapolis, Minnesota
1914	Brite Divinity School	Fort Worth, Texas
	Central Christian College	Kelley, Kentucky
1915	Harper College	Harper, Kansas
	Monea College	Rector, Arkansas
	Southeastern Christian College	Auburn, Georgia
	Tennessee Christian College	Jonesboro, Tennessee
1919	Kentucky Christian College	Grayson, Kentucky

Compiled from State histories and from the 1964 Claude Spencer list.

ASSETS OF COLLEGES AT CENTENNIAL CELEBRATION IN OCTOBER, 1909

NAME OF COLLEGE	Number in Faculty	Number of Students			Value of Property	Endowment	Location	President
		Male	Female	Ministerial				
Addran-Jarvis College							Thorp Springs, Tex.	
Atlantic Christian College	14	40	86	14	$ 40,000.00	$ 3,000.00	Wilson, N.C.	Jesse C. Caldwell
Berkeley Bible Seminary	4	14	3	14	20,000.00	20,000.00	Berkeley, Calif.	H. D. McAneney
Bethany College	18	198	72	88	200,000.00	135,000.00	Bethany, W. Va.	Thos. E. Cramblet
Bible College of Missouri	3	97	88	18	40,000.00	55,000.00	Columbia, Mo.	W. J. Lhamon
Butler College	17	116	132	35	250,000.00	450,000.00	Indianapolis, Ind.	Thomas C. Howe
Carlton College	12		100		45,000.00			
Christian University	14	102	56	72	75,000.00	20,000.00	Canton, Mo.	Carl Johann
Drake University	120	772	1074	173	403,804.00	432,351.00	Des Moines, Iowa	Hill M. Bell
Eugene Bible University	6	70	32	45	50,000.00	35,000.00	Eugene, Ore.	E. C. Sanderson
Eureka College	17	131	72	45	110,000.00	50,000.00	Eureka, Ill.	R. E. Hieranymus
Hiram College	21	156	118	57	150,000.00	100,000.00	Hiram, Ohio	Miner Lee Baton
Kentucky Female Orphan School	11		150		75,000.00	282,063.00	Midway, Ky.	Miss Ella Johnson
Milligan College	12	111	67	11	25,000.00		Milligan, Tenn.	F. D. Kershner
McLean College								
Nebraska Christian University	24	*377		65	75,000.00	40,000.00	Bethany, Neb.	W. P. Aylsworth
Oklahoma Christian University	20	*260		54	150,000.00		Enid, Okla.	E. V. Zollars
School of the Evangelists	9	131		125	75,000.00		Kimberlin Hts., Tenn.	Ashley S. Johnson
Texas Christian University	28	200	140	30	250,000.00		N. Waco, Tex.	Clinton Lockhart
Hamilton College	25		302		100,000.00		Lexington, Ky.	Mrs. Luella W. St. Clair
Transylvania University	30	765	364	174	800,000.00	225,000.00	Lexington, Ky.	R. H. Crossfield
College of the Bible	6	93	3		26,000.00	143,835.00	Lexington, Ky.	John W. McGarvey
West Kentucky College	11	132	120	4	60,000.00	5,000.00	Mayfield, Ky.	G. A. Lewellen
William Woods College for Girls	20		250		150,000.00	21,500.00	Fulton, Mo.	J. B. Jones
Sinclair College	6	11	4	6	3,500.00		St. Thomas, Ont.	John L. McLarty
Mo. Christian College for Girls	10	1	95		40,000.00	20,000.00	Camden Pt., Mo.	E. L. Barnham
Washington Christian College	11				55,000.00		Washington, D.C.	D. E. Modey
Louisville Christian Bible School	2	16		16	6,000.00		Louisville, Ky.	A. J. Thomson
Virginia Christian College	15	128	100	15	145,000.00		Lynchburg, Va.	Josephus Hopwood
Campbell-Hagerman College	21		252		125,000.00		Lexington, Ky.	B. C. Hagerman
Carr-Burdette College	5		40		75,000.00		Sherman, Tex.	O. A. Carr
Christian College	28		260		300,000.00		Columbia, Mo.	Mrs. W. T. Moore
Disciples Divinity House	2	28		4	30,000.00	30,000.00	Chicago, Ill.	Herbert L. Willett
Totals	542	*7658		1065	$3,936,304.00	$2,067,749.00		

*Total number.

62

Two hundred and eighteen students enrolled to study with a faculty of six during the first year of Atlantic Christian's history.[63]

The year was 1903. The season was winter. On a crisp February morning somewhere amid the seven hills of Lynchburg, Virginia, a compelling Disciples minister-educator named Josephus Hopwood announced to friends that he was preparing to found a college. The community of Lynchburg offered the Westover Hotel at the low price of $13,000, which Hopwood and his friends purchased and transformed into Virginia Christian College (later renamed Lynchburg College). By the fall of 1903, the little college had recruited 155 students, employed a faculty of ten, and designed a curriculum containing forty-two courses.[64]

The year was 1906. The season was fall. The indomitable Ely Von Zollars, a minister-educator who had served as president of Hiram College and Texas Christian University, was lobbying the Missionary Societies of both Oklahoma and Indian Territories to assist him in founding a new school. The societies accepted Dr. Zollars' eager challenge and jointly issued an invitation to the communities of the territories to bid for the college. Seven cities responded. The Chamber of Commerce from Enid, Oklahoma, a community barely fourteen years old with 12,000 people and twenty-six saloons, instructed their negotiating committee to "Promise them anything. Get the School." Enid presented itself as "free of malaria" and made an offer of forty acres of land, four scholarships valued at $20,000, free sewer and water mains, five years of free water supply, a paved street to within one mile of the campus, the extension of streetcar lines with guaranteed charge of 5 cents—a total package valued between $80,000 and $135,000. Enid was selected as the most suitable location for an educational enterprise; and a new Disciples school was founded there, Oklahoma Christian University (known today as Phillips University).[65]

The three stories recited here had been re-enacted many times in every quarter of Discipledom. While the setting of geography, the cast of characters, and the seasons changed, the essentials of founding remained the same. These institutions were creations of denominational initiative, community speculation, and the drive of dedicated individuals.

Daniel Boorstin observed of the early days of college founding that "American colleges were emphatically institutions of the local community."[66] This statement is particularly relevant to those institutions of learning in the Disciples tradition. The boom communities of the border states, the Midwest, and Far-West somehow seemed incomplete without a college; and, while Disciples clergy took the initiative to establish the institutions, it was the community which provided the backing. Enid, with her land, sewer lines, and free water supply; Lynchburg with her Westover Hotel; Wilson with her parcel of property—all illustrate this point. Very often, as in the cases of Hiram, Eureka, Bethany, and Lynchburg, the college actually took the name of the community it was to glorify. The boards of trustees, heavily Disciples during the nineteenth and early twentieth centuries, were, and continue to be drawn in significant numbers, from the local community in order to marshal resources and to insure that a part of the college mission matched community needs. Very early the community promoters prevailed over the academies in the governance of the schools and also influenced the design of the curriculum toward practical subjects. Disciples colleges and universities are just as accurately identified as community institutions as they are church-related.[67]

The third and last great period of college founding among Disciples was 1900 to 1920 when the fifty-two institutions cited above took root, including Atlantic Christian College (1902), Lynchburg College (1903), and Phillips University (1906). Jarvis Christian College is the only institution founded since that time which remains in covenant with the Christian Church (Disciples of Christ).

Entering the twentieth century, Disciples institutions were still under the influence of Campbellian educational philosophy, but with a stronger sectarian tone. In fact, most of them were best characterized as Bible colleges with significant numbers of their students preparing to enter some form of ministry. The average enrollment per institution during the first two decades of the century was just over three hundred students.

EARLY TWENTIETH CENTURY ENROLLMENT AND ENDOWMENT

Institution	Enrollment		Endowment in Millions	
	1912	1919	1913	1920
Atlantic Christian	155	189		
Bethany	346	398	.4	.5
Butler	296	963	.4	.4
Columbia	237	256		
Cotner	351	357		.2
Culver-Stockton	145	158	.2	.2
Drake	1544	1460	.8	.8
Eureka	187	383	.2	.2
Hiram	231	354	.2	.5
Lynchburg	130	197		
Midway	145	149	.2	.3
Phillips University	387	1015	.1	.2
Texas Christian	770	925		
Transylvania	290	473	.3	.7
William Woods	170	231	.1	.3 [68]

The presidents were, almost to a person, ordained Disciples ministers, recipients of undergraduate degrees from other Disciples-related colleges, recipients of advanced degrees in theology, and recipients of their first administrative experience at still another Disciples college. The network of

Disciples institutions tended to produce its own leadership, which often isolated it from the main currents of educational reform. Early in the twentieth century, the list of presidents included W. E. Garrison, Ely Von Zollars, Richard Crossfield, Thomas E. Cramblet, Harry O. Pritchard, Jesse Caldwell, Miner Lee Bates, Issac Newton McCash, John Hepler Wood, and Joseph Garvin. A notable exception to the pattern was Luella St. Clair Moss, who became president of Columbia College in Columbia, Missouri at age twenty-eight, uncredentialed, inexperienced, and unordained. She was one of only four women (Ella Johnson, Mrs. W. T. Moore, Meta Chestnutt) ever to serve as a chief executive officer in the Disciples network of colleges, and she rendered one of the most controversial, flamboyant, lengthy, and successful presidencies in the annals of Disciples' higher education.[69]

CREATION OF A NATIONAL SERVICE AGENCY
For the want of some central directing superintendency . . .
W. T. Moore, 1909

The first "faint beginnings" of any general service or coordination for higher education institutions came in 1894 when the national convention at Chicago created a Board of Education under the aegis of the American Christian Missionary Society. Provision for funding did not accompany its formation, thereby rendering the early years of the Board deficient on accomplishment and influence. Mrs. Albertina Allen Forrest was appointed to the office of secretary and worked heroically under impossible financial contraints. Circulating occasional questionnaires to the institutions and analyzing the data, Mrs. Forrest published articles in various Disciples journals in an attempt to promote higher education and generate a deeper sense of responsibility within the membership for sustaining the colleges. Her efforts stand as the first attempt to gather some statistical understanding of the Disciples colleges, to consider the schools as a distinct network of higher education institutions, and to create the beginning of a literature on Disciples higher education.[70]

Forrest's article, "The Status of Education Among the Disciples," is a ground-breaking work in statistical research on the nature and character of Disciples colleges. It contained seven statistical tables from which the following abridged and consolidated chart is drawn as a representative sample of her research:

Forrest observed that the unique place of the Bible in Disciples college curriculum and the quality of biblical teaching were exceptionally good. She also pointed out that the distinctive presence of the Bible at Disciples colleges did not compensate for a multiplicity of other deficiences. It was equally

REPORTING DISCIPLES COLLEGES-1896

REPORTING INSTITUTIONS	ENROLLMENT				FINANCIAL DATA				FACULTY		LIBRARY	
	Male	Female	Min STD	STD Rec Fin Aid	Endowment	Debt	Tuition Income	Annual Contributions	Professors	Avg. Salary	Hrs. per Week	Volumes
Kentucky University	227	49	22	0	$201,000	$ 0	$ 5,476	0	14	$1,750	16	14,672
Butler College	156	78	24	0	253,000	0	5,200	0	11	1,100	16	12,000
Eureka College	131	115	43	20	37,453	19,000	—	—	7	900	20	4,692
Christian University	60	50	25	2	16,000	0	3,000	1,500	10	800	20	1,000
Oskaloosa College	60	70	8	0	30,000	5,000	2,000	0	6	500	25	4,000
Kentucky Bible College	155	0	155	23	73,000	0	3,250	0	4	1,400	15	2,000
Hiram College	252	143	50	20	125,000	0	8,145	1,575	12	1,200	21	6,120
Add Ran Christian Univ.	—	—	40	25	0	15,000	10,000	0	13	765	—	2,100
Fairfield College	55	20	11	0	0	9,000	2,000	0	5	—	18	250
Cotner University	160	190	35	5	0	50,000	6,000	2,000	6	1,100	22	1,000

71

necessary, she said, to stay apace with the new order of sciences and languages as it was to teach the Bible properly.

Based upon her analysis of Disciples college's statistics, Forrest formed a number of helpful insights: (a) None had sufficient endowment, which she suggested should be at least $500,000, and only Butler and Kentucky University approached comfortable levels. (b) Where indebtedness exceeded endowment, Forrest believed that irreparable damage had been done to the institution and it would soon close. (c) It was inappropriate, in her judgement, for the colleges to depend so heavily upon outside contributions from year to year for operating expenses. She expressed pleasure that the practice was falling into disfavor, adding that "the promiscuity of such appeals upon the different churches is closely allied to the house to house tramp charity . . . so roundly condemned by social reformers of our day." (d) Disciples campuses were well improved with excellent buildings, but the adaptation of these buildings to the needs of the school was inadequate. Laboratories and equipment for chemistry and physics were woefully insufficient and there were no facilities whatever for experimental psychology. (e) In most cases the student-teacher ratios were much too high when measured against the 1890's national average of fourteen to one. (f) On the work and remuneration of faculty, only Butler, Kentucky University and the College of the Bible approached the national standard of eight to fifteen hours of classroom work per week and salaries were well below the church-related college average of $2000-3000. Forrest also pointed to the weaknesses in graduate education of Disciples professors. Only one professor among all Disciples professors had a Ph.D. and 42 percent had no graduate training at all. Of those who did, 31 percent received it from our own colleges, which were not prepared to offer such a program. Many Disciples institutions hired sizeable numbers of their own graduates. At Hiram College, eight of twelve faculty were Hiram graduates and four of those had not attended any other school, thus giving Disciples faculty a significantly provincial character. (g) Requirements for degrees in Disciples colleges were vastly different. Forrest called for some uniform standard so that "degrees" would have a basis of comparison and not be misused. Butler and Add Ran, for example, were operating Ph.D. programs, yet were not anyway equipped to offer such a degree. (h) Ministry was a predominant field of study with 30 percent of all male students preparing for a career in religious service.[72]

Forrest capped her statistical summary with a practical plea to the Movement:

No compiled statistics of our educational interests have been printed before. They are not complete in every respect, but if the same line of work can be carried out each year it can be greatly enlarged and improved. The purpose has proved to be, in some respects, to criticize, but in another respect it has been to bring to the appreciation of the Disciples the worth of our schools.

> No one can fail to see that the Disciples are doing a great work with small means. Ought this not to arouse us to a deeper appreciation of the needs of our colleges? We cannot divorce our education from our religion, and if we would become a power in the religious world we must become a power in the educational world.[73]

Another contribution of the Board during these early years, aside from Forrest's research and publications, was its recommendation that the first Sunday in July be recognized as Education Sunday by all congregations. Voted at the 1898 Chattanooga, Tennessee convention, it represented an important achievement in gaining church-wide recognition of a common ministry in higher education.

The orginal purpose of the Board of Education contained three elements:

1. To collect and distribute information concerning educational institutions of the Disciples of Christ.
2. The endowment of chairs in the different colleges for instruction in the history and science of missions.
3. The raising of funds for scholarships to aid students preparing for religious work.[74]

Albertina Forrest served as Secretary until 1900, when she recommended that the Board be dissolved and a National Education Society organized to replace it. Adopting her suggestion, the American Christian Education Society was formed in 1901 with its office in Washington, D.C. and F. D. Power as president. The following year its headquarters were transferred to Indianapolis and A. B. Philputt was named president. By 1903, a full-time secretary, Harry G. Hill was employed; but the position was soon phased out for lack of funds. In 1910, the Association of Colleges of the Disciples of Christ was organized under the presidency of the venerable Richard Crossfield, then president of Transylvania University. This Association was replaced September 4, 1914, at the St. Louis national convention, with the formation of the Board of Education of the Disciples of Christ in order to participate effectively in the church-wide "Men and Millions" capital drive. Crossfield continued as president of the new board of thirty-seven members which paid dues of $100 or $50, depending on the size of the school.

The new Board was created with a two-fold purpose: to train leaders for the church (the ministry, the mission field, and lay service); and to assist the colleges in fund raising (gifts and endowments, legacies and annuities, and education day). In its broad outline, this plan represented the first comprehensive program for higher education ministry developed by a service agency of the Disciples.

Some evidence exists to demonstrate that a deeper sensitivity to higher education was engendered throughout the Movement as a result of the Board's work. Education Sunday netted $19,000 in 1915; in 1916, it rose to

$31,000, nearly double what it had been two years before. Part of the increase was no doubt due to war-time prosperity, but part of it was also due to the work of the Board. Opening enrollments in the fall of 1918 had grown to 7,839 students in the network of thirty-seven Disciples colleges.[75]

Continued economic growth following World War I spurred Disciples colleges and generated enough funds to appoint a full-time general secretary to head the Board. Harry O. Pritchard, president of Eureka College, was elected to the position in 1919. With Pritchard's arrival the Board expanded its vision to include a six part program:

1. To bring all colleges up to as high standards educationally as their resources will permit.
2. To give advice on the best business methods for conducting colleges.
3. To provide assistance in the conduct of capital campaigns.
4. To assist in a nation-wide recruitment campaign for students for ministry.
5. To nationalize the appeal for Higher Education and create among Disciples an educational conscience.
6. To keep in touch with educational movements in other religious bodies.[76]

A graduate of Butler University, Indiana University, and Yale Divinity School, School, the highly skilled and nationally respected Pritchard presided over a "golden age" in the life of the new Board which would last until 1934.

Across the eighty-three years from the founding of Bacon College to the 1919 election of Harry O. Pritchard, Disciples made four distinct and unique contributions to American Higher Education: 1. The significant place given to the study of the Bible in the undergraduate curriculum was unique to Disciples colleges. Even in the twentieth century the emphasis upon biblical study in Disciples college has remained greater than in the majority of their counterparts. 2. Disciples colleges pioneered in co-education. While they were not the first to *admit* women, they were among the very first in *founding outright* a number of co-educational institutions—Eureka, Hiram, Butler, and Culver-Stockton—while also leading in the establishment of schools for females. 3. The third contribution, considered by many as the most original, was the establishment of Bible chairs, divinity houses, and schools of religion at tax supported colleges and universities. The Disciples were first to implement this concept and founded a greater number than any other religious body. 4. Finally, the Disciples were first to advance and implement the concept of campus ministry on state-owned campuses, leading the way in 1894 at Ann Arbor, Michigan. When Harry Pritchard took the reins of leadership in 1919, one of his initial tasks was to publicize this legacy among the congregations in the Restoration Movement.

References

1. D. Duane Cummins, *A Handbook for Today's Disciples.* Christian Board of Publication, 1981, pp. 12-13.
2. *Ibid.*
3. *Ibid.*
4. Leo Marx, *The Machine in the Garden.* Oxford University Press, 1964, pp. 3, 13-17, 250-265.
   Roderick Nash, *Wilderness and the American Mind.* Yale University Press, 1967, pp. 84-95.
5. *Ibid.*
6. *Ibid.*
7. Commager, *Documents in American History*, p. 413.
8. Rudolph, pp. 292-300.
   Hofstader, pp. 30-37.
9. *Ibid.*
10. *Ibid.*
11. John Henry Newman, *The Idea of a University*, 1959 Edition. Doubleday, p. 138.
12. *Ibid.*, pp. 171-172.
13. *Ibid.*, pp. 138-139.
14. *Ibid.*, p. 139.
15. *Ibid.*, p. 135.
16. *Ibid.*, p. 139.
17. Minutes of the Board of Kentucky University, June 20, 1865; cited in John D. Wright, *Transylvania: Tutor to the West.* 1975, p. 198.
18. Dwight E. Stevenson, *Lexington Theological Seminary.* Bethany Press, 1964, pp. 23-43.
    Wright, *Transylvania*, pp. 190-211.
    A. W., Fortune, pp. 259-287.
19. John W. McGarvey, "Ministerial Education." *Lard's Quarterly*, April, 1865, pp. 239-250.
20. *Ibid.*, p. 242.
21. *Millennial Harbinger*, Vol. XXXVI, No. 8 (August 1865), pp. 364-365.
22. *Ibid.*, p. 371.
23. *Ibid.*, Vol. XXXVI, No. 9 (September 1865), p. 416.
24. *Ibid.*, Vol. XXXVI, No. 10 (October 1865), p. 450.
25. *Ibid.*, p. 451.
26. *Millenial Harbinger*, Vol. XXXVI, No. 11 (November 1865), pp. 495-496.
27. George L. Peters, *Disciples of Christ in Missouri.* Missouri Convention, 1927, pp. 116-117.
28. *Ibid.*, p. 118.
29. Stevenson, pp. 30, 55.
30. G. T. Carpenter, "Our Colleges." *The Christian Quarterly Review*, Vol. IV, (July 1985), p. 388. (374-388).
31. Leon A. Moomaw, *History of Cotner University.* 1916, pp. 40-45.
32. Colby D. Hall, *History of Texas Christian University.* TCU Press, 1947, pp. 35-36.
33. E. B. Ware, *History of the Disciples of Christ in California.* 1916, p. 165.
34. Moomaw, p. 39-42.
35. Charles Richey, *Drake University Through 75 Years.* Drake University, 1956, pp. 35-51.
36. Adal Forster, *A History of the Christian Church & Church of Christ in Minnesota.* Christian Board of Publication, 1953, pp. 19-22.
37. Shaw, *Hoosier Disciples*, pp. 215-216, 234.
38. Green, *History of Hiram*, p. 255.
39. Truedly, Hiram, pp. 150-170.
40. Colby Hall, *Texas Disciples*, pp. 248-249.
41. *Ibid.*
42. Reuben Butchart, *The Disciples of Christ in Canada Since 1830.* Ontario: Richardson, Bond & Wright, 1949, p. 151.
43. *Ibid.*, pp. 148-153.
44. Woolery, *Bethany*, p. 112.
45. Carpenter, "Our Colleges," p. 378.

46. Watson, *Christian Churches in Alabama*, p. 117.
47. Green, *Hiram*, p. 243.
48. Hall, *Texas Christian University*, pp. 117-161.
    Ritchey, *Drake University*, pp. 37-51.
49. Hap Lyda, "Black Disciples in the Nineteenth Century," W. A. Welsh, *The Untold Story*. Christian Board of Publication, 1976, pp. 9-19.
50. *Ibid.*
51. David E. Harrell, *The Social Sources of Division in the Disciples of Christ 1865-1900*. Publishing Systems, 1973, p. 170.
52. Cited in Harrell, p. 172.
53. *Ibid.*, p. 180.
54. *Gospel advocate*. March 12, 1868; cited in Herman Norton. *Tennessee Christians*. Reed & Co., 1971, p. 132.
55. *Millennial Harbinger*, Vol. XXXIX, No. 4 (April 1868), pp. 227-228.
56. Elmer C. Lewis, "A History of Secondary and Higher Education in Negro Schools Related to the Disciples of Christ," 1957. (Unpublished Doctoral Dissertation, University of Pittsburgh), pp. 28-30, 49-50.
57. Lewis, p. 41-48.
    Clarice Campbell and Oscar Rogers, *Mississippi: The View From Tougaloo*. University of Mississippi Press, 1979, pp. 181-182.
58. Colby Hall, *History of Texas Christian University*, p. 330.
    Clifford Taylor, "Jarvis Christian College," 1948. (Bachelor of Divinity Thesis, Brite Divinity School), pp. 4-17.
59. *Ibid.*
60. Lyda, pp. 12, 15, 18. *Disciples of Christ Year Book, 1899*, American Christian Missionary Society.
61. C. C. Ware, *A History of Atlantic Christian College*. Bethany Press, 1956, p. 62.
    D. Duane Cummins, "The Preacher and the Promoter." *Discipliana*, Vol. 44, No. 1 (Spring 1984), pp. 3-7, 14.
62. *Survey of Service*. Christian Board of Publication, 1928, p. 604.
63. *Ibid.*
64. Orville W. Wake, "A History of Lynchburg College, 1903-1953," 1957. (Unpublished Doctoral Dissertation, University of Virginia), pp. 63-66.
65. Frank H. Marshall, *Phillips University's First Fifty Years*. Phillips University, Vol. 1, 1957, pp. 21-31.
    Ronald E. Osborn, *Ely Von Zollars*. Christian Board of Publication, 1947, pp. 197-211.
66. Daniel Boorstin, *The Americans: The Colonial Experience*. Alfred Knoff, 1958, p. 181.
67. D. Duane Cummins, pp. 3-7.
68. *Disciples of Christ Year Book, 1915, 1920*, American Christian Missionary Society.
69. Allean L. Hale, *Petticoat Pioneer*. Artcraft Press, 1956, pp. 114-152.
70. Griffith A. Hamlin, "The Origin and Development of the Board of Higher Education of the Christian Church (Disciples of Christ) 1894-1968," 1968. (Masters Thesis, Southern Illinois University), pp. 23-42.
71. Albertina Allen Forrest, "The Status of Education Among the Disciples." *The New Christian Quarterly*, Vol. V. (October 1896), p. 412.
72. *Ibid.*
73. *Ibid.*, pp. 415-416.
74. *Disciples of Christ Year Book, 1897*. American Christian Missionary Society, p. 50.
75. Hamlin, pp. 26-42.
76. *Disciples of Christ Year Book, 1920*. American Christian Missionary Society, p. 84.

Chapter 4

DISCIPLES COLLEGES IN THE TWENTIETH CENTURY

EDUCATIONAL CURRENTS BETWEEN THE WORLD WARS

> The Wisdom of all ages is to be naught compared with the inclination of a sophomore.
>
> Irving Babbitt, 1929

Spread across the twenties and thirties was a growing challenge to the university pre-occupation with practical and professional education, to the excessive emphasis upon the individual, and to the "undisciplined chaos" of the elective principle. The intellectual and moral crises, created by the shattering experiences of world war and economic depression, turned the thought of educators more toward what is human about persons rather than what is merely individual about them, toward intellect rather than utility, toward wisdom and character rather than scientific materialism and power. Specialization and science were widely thought to be the chief contributors to the brutal human condition of war and depression. In light of that belief there was a new demand for persons with wisdom and breadth of vision, capable of thinking holistically, persons who could understand the inter-relatedness of past, present, and future, of institutions, values, and traditions, and how all of these elements coalesced into a definition of the new day.

Symbolic of this turning of mind was the General Education Movement begun at Columbia University in 1919. The Columbia planners developed a core-course model, designed to restore the concept of a body of thought and of a continuing intellectual heritage, that would be a general education requirement of all students, serving as context and balance to the existing preference for specialization. Under the Columbia plan, humanities courses— philosophy, history, literature, art—enjoyed a new vitality in the collegiate curriculum. Efforts to reconcile humanities and science in the university course of study became current fare across the country.

It was also a time that saw the philosophies of Alfred North Whitehead, William James, and John Dewey gain influence with curriculum builders. James believed one of the most essential parts of a liberal educational was "to know the chief rival attitudes towards life." A person with no philosophy, he wrote, "is the most inauspicious and unprofitable of all social mates."[1] Whitehead argued that "you may not divide the seamless coat of learning," and that the subjects of "general education are special subjects specially studied."[2] Dewey in his *Democracy and Education: An Introduction to the Philosophy of Education* wrote that education and experience were synonymous and that education should not be segregated from society. With war and depression charging through the American experience, people renewed their quest for a philosophy of life, sought a larger context for their specialized knowledge, and attempted to integrate their experience with education. Academia developed a deeper appreciation for economics, political science, sociology, and psychology—a body of courses known as the Social Sciences, designed to strengthen the relationship between education and society by providing, through scholarly study, a greater breadth of understanding of people and institutions.

Administratively, colleges and universities had become complex organizations with sophisticated managerial apparatus and hierarchical corporate structures. Before the Civil War most colleges were managed with a president, a treasurer, and a librarian, although many early Disciples colleges had only a president. A 1938 study of higher education administration revealed the median number of administrators at a typical college in 1860 was four; but by 1933 the median figure had grown to 30.5.[3] Institutional and curricular expansion along with increased numbers of students created a demand for new services, which in turn called for more administrators, a proliferation of officers that included registrars, directors of admissions, business officers, deans and assistant deans of faculties, women, and men, and a full range of presidential assistants in charge of everything from public relations to church relations.

The inexorable growth of organizational complexity summoned forth a new breed of president with a predominant leadership style of technical and professional managerial skills rather than the minister-philosopher qualities of an earlier time. In a world grown secular and less responsive to religious influences, the tradition of clergymen as presidents was fast disappearing from the university scene while remaining very much a staple at Disciples colleges.

Hereditary wealth had been unable to wield any undue authority in setting educational ideals during the nineteenth century because of the disjunctive and fluid nature of the age. It was in the twentieth century that benefactors with immense fortunes began to exert major influence on the life of colleges. During the 1920's and 1930's most private institutions depended for their very existence upon the material wealth and generosity of philanthropists. When the contributions were given directly, the benefactor often became a powerful voice on the board of trustees. Gifts granted by a foundation were accompanied with a set of criteria that had to be satisfied before the grant was awarded. Foundations became an influential force in shaping the life of many campuses, effecting budget management and admissions standards, determining research subjects, and even weakening the relationship with the church. Many colleges were quite willing to drop the church-relationship to qualify for foundation support. Disciples colleges, by contrast, were neither experienced nor staffed to raise major capital dollars, which caused their endowments to remain exceedingly modest and their dependence upon the church relatively strong.

DISCIPLES COLLEGES: 1920 - 1949

The most important single aim of the Colleges and Universities of the Disciples of Christ appears to be the continuation and extension of the faith of the communion.

H. O. Pritchard, 1928

College founding within the movement between 1920 and the time of restructure in the late 1960's produced fifty-eight colleges along with an assorted list of twenty-nine Bible institutions, schools, academies, and seminaries. Overwhelmingly, the twentieth century colleges were founded by the Church of Christ sector of the Restoration Movement, primarily in the trans-Mississippi West and the Old South. The Disciples branch of the Movement decelerated its efforts to establish new institutions and concentrated its educational energy on developing cooperation among the existing institutions through the new Board of Education. Disciples have not established a new four-year college since the appearance of Jarvis Christian College in 1913. Chapman College was created in the 1920's from a lineage of three previous Disciples institutions. The same was true of Northwest Christian College (1934), which continues a unique relationship with two segments of the reformation Movement. The last higher education institution of any kind to be established by Disciples as of this writing was the Disciples Seminary Foundation at Claremont, California, in 1960. It is not included in the list of "colleges" for this period.

Canada was also engaged during these years in the founding of two new colleges. With the urging of Harry Pritchard an All Canada College, incorporated as *College, Churches of Christ in Canada*, was established in October, 1927 at Toronto, but was forced to suspend operations at the beginning of the depression in 1929. Alberta Bible College, a ministerial training school founded by C. H. Phillips, was incorporated in 1936 at Lethbridge and two years later moved to Calgary.[4]

COLLEGES FOUNDED BY THE MOVEMENT 1920-1968

(Excluding Bible institutes, Bible schools, Bible academies, Bible seminaries, Bible chairs, divinity houses, seminaries)

Year	Institution	Location
1920	*California Christian College (Chapman)	Orange, California
	Colorado Christian Bible College	Denver, Colorado
	Midland College	Midland, Texas
	Seattle Bible College	Seattle, Washington
1922	Harding College	Searcy, Arkansas
	Randolph College	Cisco, Texas
1923	Central Christian College	Centerville, Iowa
	McGarvey Bible College	Louisville, Kentucky
1925	Atlanta Christian College	Atlanta, Georgia
1927	Christian Workers University	Manhattan, Kansas
	College, Churches of Christ in Canada	Toronto, Canada
	Colorado Bible College	Fort Collins, Colorado
	National Bible College	Wichita, Kansas
	Northern Bible College	Pierre, South Dakota
1928	Pacific Christian College	Long Beach, California
1930	Eugene Bible College	Eugene, Oregon
	Ozark Christian College	Harrison, Arkansas
1932	San Jose Bible College	San Jose, California
1934	*Northwest Christian College	Eugene, Oregon
1936	Alberta Bible College	Lethbridge, Canada
1937	Pepperdine College	Los Angeles, California
1942	Dakota Bible College	Arlington, South Dakota
	Ozark Bible College	Joplin, Missouri
1945	Boise Bible College	Boise, Idaho
	College of the Scriptures	Louisville, Kentucky
	Winston-Salem Bible College	Winston-Salem, North Carolina
1946	Florida Christian College	Tampa, Florida
	Midwest Christian College	Oklahoma City, Oklahoma
1947	Dasher Bible College	Valdosta, Georgia
	Intermountain Bible College	Grand Junction, Colorado
	Mars Hill College	Florence, Alabama
	Southern Christian College	San Antonio, Texas
1948	Roanoke Bible College	Elizabeth City, North Carolina
1949	Central Christian College	Bartlesville, Oklahoma
	*Christian College of Georgia	Athens, Georgia
	Four-State Christian College	Texarkana, Arkansas
	Great Lakes Bible College	Vestaberg, Michigan
	Kentucky Bible College	Winchester, Kentucky
	Louisville Bible College	Louisville, Kentucky
	Mexican Bible College	Nogales, Arizona
1950	Dallas Christian College	Dallas, Texas
	Puget Sound College of the Bible	Seattle, Washington
1951	Platte Valley Bible College	Scottsbluff, Nebraska
1953	Chattanooga Bible College	Chattanooga, Tennessee
	Gulf States Christian College	Baton Rouge, Louisiana

*Functioning and related to the Christian Church (Disciples of Christ) in 1986.

Year	Institution	Location
1956	Columbia Christian College	Portland, Oregon
	York College	York, Nebraska
1957	Central Christian College	Moberly, Missouri
	Chillicothe Bible College	Chillicothe, Missouri
	Lubbock Christian College	Lubbock, Texas
1958	North Central Christian College	, Ohio
	Ohio Valley College	Parkersburg, West Virginia
1959	Memphis Christian College	Memphis, Tennessee
	Northeastern Christian College	Villanova, Pennsylvania
1960	Fort Worth Christian College	Fort Worth, Texas
	Maritime Christian College	Charlottetown, Prince Edward Island, Canada
1961	Paducah Christian College	Paducah, Kentucky
1964	College of the Southwest	Dallas, Texas

Compiled from state histories and from the 1964 Claude Spencer list.

Viewing the company of Disciples colleges as a single network rather than a scattering of thirty-seven fugitive institutions unconnected and totally independent, H. O. Pritchard took the first steps in 1923 toward some form of denominational coordination of its higher education institutions. Through the Board of Education, Pritchard designed a series of territorial assignments, which were set in place with the mutual consent of the cooperating institutions. The assignments were carefully determined by geography and by demographic studies of church membership in relation to their financial ability to support educational institutions. Each college or university was given the responsibility for cultivating the territory assigned to it. Those institutions, planning campaigns for funds, were expected to limit their *general* solicitation of congregations to the territory assigned them, but they were not restricted from soliciting individuals wherever they were residing.

This early "territorial allotment" plan was the first significant attempt at coordination among Disciples higher education institutions and is the immediate ancestor of the present "comity relationships" coordinated by the Division of Higher Education.[6] The current relationships contain essentially the same provisions and geographic assignments as the original 1923 plan.

The most important contribution of the Pritchard era of institutional coordination was arranging for the research and publication of *College Organization and Administration*, authored by Floyd Reeves and John Russell. The book was a pioneer study in the field of quantitative measurements for institutional analysis and became widely used as a text in higher education classes at graduate schools, including the University of Chicago. Due to Pritchard's foresight, Disciples were among the Protestant leaders in quantitative evaluation of institutions. The authors of the study were soon asked by the United Methodists and other denominations to prepare a similar analysis of their affiliated colleges.

1926

TOTAL CHURCH MEMBERSHIP, CHURCH MEMBERSHIP PER DISCIPLE INSTI-
TUTION, AND INDEX OF ECONOMIC ABILITY PER CAPITA OF THE POPULATION
OF THE STATE IN WHICH THE INSTITUTIONS ARE SITUATED*

INSTITUTION OR GROUP OF INSTITUTIONS	Total Church Membership in the Territory Assigned	Average Church Membership Per Institution	Index of Economic Ability Per Capita of State	
Hiram College	106,680	106,680	$1,010	
Phillips University	122,268	122,268	701	
Cotner College	80,486	80,486	965	
Indiana Institutions	160,436	80,218	871	
Drake University	77,715	77,715	1,000	
Bethany College	73,276	73,276	807	
Illinois Institutions	133,003	66,501	1,112	
Lynchburg College	51,200	51,200	615	
California Christian College	51,071	51,071	1,338	
Kentucky Institutions	145,844	48,614	528	
School of Religion at Tuscaloosa	41,238	41,238	434	
Atlantic Christian College	35,785	35,785	530	
Spokane University	29,561	29,561	1,079	
Texas Institutions	78,980	26,326	723	
Missouri Institutions	153,921	25,653	844	5

*The data for church membership are taken from the *1926 Disciples of Christ Year Book*.
The index of economic ability for the United States is $926.

Reeves and Russell declared that Disciples institutions had developed as result of a conviction on the part of religious leaders that religion should be an intrinsic part of the educational experience of each individual. One of the fundamental objectives of Disciples institutions had always been to provide a religious environment and religious training for youth while they were students. The complete separation of church and state, in the authors opinion, had made it impossible to provide direct religious instruction at state schools and the responsibility for religious instruction, therefore, fell almost entirely upon the church.

Reeves and Russell accumulated an abundance of statistical data through which they were able to determine a general identification of the student clientele at Disciples colleges. Typically, student enrollment during the 1920's was 60 percent Disciples and predominantly from villages, small town, and open country within a fifty mile radius of the college.

On most of the Reeves-Russell statistical charts, there are three institutions which consistently defy all patterns. They are Drake University, Butler University, and Texas Christian University. All three had enrollments between 1400 and 2000, all three were located in cities, and all three were taking on the form of municipal universities. They stood as anomalies in the midst of the Disciples 1920's network of country colleges with enrollments of three to five hundred students.

PER CENTS OF COLLEGE STUDENTS RESIDING IN THE OPEN COUNTRY, IN VILLAGES, IN SMALL TOWNS, AND IN CITIES, FOR NINETEEN INSTITUTIONS 1921-1922

	Open Country (Population Below 250)	Village (250-2500)	Small Town (2500-5000)	City (Over 5000)	Disciples Students Percent of Entire Enrollment	Percent of Students Residing Within a Radius of Fifty Miles of the Institution Attended
Atlantic Christian College	10%	48%	2%	40%	58.3%	83%
Bethany College	4	44	10	37	77.9	50
Butler University	1	13	—	85	—	—
California Christian College	—	—	—	—	—	62
Carr-Burdette College	1	52	7	37	33.8	—
Christian College	—	44	13	42	56.7	41
Cotner College	8	66	6	13	85.6	40
Culver-Stockton College	6	83	3	8	63.7	72
Drake University	3	33	7	55	—	—
Eureka College	4	65	3	26	71.2	—
Hamilton College	—	—	—	—	—	59
Hiram College	4	40	8	48	66.5	68
Lynchburg College	—	—	—	—	69.3	43
Phillips University	—	—	—	—	54.2	62
Randolph College	—	—	—	—	58.4	50
Spokane University	12	46	9	32	65.4	32
Texas Christian University	3	29	7	59	—	—
Transylvania College	6	38	10	44	71.0	55
William Woods College	4	36	12	47	53.0	32

From a sample of seven institutions, Reeves and Russell determined that among the students attending Disciples colleges in 1920, more were preparing for a career in teaching than any other profession and the number of graduates entering teaching outnumbered graduates entering ministry by roughly two to one. "Disciples institutions," wrote Reeves, "are teaching institutions." He might also have added that Disciples institutions had become an important network of teacher training institutions.

The $273 per year cost of educating a student at a Disciples college was a matter of special interest to the authors. They demonstrated that a student is an economic liability rather than an asset. At Disciples colleges during the 1920's, student tuition covered, on the average, 61 percent of the cost; endowment income underwrote an average of 27 percent of the cost; the remaining 12 percent had to be solicited from congregations and individuals. The $273 cost per student in Disciples colleges was a shade above the 1920's national average of $266 for similar size instituions.

Disciples institutions were more heavily dependent upon gifts from congregations and individuals than other institutions of other denominations. Reeves and Russell calculated that, in aggregate, the Disciples colleges at that time needed additional endowment in the amount of $13 million to cover the costs and avoid deficits.

PER CAPITA CURRENT EXPENSE FOR EDUCATIONAL PURPOSES AT THIRTEEN COLLEGES OF THE DISCIPLES OF CHRIST

Institution	Year	Expenditures For Educational Purposes*	College Enrollment	Cost Per Student
Phillips University	1925-26	$101,477.82	581	$174
Transylvania College	1924-25	65,723.00	310	212
Atlantic Christian College	1924-25	30,643.51	137	223
Cotner College	1925-26	64,065.50	277	231
Christian College	1925-26	54,284.27	232	234
Spokane University	1926-27	26,504.71	102	260
Lynchburg College	1924-25	54,650.64	207	264
California Christian College	1926-27	45,661.74	172	265
Hiram College	1923-24	111,325.55	387	288
William Woods College	1925-26	54,886.72	182	301
Culver-Stockton College	1924-25	79,816.09	245	326
Eureka College	1924-25	114,600.00	300	382
Bethany College	1925-26	129,527.00	290	447
Total	---------	933,166.55	3,422	273 [9]

*The expenditure for educational purposes as classified in this table includes (1) administration and general expenses, (2) operation and maintenance of physical plant, and (3) instructional expenditures.

OCCUPATIONAL DISTRIBUTION OF ALUMNI OF FOUR INSTITUTIONS, FROM 1860 TO 1919.
(BUTLER UNIVERSITY, TRANSYLVANIA COLLEGE, HIRAM COLLEGE, AND EUREKA COLLEGE)

Year	Total Number	Religious Service Number	Percent	Education Number	Percent	Others Number	Percent	Dead and Unknown Number	Percent
1860-69	289	19	7	14	5	142	49	114	39
1870-79	344	32	9	17	5	186	54	109	32
1880-89	389	65	17	47	12	187	48	90	23
1890-99	932	185	20	132	14	432	46	183	20
1900-09	785	180	23	190	24	351	45	64	8
1910-19	1012	212	21	365	36	398	39	37	4
Total	3751	693		765		1696		597	
Average			19		20		45		16

OCCUPATIONAL DISTRIBUTION OF THE GRADUATES OF THREE DISCIPLE COLLEGES IN TERMS OF PERCENTAGES.
(EUREKA, CULVER-STOCKTON, AND LYNCHBURG COLLEGES)

Occupation	Averages For Three Colleges From 1900 to 1909	Averages For Three Colleges From 1910 to 1919	Averages For Three Colleges From 1920 to 1924
Commercial Pursuits	5.6	4.9	7.7
Education	14.3	26.9	49.4
Law	5.1	2.3	.3
Religious Service	23.9	22.8	18.8
Physicians	.5	1.6	.3
Other Professions and Occupations	51.6	41.5	23.5

Reeves and Russell concluded from their quantitative analysis that Disciples institutions in the 1920's had as their fundamental objective the "continuation and extension of the faith of the communion." They found evidence of this objective in the percentage (18 to 19) of students preparing for ministry, in the high percentage (60) of Disciples students on the campuses, in the high percentage of faculty who were Disciples, in the large number of presidents and other administrators who were Disciples and moved from one Disciples institution to another, and in the fact that all the newer Disciples institutions were founded by graduates of older Disciples colleges.[10] All of these evidences represented an attempt to preserve a tradition, produce leadership for the communion, and to extend the faith. It also reflected a tendency toward inbreeding which would not be modified in any substantial way until after World War II.

Reeves and Russell also concluded that several significant improvements were apparent in the life of Disciples colleges. These included improved physical facilities and expanded curriculums which were offering a solid range of social sciences. An increasing number of the colleges were gaining accreditation with ten of the four-year institutions and two of the junior colleges holding membership in either the North Central Association or Southern Association of colleges. Improved education among faculties resulted in a 100 percent increase in the number of Ph.D. degrees between 1921 and 1928 along with a drop from 25 to 0 percent in the number of faculty without any degree at all during the same seven years. Other improvements included the discontinuation of preparatory departments and vastly improved business management techniques, from a point in 1923 when only two of the institutions operated under a budget plan and only one-half performed audits to a point in 1928 when one-half of the institutions had adopted budget plans and all but two conducted official annual audits by a certified public accountant. These advances reflected a new academic maturity. They were largely due to the cooperative and coordinative efforts engendered by the Board of Education under the leadership of H. O. Pritchard. It was the Board that offered counsel and assistance to the colleges in endowment growth and constantly urged higher standards through accreditation, better educated faculties, and better fiscal management practices. The work of the Board during that early period, toward enhancing the quality of existing colleges rather than expanding a network of mediocre colleges, was an invaluable contribution. In the tenth annual report to the Board of Directors of the Board of Education, H. O. Pritchard declared:

I believe with all my heart in this organization. I believe that without it we never would have been where we are today educationally. I believe that without the cooperation for which it stands there are institutions represented in this room tonight that would now be out of existence.

I have given more than ten years of the best part of my life to this cause. I am willing to continue in work, if desired, and to give to it all that I am, but if I am to do so, there must be a program which is eminently worth while, which will challenge the best that is in all of us, and which will be practicable in meeting the needs, demands and conditions of this hour.[11]

In 1934, near the height of the Great Depression, dwindling congregational income forced the total church into a retrenchment of its operations. Upon the recommendation of a survey commission, a number of boards, including the Board of Education, were consolidated into the United Society of Christian Missions and Education. H. O. Pritchard, until his death in 1936, assisted with this transfer process. Matters pertaining to higher education were administered by the *Department of Higher Education* and by an agency totally separate from the Society called the *College Association of the Christian Church.* The coordination of purpose and program between these two organizations lacked precise definition, and it was soon apparent that the dual existence should be terminated. At the 1938 International Convention in Denver, a recommendation was approved which changed the College Association into the *Board of Higher Education of the Disciples of Christ.* While the work of campus ministry remained with the United Society, most functions of the Department of Higher Education were also transferred to the new Board.[12]

Growing enrollments and endowments, construction of new buildings and expanded curricula were hallmarks of Disciples colleges during the postwar boom years of the 1920's. The Stock Market crash of 1929 transformed those conditions into a world remarkably opposite and opened a period of sharp enrollment declines; accumulating operational deficits; dwindling sources of financial support; huge, unpaid construction debts from the 1920's expansion; and reduction of faculties—a period of severe institutional retrenchment. Preventing closure, an unremitting threat, was once again the highest priority of nearly every Disciples institution. Of the seventeen colleges related to the Disciples during the 1920's all survived the 1930's except Spokane Bible College, which merged its assets with Eugene Bible College to become Northwest Christian College in 1934. Parsimony and frugality had shaped the souls of Disciples institutions for an entire century. Dealing with the experience of economic depression in the 1930's was something less than extraordinary.

The story of Disciples colleges from 1940 to 1980 is partially reflected in the enrollment chart which appears above. The wake of World War II swept through the little network of Disciples colleges on the very heels of economic depression, further reducing enrollments as male students were conscripted for military service. War mobilization meant educational disruption. Army Specialized Training Programs and Navy V-12 Programs were operated at five hundred colleges across the nation, providing training for 300,000 persons.

TWENTIETH CENTURY
ENROLLMENT TRENDS

Institution	1913	1918	1923	1928	1931	1944	1948	1953	1958	1963	1974	FTE 1979	FTE 1984-85
Atlantic Christian College (1902)	170	118	173	187	168	293	850	706	1,267	1,769	1,708	1,566	1,232
Bethany College (1841)	320	440	358	334	363	269	860	480	619	797	1,150	892	776
Chapman College (1919) (California Christian College)			96	410	354	54	290	315	516	1,197	2,983	1,142	1,420
Columbia College (1850)		248	363	230	262	333	360	327	374	372	685	814	591
Culver-Stockton College (1853) (Christian University)	156	112	304	425	420	130	527	371	627	954	646	466	766
Eureka College (1848)	222	286	329	273	268	78	399	181	296	347	544	411	512
Hiram College (1850)	300	325	380	310		192	760	658	641	897	1,200	1,070	1,074
Jarvis Christian College (1912)								147	226	350	640	612	522
Lynchburg College (1903) (Virginia Christian College)	169	130	221	258	256	180	880	601	856	1,311	1,614	1,741	1,518
Midway College (1849) (Kentucky Female Orphan School)	140	150					101	100	116	265	252	283	314
Northwest Christian College (Eugene Bible College) (Spokane Bible College)	136	332	158	155	177			384	387	370	344	217	188
Phillips University (1907) (Oklahoma Christian University)	350	756	1,260	879	901	610	1,209	1,061	1,226	1,307	1,297	786	638
Texas Christian University (1873)	528	657	813	1,528	1,392	2,142	9,916	4,689	7,483	7,790	4,874	4,333	5,159
Tougaloo College (1869)								182	529	760	929	829	627
Transylvania University (1798)	615	361	411	352	431	161	584	373	523	692	732	771	752
William Woods College (1890)	140	190	212	273	258	351	402	314	334	544	852	996	743
Totals	3,246	4,105	5,078	5,614	5,250	4,793	17,138	10,889	16,020	19,722	20,450	16,929	16,832[13]

The draft, military training programs, and weapons research changed permanently the whole higher education system as government assumed a more prominent voice in determining the role and responsibility of higher education in American society. All colleges, in a sense, became public institutions, reorganizing themselves in lasting ways.

Of the twelve institutions submitting statistical data in 1944, eight reported substantial declines during the war years, while four reported increases. William Woods College and Columbia College enjoyed increases because they were women's colleges. Texas Christian University was a large enough institution to attract government subsidy and quickly became a center for several service training programs, including the Civil Aeronautics Authority for the Air Force, the Special Flight Instructors and V-12 programs for the Navy, the Enlisted Reserve Corps for the Army and Marines, and the Engineers, Science and Management Defense Training Program.[13] These programs brought sustained enrollment increases to TCU during the war years. Drake University was similarly assisted by serving as a location for the Women's Army Auxiliary Corps (WACS) and the Army Air Corps training crew. More typical of the dramatic change in configuration of student populations were the convulsive enrollment shifts at Hiram College where the number of male students dropped from 210 in 1938 to thirty-nine in 1945, then surged to 238 in 1946.

HIRAM COLLEGE

Year	Male	Female	Total
1938-1939	210	168	378
1939-1940	187	156	343
1940-1941	180	146	326
1941-1942	137	133	270
1942-1943	156	128	284
1943-1944	54	145	199
1944-1945	39	163	202
1945-1946			
1st quarter	44	191	235
2nd quarter	64	194	258
3rd quarter	176	202	378
4th quarter	238	205	443[15]

Each campus, large or small, contributed to the war effort in a far more costly way than enrollment decline. At Texas Christian University, for example fifty-nine of its students were killed in action between 1941 and 1945.

Higher education literature in the early 1940's, such as *The University and the Modern World* written by Arnold Nash in 1943, was highly critical of the increasing fragmentation of the universty and of learning, the intellectual isolation of each discipline, the false notion of the autonomy of each discipline, and the failure to provide a unifying philosophy of the university or of knowledge. John Dewey's philosophy, so popular in the 1920's, fell out of favor in postwar America and was blamed for the diffuseness and fuzziness of learning. In 1943, Harvard University appointed a "University Committee on the Objectives of a General Education in a Free Society." The committee struggled to find threads of coherence for a common body of knowledge, and ended up rejecting four possible unifying principles as insufficient: Christianity, Western Culture, Pragmatism, and Change. Education, they suggested, must aim "to prepare an individual to become an expert in some particular vocation or art and in the general art of the free man and the citizen," which was hardly an improvement on Newman's description a century before. Interesting as the national debate was, the effort to survive the wide swings in enrollment left little energy on Disciples campuses in the 1940's to discuss the changing philosophies of education. Furthermore, Disciples colleges, at that time, still maintained a tenuous sense of knowledge being unified around the basic theme of Christianity.

During the immediate postwar period, a huge upsurge in enrollment inundated Disciples campuses. President Franklin D. Roosevelt appointed a committee in 1942 to fashion a program of postwar veterans' benefits; and, in 1944, Congress enacted the "G. I. Bill of Rights." The G. I. Bill allowed returning veterans, desiring to pursue an education, a tuition grant of up to $500 for one year plus time served up to four years, and a monthly living allowance of $65 to $90. Enormous student enrollments flooded the campuses in the late 1940's. Students were much more diverse in age, sex, religious preference, and their choice of career goals—all of which resulted in a transformation of the traditional Bible college curriculum to a liberal arts design more in concert with the needs of urban-industrial communities at mid-century. The little church-community colleges were evolving into autonomous institutions with a life and growth of their own.[16]

Everything was in short supply, from classrooms and faculty to dormitories. Phillips University, in its effort to accommodate the unprecedented growth, acquired recently vacated war surplus buildings and moved them to campus; converted one army barracks into a men's dormitory and christened it "East Hall;" and modestly renovated another one which was placed in the center of the campus for classroom use and appropriately named the "Government Building." Near the gymnasium several rows of Quonset huts were set in place to house married students, most of whom were returning G. I.'s Phillips University's acquisition of vacant army barracks was typical of Disciples campuses. Culver-Stockton and Eureka both brought in clusters of pre-fab trailers to house returning G. I.'s.

John L. Davis, executive secretary of the Board of Higher Education, surveyed Disciples colleges as they emerged from the dislocation of war and reported in the summer of 1945 that these institutions had "come through the war in far better material condition than anyone dared hope in the ominous days of 1942."[16]

STATISTICAL REPORTS

Institutions Affiliated With the Board of Higher Education, 1944-45

Colleges and Foundations[1]	Income From Churches	Total Income	Expenditures	Endowment	Gross Assets	All Students U.G.	All Students G.	Ministers[4] U.G.	Ministers[4] G.
Atlantic Christian	$ 8,456.42	$ 82,553.08	$ 82,933.94	$ 321,277.42	$ 731,864.87	261		14	
Bethany College	3,688.83	644,913.33	624,768.29	2,981,600.14	4,391,196.70	317		10	
Chapman	12,198.13	109,049.31	58,891.72	140,000.00	438,205.51	67	1	32	
Culver-Stockton	239.48	116,491.76	153,923.46	838,750.87	1,510,491.10	170		3	
Eureka College	11,226.05	85,902.20	67,212.96	165,001.80	658,484.24	94		21	
Hiram	2,145.70	217,264.49	244,752.03	1,017,534.56	2,276,310.01	202		8	
Lynchburg College	74,210.75[2]	203,945.92	219,592.89	294,406.33	1,069,064.20	226		44	
Transylvania	8,333.21	88,090.11	132,438.81	708,726.06	1,496,913.82	151		38	
Butler	189.15	688,591.15	553,258.66	3,246,827.52	7,168,162.00	1,478	379	49	114
Drake	8,032.71	573,748.68	573,748.08	1,330,340.03	4,116,249.35	1,376	93	34	37
Phillips	44,073.34	228,012.60	210,478.28	626,314.73	1,381,038.97	658	93	238	79
Texas Christian	22,112.17	943,795.01	730,425.18	4,000,000.00	6,822,443.66	2,294	195	87	38
Christian		348,234.73	301,352.96	[3]	1,075,198.88	360			
William Woods		285,028.49	278,981.87	531,794.11	1,369,199.48	320			
College of the Bible	7,042.45	58,797.15	57,001.71	506,533.56	731,603.15		84		84
Disciples Divinity House	[3]	30,105.82	27,282.18	[3]	1,043,050.21		26		26
Disciples House (Vanderbilt U.)	5,032.19	10,555.38	10,150.90		47,000.00	1	25		25
Bible College of Missouri	1,762.93	12,016.03	11,483.48	201,199.08	304,634.09	207	1	1	
College of Churches of Christ of Canada	1,000.00	2,628.00	2,490.00	22,000.00	25,000.00	9		5	
Illinois Disciples Foundation	625.03	4,825.97	5,372.94	65,000.00	91,327.08			9	
Indiana School of Religion	1,292.63	7,080.99	7,556.74	25,000.00	150,000.00	67		4	
Kansas Bible Chair	2,816.29	8,952.34	8,690.55	17,650.97	77,650.97	121			
Student Centers Foundation	85.00	85.00	34.35						
Nebraska Christian Foundation	812.62	812.62	395.26		39.00	117	17		
Drury School of the Bible	812.62	1,907.14	1,907.14	18,000.00	18,000.00	60		13	
Totals	$215,672.58	$4,753,418.20	$4,365,087.98	$18,246,357.01	$37,029,127.29	8,556	914	613	403
							9,470		1,016

[1]No report received from Purdue Christian and Oklahoma Christian Foundations.
[2]Includes contributions for debt retirement.
[3]Not itemized but included in total.
[4]Includes all full-time Christian service students.

Henry Noble Sherwood, who became the new executive for the Board of Higher Education in 1946, observed that two world wars and a depression in one generation could not snuff out the life of Disciples colleges, and as they entered a new era of unprecedented growth, they would continue to:

> free the human spirit from the dross of ignorance, intolerance and prejudice. . . . [Disciples] Colleges are summoned to mold a new [person] to fit the challenge of this generation.[19]

Preparing persons to meet the challenge of a new age did not immediately displace the preparation of ministers. The colleges continued to produce sizeable numbers. Statistics submitted in 1950 revealed that 6 percent (1556) of the total undergraduate enrollment (25,278) in the network was preparing for a career in ministry.[20]

DISCIPLES COLLEGES: 1950-1980

> "Church-related institutions of higher education have had and should continue to have a crucial role in the Church mission. The Christian Church (Disciples of Christ), desiring to reaffirm its commitment to the role of higher education in the fulfillment of its total mission, and this institution of higher education related to the Christian Church (Disciples of Christ), desiring to reaffirm its role and relationship to the total mission of the Church, do voluntarily enter into covenant."
>
> Preamble to the Covenant

War in Korea between 1950 and 1953 reduced enrollments once again, but only for the short term. Prosperity, leisure, and the increasing value placed upon a college education all combined with a new "Korean" G. I. Bill to make education a major growth industry for the next twenty-five years. In the late 1940's, the Truman Commission on Higher Education had declared that education should be accessible to everyone; and the federal government gave impetus to that vision by making available huge amounts of aid to the educational enterprise. Enrollments exploded. In 1920, total college enrollment in the United States was less than 600,000 students. By 1960 it stood at 3,600,000 and by 1970 it had exceeded 8,000,000, then topped 12,000,000 in 1980. Having absorbed the postwar surge, Disciples colleges' enrollments remained relatively stable between the mid-1950's and the mid-1980's, with the peak years between 1967 and 1974.

Pervasive changes in higher education, engendered by the mid-century wars, caused all church-related colleges to seriously examine their institutional purpose. Quadrennial convocations of Christian colleges were held at Denison University in 1954, at Drake University in 1958, and at St. Olaf College in 1962 to probe the meaning of the small church-related college and the role of higher education in American society. The earlier conferences, attended by persons representing 450 colleges, focused upon the definition of being a church-related college in a secular age and advanced the idea that there was no dichotomy between the sacred and the secular. A Christian college was defined as an institution open to many approaches to truth. The very act of worship, integral to a Christian college, was described as one of the means of seeking truth.[21]

Disciples hosted the 1958 Quadrennial Convocation at Drake University; but throughout the 1950's the Board of Higher Education, under the new leadership of Harlie Smith, shifted much of its emphasis to the developing theological education institutions and reduced its attention to the colleges. In 1952, the Board designed a program of ministerial recruitment and in 1953, conducted a study of the teaching of stewardship and "churchmanship" in seminaries along with a study of "The Seminary Student." The board organized the first national seminarian's conference in 1955 and went on to declare the 1957-1958 academic year the "Year of Ministry," which was then followed by a new ministerial enlistment program in 1958. Formerly, *all* energy and resources had been directed toward the colleges. A marked characteristic of the Board's work in the 1950's was the division of its responsibility and resources to encompass the developing seminaries. In the process, groundwork was laid for a weakening of the relationship with the colleges.[22]

As the 1950's drew to a close concern was expressed about the faceless, voiceless conformity of the new college graduates. An article in *Life*, published in June of 1957 and entitled "Arise, Ye Silent Class of 1957!", reviewed the commencement addresses given in the previous weeks, all of which were warning of a "collective sterility," "unprotesting conformity," "prefabricated organization men," "a silent generation more concerned with security than integrity." Graduates of 1957 had attended college in the shadow of the G.I.'s and were described as a group of young people who:

> will not sign a petition for pink raspberry ice cream in the dining hall commons for fear that someday they may have to explain their color predilections to zealous congressional committees.

and as a generation:

> forced from childhood directly into adulthood living in a world balanced precariously on the edge of an apocalypse.[23]

These same 1957 college graduates were also described as the "forerunners of a major cultural and ethical revolution, the unconscious ushers of an essentially secular, self-oriented society."[24]

The postwar baby boom descended upon the colleges in the 1960's, bringing a 19 percent increase in enrollment to Disciples campuses between 1958 and 1963, a modest increase when compared with the public sector. To accommodate the expanded enrollments, building programs were launched on virtually every Disciples campus to provide dormitories, gymnasiums, and additional classroom space. Construction costs were heavily subsidized through the federal government, which unleashed a body of educational legislation unequalled in volume by any decade in American history. Included in the long list of acts was the Higher Education Act of 1963, providing grants and loans for classroom and laboratory construction; the Health Professions Education Assistance Act of 1963; the Economic Opportunity Act of 1964, offering "work-study" incentives; the Higher Education Act of 1965, with its special entitlement programs to assist developing institutions; and the International Education Act of 1966.

It was a period of expanding the physical facilities at Disciples colleges for which they received millions of dollars through the federal government, subsidizing both construction and student tuition costs. Meanwhile, the size of church financial support paled in comparison to the federal largesse. Larger enrollments, larger faculties, and expanded facilities substantially increased operating budgets of the colleges, sending tuition costs to student beyond all forecasts. As Disciples colleges acquired government loans, tuition subsidies, foundation grants, and corporate gifts to meet the financial challenge, they decreased their dependency upon the church. In 1963, for the first time since 1945, Disciples financial support fell below 5 percent of the operating budgets and has continued downward until today it is less than one-half of one percent.[25]

As the decade of the 1960's unfolded, Disciples began to lose confidence in their church-related colleges, which were widely viewed as falling victim to secular influences. Fewer faculty and administrators were members of Disciples congregations, and the percentage of Disciples students within the ballooning enrollments was diminishing from 12 percent in the late 1940's to 10 percent in the 1960's. Student protests against curriculum requirements, the Vietnam War, and traditional campus authority soured many church members; and the elimination of required chapel on nearly every campus, along with many rules governing the use of alcohol and social behavior, further alienated many within the church. The 1960's generated more tension in the relationship between the Disciples colleges and the church than any other period in the history of the Movement.

A note of skepticism and doubt regarding the need for church-related colleges was voiced in the 1962 Quadrennial Convocation of Christian Colleges. Edward Eddy, a college president, proclaimed to the gathering through his address that he was not sure that he really believed in church-related colleges. He described their programs as diffuse, meandering, no different than American Protestantism—not really knowing what they believe and allowing their faith to become a conservator in society rather than a progressive.[26] John Dillenberger argued that it was time to stop berating the fragmentation of knowledge and move beyond the Protestant obsession for the unity or comprehensive system of knowledge, particularly a Christian one.[27] The conference proceeded, however, to affirm the need for church-related colleges, their freedom to use resources of Christian tradition, their role as one of the culture-forming forces in society, their "lively awareness" of religious influence which has shaped Western Civilization, and their motivation for the use of knowledge in the interest of others.[28] Disciples colleges participated actively in this convocation, as well as the previous ones; and a few campuses even carried out introspective evaluations of their own. All remained loyal to their Disciples heritage throughout the 1960's.

A landmark study of church-related higher Education appeared in 1965 under the title *Church-Sponsored Higher Education in the United States*.[29] It reported that Disciples claimed eighteen of 817 church-related colleges and universities.

Religious Body	Number of Institutions	Percentage of Institutions
Roman Catholic Church	339	41.5
Methodist Church	102	12.5
Southern Baptist Convention	52	6.4
United Presbyterian Church in U.S.A.	51	6.2
United Church of Christ	24	2.9
American Baptist Convention	22	2.7
Presbyterian Church in the U.S.	20	2.5
Lutheran Church in American	19	2.3
Disciples of Christ	18	2.2
American Lutheran Church	13	1.6
Lutheran Church-Missouri Synod	12	1.5
Seventh-day Adventist Church	12	1.5
Episcopal Church	11	1.3
Society of Friends	11	1.3
Other (50 religious bodies)	111	13.6
Total	817	100.0

Having studied the curriculums of the institutions and lamenting the "vacuity which comes from not having a coherent philosophy to tie the separate activities together and make them a rational whole," the authors of the study presented their vision of what a church-related college ought to be:

Viewed in historical perspective, the church-sponsored institutions belong to the great tradition of collegiate education in the arts and sciences illuminated by Christian faith. It is a conception of education which, in its essentials, has stood the test of some fifteen centuries. It combines learning in the fundamental fields of knowledge with the insights of the Christian faith, the aim being to cultivate the *humane person*. Its subject matter changes, but its purposes are fairly constant. At its best it is a broad and general education in that it stresses the arts of thought and communication and the principles which should govern personal and public affairs. It is the most useful kind of education, in the best sense of the word "useful," for its worth is not restricted to a particular occupation, a particular time or place, a particular stratum of society. It should be a liberating, a freeing education. It should provide good preparation for responsible living in a rapidly changing world such as ours. Soundly conceived, it gives the student an understanding of the values that are most worth conserving in our heritage and of how they may be the guiding principles of the future. If there is a single word that describes the highest aspiration of colleges of this type for their graduates, that word is probably "wisdom."[30]

Drawn from the frame of vision of the "humane person" and the seeking of wisdom, an abiding sense of social justice has always been part of the substantive nature of Disciples campuses. In 1942 philosophy professor Paul Delp, three Black students, and two white students—all from Chapman College—engineered the first non-violent, inter-racial sit-in on the West Coast. The incident occurred at a segregated lunch counter in Bullock's Tea Room in a Los Angeles department store. In 1955 students at Phillips University organized a non-violent boycott of the Red Feather Cafe in Enid, Oklahoma which had refused service to a Black student. Several Disciples campuses, such as Culver-Stockton in October of 1969, held formal symposiums on the Vietnam War; while other Disciples campuses organized peace marches, peace demonstrations, and war moratoriums during the late 1960's to protest war.[31] For the most part, they were orderly and mild. The October 1968 march at Drury College, for example, carried the full sanction of the college administration.[32]

Receiving more attention on Disciples campuses was the issue of civil rights. Nearly every college formed a Black caucus to deal with issues of full campus social integration. Black History Week became a standard feature on most campuses with its films, lectures, Black poets, and African dance troupes; and by the late 1960's, the majority of the catalogues contained courses on Black history and culture. The most dramatic involvement, however, occurred at Tougaloo College which gave leadership to the civil rights movement throughout Mississippi. Tougaloo students, faculty, and administrators participated in sit-ins at segregated lunch counters, cafeterias, and libraries; organized a cultural committee which succeeded in cancelling several guest artist appearances in the Jackson community where Blacks were disallowed; and worked toward the integration of several local congregations. One of the first two students to be enrolled at the University of Mississippi was Cleveland Donald, who had taken his freshman year at Tougaloo. Campus chaplain, Ed King, was part of the delegation which went to the 1964 Democratic National Convention to contest the seating of the regular Mississippi delegates. Examples of Tougaloo's civil rights leadership are abundant, and it should be further noted that violence was frequent with cars racing through the campus firing guns at houses, blazing crosses placed at the gates of the college, and the continual run of vandalized property. A sense of social justice was firmly present on the Tougaloo campus; and it was never deterred in giving leadership to that cause.[33]

The Disciples Board of Higher Education continued its emphasis upon seminary education in the 1960's, beginning with the establishment of the Disciples Seminary Foundation in 1960 at the School of Theology in Claremont, California; a seminary education study launched in 1963; and in 1964, a study of ministerial supply. Enrollment and financial statistics of the colleges were no longer reported in the *Disciples of Christ Year Book* after 1967. The Board itself experienced a steady attrition of budgetary support which curtailed its programming and limited its ability to serve multiple networks of institutions.

Survival became the catchword of the 1970's. Included among the literature appearing at mid-decade was the Carnegie Foundation's *More Than Survival* in 1975 and Leslie and Miller's *Higher Education and the Steady State* in 1974, both forecasting difficult times. The Vietnam War, with its academic deferments, had helped college enrollments remain stable through the early 1970's; and the 1972 Basic Educational Opportunity Grants Act (now the Pell Grants) provided subsidies which also contributed to enrollment stability, although it created further institutional dependency upon the government.

Beginning in 1974, enrollment at Disciples colleges commenced a modest, but steady decline which lasted through the remainder of the decade. Part of the decline was due to the slippage in the ranking of social priorities of a college education because of waning evidence of its economic advantages; part of it was due to declining numbers in the traditional college-age group because of lower birth rates; and part of it was due to an increasing percentage of persons choosing to attend a public rather than a private college. In 1950, 50.3 percent of the college students were enrolled at private institutions, and 49.7 percent were enrolled at public institutions. In 1960, the ratio was 59 percent public to 41 percent private; in 1970, 75 percent public to 25 percent private; and in 1975, 78 percent to 22 percent in favor of the public institutions. To remain competitive, Disciples colleges, like all church-related colleges, invested considerable time in mission studies re-defining their distinctive purpose and calling forth new leadership styles.

By the end of the 1970's, the predominant leadership mode for Disciples institutions was one of technical and profession administrative skills. The educational preparation of the presidents tended toward the new twentieth century disciplines, rather than theology. Only four of the current assemblage of presidents are ordained ministers, and only two hold degrees from another Disciples institution. The expertise possessed by the educational leadership in our day is most often lodged in capital development, financial management, technical administration, and institutional promotion. While academic and theological attributes certainly remain important, they are of lesser priority than in earlier years. A study of administrative flow charts over the last quarter century reflects the dynamic of this change as staff has been enlarged to include a rich variety of managerial specialists including institutional planners, development officers, and recruitment specialists.

The shift in leadership style is also reflected in the pattern of capital funding. Across the last seventy years, endowments have experienced gargantuan growth from an aggregate of $2 million for all institutions in 1915 presently in covenant with the church, to a total in excess of $310 million in 1985.[34] The small capital aggregate of 1915 came almost exclusively from the church. The new capital, more than two-thirds of which has been accumulated since 1978, was generated largely from trustees and corporations; and along with the funds came the voice of influence. The costs of operating a college have grown in similar proportion so that the interest income from the $310 million underwrote the same percentage of the combined operating budgets in 1984-85 as the interest income from $2 million underwrote in 1914-15.[34]

The relationship between the colleges and the church continued to weaken during the early 1970's, reaching a point in 1973 when a coalition of Disciples colleges in Missouri appealed their financial allocation and called for arbitration. In response, the General Board of the Christian Church (Disciples of Christ) at its May 1975 session, appointed a special Higher Education Evaluation Task Force of six persons (C. C. Nolen (Chair), William C. Howland (Staff), James I. Spainhower, Robbie N. Chisholm, Ann E. Dickerson, and D. Duane Cummins) which was commissioned:

> . . . to make an evaluation of colleges, universities, schools of religion and Bible chairs that are member institutions of the Board of Higher Education, taking into account such factors as the depth of church relatedness and the contribution of the institution to the church; the fairness and equity of funding; the quality of the education experiences provided; total financial support; and other matters relating to funding by the Christian Church (Disciples of Christ).[36]

The task force performed a comprehensive analysis of institutional audits, HEGIS reports, AAUP reports, and interpretative literature, circulated a survey instrument of its own, and conducted a series of on-site interviews at every campus. From its huge data base, the task force concluded that there was not a precise quantitative measurement that could be used for gauging the degree of church-relatedness. Whether a school receives funds from the church, holds chapel, retains a chaplain, has a chapel building, requires courses in religion, has a high percentage of trustees, administrators, students, and faculty who are church members are all indicators of church-relatedness; but assigning weights to these indicators to arrive at a calculated degree of church-relatedness for an individual institution is not exclusively indicative. Struggling with the issue of church-relatedness, the task force reached four conclusions about the characteristics of a church-related college:

First, a pivotal determinant is the active involvement of committed leadership.
Second, a church-related institution is characterized by a critical mass of people who share a common tradition.
Third, a church-related institution provides an environment in which the campus community may clarify and reinforce its values.
Fourth, a church-related institution is characterized by the way in which people on a campus express their concern for other human beings.[37]

Regarding the second characteristic, it was disclosed in the 1976 report that 11 percent of the student population in the thirteen institutions, were Disciples, approximately 50 percent of the administrators, and approximately 40 percent of the trustees.

On the basis of its comprehensive evaluation the task force presented nine recommendations to the church, two of which offered profound change. The first recommendation outlined the development of a formal covenantal relationship between the educational institutions and the church. In its final form the Covenant embodied the principles of mutual interpretation, a mutual supportive services relationship, a mutual community of faith and reason, and a mutual acceptance of the Campbellian philosophy of wholeness of person.[37] It required eighteen months to develop and implement the Covenant which fifteen colleges eventually entered, creating the strongest structural relationship between the colleges and the church in the Movement's history.

The second recommendation was equally revolutionary, setting forth a means of distributing financial allocations to the institutions by formula. Believing that it was critical for a new understanding to emerge regarding the financial relationship between the church and higher education institutions and that in the past many had looked to the church to do something it had been incapable of doing because of the limitation of resources and its other priorities, the task force asserted that

> . . . the view of financial distributions from the church must now shift to a concept of an investment in the total mission of the church rather than as a response to financial need or as a means of saving institutions. . . . The dollars distributed express relationship and an authentic investment in mission.[39]

In this context the task force recommended a four-part formula to be used for the distribution of funds to college.

A. *$30,000 as the base figure:* Tangible evidence of Disciples commitment to undergraduate higher education as a significant part of the total church mission.

B. *$10 for every full-time undergraduate:* demonstrates a fundamental commitment to society by recognizing the importance of educating all students.

C. *$100 for every Disciples full-time undergraduate:* reflects an abiding educational concern the church has always held for its own youth and demonstrates the church's desire to encourage the recruitment of its youth into church-related institutions.

D. *$500 for each Disciples graduate matriculating into an accredited seminary:* encourages the recruitment of ministerial students.[40]

These two recommendations constitute a landmark change in the historic relationship between Disciples colleges and the church, a landmark made even more significant in the light of the reformed structure of the Board of Higher Education.

Dr. William L. Miller became president of the Board of Higher Education in 1968 and, across the ensuing nine years of his presidency, he guided the Board toward a new vision of its ministry. Convinced that the work of the Board should be more integral to the life and mission of the whole church, Dr. Miller advocated that redesigning the Board into a "Division" of the church would provide a more effective and responsible structural expression for the higher education ministry of the church. In March, 1977, the seventy-seven member Board voted in principle a radical reorganization transforming the Board of Higher Education into a Division of Higher Education, moving from an association of institutions to become an administrative unit of the church. Approved by official vote the following October, the board of directors of the new division contained twenty-four members including three from the colleges, three from the seminaries, three from campus ministries and fifteen at large. The representative and participatory voice of the colleges was lodged in a council of colleges and universities, one of three councils under the aegis of the new Division of Higher Education. The Division was designed to service the colleges on behalf of the church and to interpret the colleges and educational environment to the church. Dr. Miller's vision had become a reality.

Reconstituting the Board into a Division combined with the new covenantal relationship and formula funding represented a fundamental shift in denominational polity toward higher education institutions. On January 1, 1978, a new president of the new Division of Higher Education, D. Duane Cummins, was charged with the responsibility of guiding the colleges and the church into a new covenantal relationship, guiding the colleges, seminaries, and campus ministries into a new divisional structure within the church, and guiding the related institutions and the church into a new concept of funding. It was a challenging moment in the long history of the church and its higher education ministry.

THE 1980'S AND BEYOND
THE SOCIETY: A QUEST FOR COHERENCE

Tis all in peeces, all cohaerence gone;
All Just supply, and all Relation:
Prince, Subject, Father, Sonne, are things forgot,
For every man alone thinkes he hath got
To be a Phoenix, and that then can bee
None of that kinde, of which he is, but hee."

John Donne, 1611
"An Anatomie of the World:
The First Anniversary."
(cited in *Habits of the Heart*)

Sociologists tell us we live in a post-industrial era. Theologians tell us we live in a post-modern era. Church historians tell us we live in a post-Protestant era. Ecumenists tell us we live in a post-liberal era. World political historians tell us we live in a post-western era. Each quarter of society and each learned discipline provide varying and disconnected definitions of our day. Few attempt synthesis or attempt to relate the myriad interpretations into any coherent pattern or holistic understanding. That fact in itself offers significant insight into our day—a day between the closing of one era in the chronicle of human history and the opening of another, a day of uncertainty which has caused individuals to withdraw and rely almost solely upon themselves.

We live in a socio-cultural milieu described as bewilderingly pluralistic, fragmented into a kaleidoscope of political, social, economic, religious, and ethnic factions. It is a time, say some, focused sharply upon *self* with slight regard for the shared needs of community. "What has failed at every level, from the society of nations to the national society to the local community to the family," it is suggested, "is integration: we have failed to remember 'our community as members of the same body.'"[41] Conciliar structures of every stripe—political (i.e., United Nations), religious (i.e., National Council of Churches of Christ), and economic (i.e., European Common Market)—have weakened while special interests have grown stronger.

To the classic question of identity, "Who are you?", contends Daniel Bell, the person of our day responds, "I am I, I come out of myself, and in choice and action I make myself."[42] This form of identity, says Bell, is the hallmark of our own modernity. In his popular work, *Megatrends*, John Naisbitt observed that during the 1970's individuals lost confidence in their institutions—government, corporations, education, religion—and "began to disengage from the institutions that had disillusioned them and to relearn the ability to take action on their own."[43] Entrepreneurship, participatory democracy, and the pervasive decentralization of American life are just three of the 1980's manifestations of that disengagement. Marilyn Ferguson writes of an Aquarian conspiracy that "promotes the autonomous individual in a decentralized society."[44] Amitai Etzioni, in his telling analysis of special political interest groups, comments that the sum of the parts of society has become greater than the whole. It is argued by these observers that the primary human reality of our age is the individual, rather than community.

In his recent publications, Christopher Lasch writes of an "atomizing individualism" and suggests that there is an increasingly beleaguered sense of *self* and a corresponding emotional retreat from the long term commitment that presupposes a stable, secure, and orderly world.[44] This retreat, in his view, fosters a survival mentality, a diminished sense of self-hood in a world without coherent patterns. Robert Bellah and his associates describe a long and rich tradition of individualism in the American experience, and declare that "individualism lies at the very core of American culture."[46] But they find in our day a destructive form of individualism, and describe our time as "a culture of separation," a period in which "self has become ever more detached from social and cultural context that embodies traditions."[47]

In his newest work, *The Cycles of American History*, Arthur Schlesinger presents a long historical view in which he sees the present emphasis upon individualism as a phase of an alternating rhythm between public purpose (civic commitment, social reform, positive government action for the whole community) and private interest (privatization, pursuit of private wealth, economic conservatism). He describes the current ethos of privatization, separation, and individualism as a form of corrective action within the body politic against excesses of public concern. "It replenishes the self, the family, the private economy," he suggests, "and renews defenses against mass society and an aggressive state."[48] Today's inward turn, in Schlesinger's view, is a natural reaction to a recent era of active public purpose.

It must be recognized that rampant individualism and separation are necessary from time to time to free humanity from the tyrannies and structures of an old order, but those impulses must be tempered by a renewal of commitment and community, a return of common comprehension, a rediscovery of the coherence that is so often lost. This is the world, argues Bellah, that is waiting to be born:

> What keeps the new world powerless to be born, is that if we give up our dream of private success for a more genuinely integrated societal community, we will be abandoning our separation and individuation, collapsing into dependence and tyranny. What we find hard to see is that it is the extreme fragmentation of the modern world that really threatens our individuation; that what is best in our separation and individuation, our sense of dignity and autonomy as person, requires a new integration if it is to be sustained.[49]

THE CHURCH: A QUEST FOR COMMUNITY

> There can be no final conclusion to restructure. It is an ongoing process and must remain fluid and flexible.
>
> Loren Lair, 1971

The Christian Church (Disciples of Christ) chose courageously to restructure its institutional life during a span of years when mainline religions found their authority weakening, their ability to develop community shrinking, and their hold on American culture waning. Increasing disengagement of religion from the public sphere and a correlating retreat into more private and secluded worlds were marks of the time. Resurgent individualism contributed to a growing preference among church members for cloistering their faith in the refuge of personal solitude rather than committing publicly to corporate or conciliar expressions of ministry and worship. Religion was described by sociologists as privatized, a personal belief accepted or rejected by individual will, with little recognition of any authority beyond self. Social fragmentation and the renewed spirit of volunteerism had weakened the ability of individuals to discipline themselves into a commitment beyond their own person. People found a reduced capacity to maintain sustained relations with each other, and the institutional frame of religion was steadily weakened by declines in participating corporate membership and corporate financial support. A 1978 Gallup Poll reported that 80 percent of the respondents supported the opinion that individuals should arrive at religious belief independent of the church. When the institutional and theological structures for religion begin to weaken, the individual need for faith becomes a search for direct experience which leads to spiritual isolation, non-rationalism, anti-institutionalism, cults, and all manner of religious mutation. Such was the religious environment between 1968 and 1986 when the Christian Church (Disciples of Christ) adopted and began to live into a massive new institutional order.[50]

It had required twenty years, but on October 1, 1968, a *Provisional Design for the Christian Church (Disciples of Christ)* was adopted at the International Convention in Kansas City. A need to reconceptualize Disciples polity had been recognized in the years immediately following World War II. At the 1948 International Convention in San Francisco, Disciples college leaders pressed for a review of the institutional order and mission of the church. In their judgment the ability of the church to respond in ministry to a highly complex world was ineffective and irresponsible because of an organizational structure grown archaic. The Convention voted appropriate machinery to begin the task. Abnormal religious prosperity during the 1950's slowed the process, but the 1960's saw the work to fruition.

A commission on restructure, appointed by the International Convention to develop the new order, cited seven motivations for the organizational reform of the church. The two essential issues were the needs (1) to bring a clear sense of coordination to the work of agencies, boards, institutions, conventions, states, and congregations—which had become a benevolent anarchy of fragmented empires, and (2) to assist the membership in understanding the wholeness of "church"—that there were several manifestations of "church"; and that state societies, general agencies, and ecumenical bodies were not merely servants of congregations, but performers of ministry beyond congregations which was more effectively and responsibly accomplished in cooperation.

Out of the long years of deliberation came a quasi-constitutional document called *The Provisional Design*, an advance in institutional structure representing the most significant internal accomplishment of the Christian Church (Disciples of Christ) in the last two decades. To enable the church to perform its wider ministry, *The Provisional Design* provided for the development of general unit and regional structures, each with its own integrity, and refined the processes of total church decision-making by creating representative plenary bodies: the General Board and the General Assembly. The unified organizational life emerging from *The Provisional Design* was a dramatic improvement over the jerry-built, pragmatic institutionalism of pre-restructure times.

The genius of *The Provisional Design* was lodged in the concept of covenant, bonding the three manifestations of church (Local, Regional, General), and defined by Loren Lair as:

> . . . [the] cement that holds the three manifestations together loose enough to permit the give and take that diversity requires, yet solid enough to hold the parts of the body together.[51]

Through covenant, the congregations, regions, and general agencies were linked in an interdependent and mutually supportive relationship—none the mere servant of the other, all accountable to each other. Covenant should not be viewed narrowly as simply an organizational model. It is imperative to the life of the Christian Church (Disciples of Christ) that covenant be understood as the fundamental nature of the church and that God's covenant with us is reflected in the covenantal life of the church. The nature of the entire religious community is covenantal and it is through that concept that we find our relationship with each other, rather than through the cold legality of an organizational system.

Through covenant, the church has been enabled to pursue more confidently its historic goal of Christian unity through free and open discussions in representative assemblies, involving all manifestations of the church. General and regional leaders of the Christian Church (Disciples of Christ) address the subject of ecumenism articulately, with broad understanding and with abiding commitment. Among Protestant denominations in the United States, the Disciples' record of bi-lateral and conciliar involvements is difficult to match. Ecumenism is deep in the grain of our history and, in fact, distinguishes Disciples from the rest of Protestantism in our day by the very emphasis it receives. For a denomination of our limited size, it just may be that our ecumenical zeal, our abiding desire for community and wholeness, is the most significant contribution we have to offer a fragmented world.

Through covenant the church was enabled to develop an order of ministry and significantly improve the means of nurture to ministers throughout the journey of their service. Disciples ministers, as a group, evolved from a moderately credentialed, freely ordained assemblage of predominantly male preachers, to a professional clergy of men and women with the multiple academic credentials required to meet an expanded criteria for ordination and ministerial standing in a formalized order of ministry. A full seminary education, often enhanced by the additional acquisition of a Doctor of Ministry degree, has become standard. Regional Commissions on Ministry have grown caringly protective of the Order of Ministry and increasingly sophisticated in managing the ordination process. The proud and happy result for the Christian Church (Disciples of Christ) is a clergy viewed with solid respect throughout the whole of Christendom.

Through covenant, the church was enabled to occasion a more equitable balance between some of its ageless polarities: "freedom and community,"

"unity and diversity," "congregationalism and catholicity." Through covenant the church was also enabled to speak and minister far more effectively in the post-industrial world. At a time when it is often fashionable to point out the imperfections of covenant, restructure, and of *The Provisional Design*, it is helpful to remind ourselves of the multitude of advancements achieved through the new order.

Determining the content of *The Provisional Design* has been described as a contest between centralized and decentralized concepts of structure. The issue was seemingly settled in the beginning on the side of the centralists, but the regional manifestation was the least articulated in the new *Provisional Design* and, therefore, enjoyed a greater freedom to develop as the church grew into covenant. With the passing of time, the regional manifestation accrued considerable polity and financial influence and today is becoming a telling voice, influencing mission and ministry beyond the congregation.

Creating the office of General Minister and President was an imaginative step toward providing a means for the three manifestations of church to have a representative presence in the cooperative witness of the larger church. Experience tells us that it may now be timely to consider investing that office with the kind of institutional authority that permits it to lead and shape Disciples' mission, as well as represent it.

Given the long Disciples tradition of the sovereignty of individual choice, the almost total autonomy and direct voice so carefully protected in every part of the Movement, this new theology of "church," with its attendant features of representative democracy and covenantal relationships was not easy to accept. Understanding and trust vary widely by geographic section yet today. Many local Disciples congregations remain relatively oblivious to or ambivalent toward restructure. Others claim to be systematically prevented from having any voice in what they perceive to be a new church structure dominated by an "exclusive leftist power structure." The majority of congregations, however, claim a far greater enlightenment and participation in total church ministry—regional, local, and general—than they have known at any time in their entire history. Some agencies of the church flourish in their preference for institutional separateness; but regions and general units claim a level of colleagueship in ministry and a common sense of mission unmatched in previous years. The experience of living together in covenant is not free of abrasion, but in the long view that experience is lifting the church above moods of privateness and fragmentation, urging the church beyond ideological and theological narrowness, and educating the church toward wholeness.

It is important to place the institutional restructure of the church in the broader context of the Movement's comprehensive quest for renewal. Reordering the structural components was merely one element of the search in recent years. Concurrent with the organizational reform, which was an effort to discover a modern institutional identity, Disciples were searching with equal intensity to renew their theological identity, their liturgical identity, their ministerial identity, their ecumenical identity, their sociological identity, their educational identity, and their identity in overseas mission. This list is not exhaustive, yet transformations occurred in every one of these categories across the same twenty-year period and illustrate the point that it should not be mistakenly believed that the exclusive agenda of the last two decades has been institutional restructure.

It was all part of a Disciples modernization, a comprehensive renewal. Among the endless examples of this renewal is the development of a covenantal design for the whole church which sparked the birth of an innovative covenant relationship with the colleges. Responding in style and form to trends both inside and outside the church, Disciples have become a more liturgical church. The growing presence of liturgical work in our day is more imitative than unique, something being experimented with in the quest for modern identity. The Panel of Scholars, in a benchmark work of the mid-1960's, gave new theological formulation to Disciples faith and thought; and it is suggested that Disciples have entered a post-rational era in their own theological evolution. Recent studies of Disciples sociological identity reveal that 60 percent of the membership resides in cities and suburbs; 27 percent in small towns; 13 percent in rural areas; 65 percent are over fifty years of age; 64 percent are female; 58 percent have some college education; 40 percent have managerial-professional employment; and that over 90 percent of the membership is white.[52] It appears that Disciples have trended from a young, lower-middle class, rural, nineteenth century movement to an aging, middle to upper-middle class, twentieth century, city church. And so the search continues.

Finally, in the quest for renewal and a modern identity, the most important issue facing the Christian Church (Disciples of Christ) in the 1990's will be a changing generation of leadership. Since 1980 more than three-fourths of the General Cabinet have retired; more than two-thirds of the Regional Ministers have been succeeded; and we are within five years of a peak retirement period among local pastors, as that enormous group entering ministry in the early 1950's reaches age sixty-five. This massive shift in leadership is far more than an ordinary succession. It heralds the changing of generations: the passing of a generation which envisioned and implemented the new institutional and theological order, and the arrival of a second generation. We hear echoes of the post-Civil War years. Nearly all studies of institutional life, including those on church organizations by David Moberg and Will Herberg, tell us that the second generation of leaders following extraordinary moments of creativity in institutional life tend to be less visionary than their predecessors, tend to crystallize the work of their predecessors, and tend to provide a leadership that is passive, placid, and transactional.

The Christian Church (Disciples of Christ) must avoid the fate of second generation atrophy. The new generation of leaders in 1990's must not be persons chosen predominantly for their organizational skills; they must not be persons who would settle comfortably into roles of functionaries; they must not be persons who would view the congregation, region, general units, or denomination as simply engines of production, sociological entities or entrepreneurial structures. The church must summon forth leaders in the next decade who are able to ignite our capacity for vision; who are molders of community, rather than ideologues; who are transcendant, rather than transactional leaders; and set them to work imaginatively in the task of ministry to humankind.

THE COLLEGE: A QUEST FOR WHOLENESS

... many of our young people are desperately seeking meaning and purpose in their lives and education ... there is a great longing for a sense of commitment in an often impersonal society. They search for guidance in their efforts to find honesty, justice and peace.

The church-related institutions, with all their diversity, have served to bring this sense of purpose and commitment to every generation of Americans, providing an opportunity for intellectual and spiritual growth as an essential part of the preparation for the challenges of life.

I do not believe the mission of the church-related college is completed. ... I must call upon you to strive even harder to uphold the intellectual, religious and humane values of your institutions. I believe you provide a needed response to the spiritual hunger of our day.

President Jimmy Carter
June 1978

Between 1836 and 1986 Disciples founded 209 colleges and universities; and a total of 485 educational institutions of all types. In 1986, eighteen colleges and universities in the United States claim identity as Disciples institutions. Fifteen of these institutions function in covenantal relationship with the church while three remain related by virtue of historic tradition.[53] One additional institution, with a rich Disciples heritage, is Butler University. Founded by Disciples and for more than 125 years sustained with Disciples resources and history, Butler severed all relationships in 1978 and claims identity today as an independent university free of any religious commitment.

January 1, 1978 opened an era for colleges in which they began relating to the church through covenant and through a Division of Higher Education. A 1985 survey of Disciples college and university presidents of the covenanted institutions revealed a unanimous opinion that the seven intervening years brought clarity and strength to the relationship between college and church.[54] The survey also acknowledged their unanimous judgment that positive advantages existed for both college and church in the new relationship. While it was believed that colleges made good use of the church as a resource, particularly in capital and endowment support, student recruitment and public relations, it was the perception of the presidents that the colleges were underused resources on the part of the church, specifically as centers for research, biblical, and religious study and pre-theological training. The presidents were near unanimous, also, in their support of the *formula* as the most equitable means of distributing the church contribution, but expressed equal unanimity on the inadequacy of the amount.[55]

The Christian Church (Disciples of Christ) in 1986 distributed $1,200,000 in direct allocations to the fifteen undergraduate institutions with aggregate operating budgets of nearly $208,000,000. Representing less than one-half of one percent of the operating budgets, the contribution was legitimately viewed from a college budgetary perspective as not maintaining pace with costs. But from the perspective of the church the $1,200,000 represented an *investment* in undergraduate education as part of the church mission, an amount equal to 7 percent of all the mission dollars available for distribution to the total ministry of the church. This placed Disciples among the top four or five Protestant denominations in the United States when the percentage of mission dollars given to undergraduate higher education is compared. Measured against the annual unrestricted gift income to the colleges, the $1,200,000 represented on average approximately 6 to 8 percent of the unrestricted gift income to each institution. Colleges and church alike agree[56] that the distribution is commensurate with the dollars currently available to the church for the financing of its total mission.[57]

Beyond the fiscal measure of the relationship, the colleges and the church have always looked carefully at the numbers of Disciples students attending the institutions. Annual surveys conducted by the Division of Higher Education report the following configuration of high school youth in the Christian Church (Disciples of Christ) during 1985: twelfth grade, 28 percent; eleventh grade, 31 percent; tenth grade, 25 percent; and ninth grade, 16 percent. By 1989 it is apparent that there will be approximately one-half as many high school seniors in the Disciples student pool as there are in 1986. This will be somewhat compounded by the fact that the total number of students in grades 9-12 between 1987 and 1991 as compared with the same group between 1981 and 1985 is 8 percent smaller. These reduced numbers suggest to the Division of Higher Education that it must develop effective programs to assist the church and the colleges with intensive recruitment and scholarship aid programs to attract the maximum number of Disciples students from what is projected to be a significantly reduced pool of traditional, Disciples college age youth by the end of the decade.

A second survey,[58] conducted in 1985, measured the post-secondary educational choices of a national cross-section of Disciples high school graduates (3,513) between 1981 and 1985. It indicated that they were divided among several options:

1. Vocational School   – 9%
2. Two-year Community College   –15%
3. No Further Education
   (marriage, service, etc.)   –25%
4. Four-year College or University –51%[59]

From the group electing to attend a four year institution, 9 percent (less than one in ten) chose a Disciples-related college. Out of the total of all Disciples high school graduates betwen 1981-1985, only 4 percent (one of every twenty-five) chose to enroll at a Disciples related college. By historic comparison since the end of World War II these figures have remained relatively unchanged. Also unchanged in that same time span has been the average figure of 10 percent Disciples students as a component of the student body on the fifteen Disciples campuses. The statistics are nearly the same in average with other mainline denominations. The Lutheran church reported recently that "4% of the youth of our Lutheran congregations attend our church colleges."[60]

DISCIPLES STUDENTS IN 15 DISCIPLES COLLEGES

Year	Total Undergraduate FTE	Total Disciples FTE	Disciples FTE As a Percent of Total
1978	18,001	1939	11%
1979	16,922	2031	12%
1980	17,356	1948	11%
1981	17,201	2001	12%
1982	16,973	1801	11%
1983	17,307	1740	10%
1984	17,363	1691	9.7%
1985	17,511	1688	9.6%
1986	17,689	1703 [61]	9.6%

Among the students who chose a Disciples college, 61 percent had been active participants in a strong Christian Youth Fellowship (CYF) program in their local congregation and 75 percent were from congregations with a pastor who was a *graduate* of a Disciples-related college. When asked how they learned of the Disciples college they chose and why they chose it, the largest number indicated they had heard of the college through their pastor and selected it because it was related to the church. CYF sponsors, church-camp, and parents were the other three most frequently cited sources of learning about Disciples colleges. Clearly, the front line interpreter for the schools is the local pastor, yet among the pastors participating in the survey, slightly more than half (52 percent) had attended a Disciples-related under-graduate college.[62] There is a declining number of ministers in the church with experience in a church-related college and a declining number of leaders in the colleges with experience in the church. This decrease in first-hand experience on both sides presents the most serious challenge to the future relationship between the two.

The survey also disclosed that teaching is still the predominant career preference among Disciples students wherever they attend college, that those attending Disciples colleges are more oriented toward service careers, and that those attending state colleges were, in substantial numbers, pursuing business and professional careers with the goal of material success.

The recruitment of all students by Disciples colleges in the next two decades will require more attention to the social environment. It is reported that only 42 percent of eighteen year old youth today live with both parents. This opens the probability that the college will increasingly become a surrogate or extended family.[63] Due to this phenomenon, the small church-related college will gain a whole new importance because students will be attracted to places of intimate community. Furthermore, it is projected for the year 2000 that one-third of the nation's population will be minority. Fluctuation in federal student aid and the elimination by many colleges of their remedial service programs, combined with recent inconsistencies of the federal government in enforcing integration laws, have significantly reduced the number of Blacks attending college. From 1975 to 1982 the number of Black high school graduates increased 29 percent while the number of Blacks attending college decreased by 11 percent.[64]

The church and the college must work together to reverse the circumstance of educationally under-served minorities. This is frequently a point of tension between the church and the colleges. While the colleges are diligent in working toward improved levels of Scholastic Aptitude Test (S.A.T.) scores and high school grade point average (G.P.A.) among newly recruited students, the church, from its commitment to social justice, supports more flexible and open enrollment policies, urging the colleges to measure themselves less by what they take in and more by what they put out. Disciples colleges' traditional homogeneity has been altered in recent years with a growing number of ethnic, intellectually educable, and economically disenfranchised students. The effort must be intensified, otherwise the campuses will become elitist enclaves and social anachronisms.

Curriculum content continues to serve as a barometer of church-relatedness. National studies, focusing upon the nature of the undergraduate curriculum, have abounded in the last two years, including *Involvement in Learning* by the National Institute of Education, *To Reclaim a Legacy* by William Bennett, *Integrity in the College Curriculum* by the Association of American Colleges, and the new Carneige Foundation report, *College: The Undergraduate Experience in America*. With a unanimous voice these reports call for the restoration of a strong liberal education with value orientation for the core of society, in order to rebuild a sense of human community. They are strongly critical of the functional, vocational tone, the narrow disciplinary orientation, and the specialized categorization of knowledge which is eroding integrated learning, general education, and the wholeness of human understanding. The reports emphasize that the very things they are calling for—value-oriented liberal arts, student involvement, integration, and coherence of learning—are the strong suits of the small church-related college. It is their heritage, what they do best, and it is "the right education for the times."

A study of Disciples colleges catalogues records a distinct pattern in all fifteen institutions of a strong, liberal arts, value-oriented, general education curriculum.[65] Six to fifteen hours of Humanities are required on every campus, the average being nine to twelve. In addition there is a requirement for religious study which varies, with six colleges requiring three hours, two requiring six hours, one requiring four hours, and six which do not require any hours of religious study but offer it on an elective basis. Four of the campuses require a foreign language for graduation and others have that matter under consideration. Disciples colleges are moving away from the concept of isolating general education in the first two years with specialized training designed as a capstone for the last two years. Instead, general education is appropriately interlaced throughout the entire four years. The strong liberal arts orientation, the opportunity for religious study, and the small departments often clustered into divisions (a configuration designed to foster integration), comprises the formula for Disciples college and university distinctiveness and educational creativity.[66]

The 1984-86 blue ribbon curriculum reports were especially critical of faculty and graduate schools, declaring that the renewed call for integrated learning and wholeness of knowledge had no effective constituency on campus. Faculty, customarily trained as specialists in research-oriented, university graduate schools, often find their education dysfunctional in their efforts to foster integration and to convey a wholeness of knowledge through their teaching. Every issue of *Liberal Education* in the last two years, however, proclaims a growing optimism that the integrity of liberal education is being restored. Liberal arts, in the sixties and seventies were misshapen by vocationalism, experienced a loss of synthesis, and fortressed themselves into undergraduate departments which came close to Robert Hutchins famous description of university departments as a "group of independent empires linked by a central heating system." Evidences abound today from many campuses that professors, students, and deans are communicating across disciplinary lines, thereby offering the best prospects in more than two decades for a new coherence in baccalaureate programs.

A study of faculty degrees at Disciples colleges discloses that by far the largest source of faculty members is a nearby state university,[67] and that overwhelmingly, the graduate degrees are earned at state-supported, research universities. At Atlantic Christian College, for example, the faculty owns 220 degrees from 104 institutions. One-fourth of those degrees are from the University of North Carolina and East Carolina University. Nearly 40 percent are from North Carolina institutions and 12 percent of the undergraduate degrees are from Disciples-related institutions with three-fifths of those from Atlantic Christian. The story is similar at Phillips University where the faculty has accumulated 159 degrees from ninety-five institutions. Oklahoma institutions granted 28 percent of all the degrees, with over one-half of those from the University of Oklahoma and Oklahoma State University. Degrees from Phillips University account of 12 percent of the full 159.[68] The predominant preparation of Disciples faculty throughout the network is in graduate schools at state universities, with slightly less than one fourth having studied in an undergraduate school that was church-related. Disciples College faculty have demonstrated an abiding understanding of the responsibility of a small church-related college to synthesize, and not to tolerate, fragmentation. They continue to make creative contributions to that end.

With only four exceptions, there is a solid contingent of faculty and staff at each of the schools who affirm membership in the Christian Church (Disciples of Christ.) There are presently 266 Disciples faculty and administrators serving at the fifteen campuses in covenant with the church, and eight of the fifteen presidents are members of a Disciples congregation.

Seeking truth is the unifying principle uniting all colleges and universities in the United States to each other, but there are salient differences. Public institutions seek truth essentially as an end in itself. Sectarian-Fundamentalist institutions are purveyors of revealed truth to serve the end of faithfulness to the revealed truth. Critical thinking in that environment is inimical to faith. The church-related institution seeks truth toward the end of wisdom. Therefore, the datum of faith receives a different affirmation than in state universities; the datum of reason is seen differently; and the reality of faith and reason in the life experience is viewed in wholeness.

There are some institutions which think of themselves more as church than college, blurring all distinctions between the community of faith and the community of inquiry. There are those colleges which have fallen into the snare of value-free inquiry and capitulate to the notion that all religious convictions are antithetical to freedom of inquiry. These colleges down-play their own religious tradition as an embarrassment. The former claim too much and the latter claim too little for the importance of religious values in the search of truth. It is the church-related institution, through its unique integrative power, which offers the blend of wisdom.

The nature of the four-year college experience at a small church-related college is distinctly different from that at a large state university. Studies reveal that decline in traditional religious attitudes and beliefs of the students is significantly less in the church-related college; that altruistic tendencies are strengthened; that interpersonal self esteem and artistic interests are increased; that involvement in campus life in a wide range of activities is much greater; and that the likelihood of graduation is higher.[69] The danger of technology triumphing over humanity at church-related colleges is remote because they remember that "a good person is a more noble work than a good technologist."

The continued presence of the church in undergraduate higher education is indispensable. It is a force that assists in the transmuting of learning and knowledge into wisdom, the integrating of pieces of knowledge with values. It is the church which recognizes humanity in people and holds us accountable for the wholeness of human community, for global awareness, for justice and peace, and for the fulfillment of others as well as ourselves. It is the presence of the church that helps build the unique blend of intellect, moral responsibility, and social justice.

Ronald Osborn, in his venerable eloquence, has described the deep interdependence of church and college in terms of divinity's need of the humanities. "Vital divinity," he writes, "requires an environment where the humanities thrive. . . . In the realm of mind and spirit, divinity and the humanities provide a striking example of symbiosis." "Ennobling religion," he continues, "requires a cultural base for the life of the mind and spirit, an atmosphere of inquiry concerning what is good, an ethos of commitment to truth and beauty."[70] Divinity and humanities are not simply backdrop for the human drama— they are infused into human experience. It is this symbiotic relationship between the humanities and divinity, which will birth the new identity of our church and which will give shape to Bellah's new world of *coherence* and, to Schlesinger's new cycle of *public purpose*—all struggling to be born.

There is a tradition of church-relatedness at Disciples colleges: there is not a tradition of sectarianism. There is a tradition of public purpose and human justice at Disciples colleges; there is not a tradition of social isolation or academic exclusiveness. There is a tradition of daring vision at Disciples colleges; there is not a tradition of educational timidity. These traditions must be taken seriously. We live in so many ways off the pioneering spirit, the expansive vision of the possibilities of education, and the daring witness to justice and educational equity of an earlier Disciples era. The very history of these colleges demands that we ask ourselves today, "What are the new frontiers and unfulfilled educational needs to which our colleges should turn their attention?" "Where should we invest our educational capital?"

The future vision of our colleges will be fashioned around two central themes—community and wholeness. In the coming age we shall find ourselves in the high technology of an informational environment with an intensified demand for the values of human dignity, spiritual repair, and the wholeness of human community. The colleges will be educating a constituency that has been deeply fragmented in recent decades and is now in search of personal moorings. This new constituency will:

— expect a synthesis of faith and culture.
— expect that faith will not wither or be intellectualized into a vapor devoid of any sense of justice or moral coherence.

— expect that the journey of their minds will occur in communities of learning which offer the wisdom of wholeness so that their lives will be deepened rather than narrowed.

— expect scholars to be leaders of integrated thought enabling specialized knowledges to converge into unity.

— expect teachers to see persons as total human beings rather than consumers of a skill.

— expect a new and more inclusive educational community that includes opportunity for the economically disenfranchised and the educationally underserved.

— expect educational leadership to have a global awareness which will recognize the need of fulfillment and dignity for the whole human family.

It is around these expectations that the future of Disciples colleges will unfold and take form. Commanding every resource and opportunity that is available they will respond to the challenge with daring new vision.

References

1. William James, *Selected Papers on Philosophy*. London: Everyman's Library, 1917, pp. 86-87.
2. Alfred North Whitehead, "The Aims of Education," in *Alfred North Whitehead: An Anthology*. McMillian, 1961, p. 97.
3. Earl J. McGrath, *Evaluation of Administrative Offices in Institutions of Higher Education*; cited in Rudolph, p. 435.
4. Butchart. pp. 155-170.
5. *Survey of Service*. Christian Board of Publication, 1929, pp. 608-613.
6. Appendix A.
7. Floyd Reeves and John Russell, *College Organization and Administration*. Board of Education, 1929, pp. 40, 41, 46.
8. Reeves and Russell, pp. 42, 44.
9. *Ibid.*, p. 224.
10. *Ibid.*, p. 26.
11. *Disciples of Christ Year Book, 1929*. United Christian Missionary Society, p. 140.
12. D. Duane Cummins, "Our 87th Year." *Church/Campus*, Vol. I, No. 1, p. 1, 4.
13. *Disciples of Christ Year Book, 1913* to *1985*.
14. Hall, *Texas Christian University*, pp. 297-303.
15. Treudley, pp. 246, 248.
16. Cummins, "Preachers & Promoters," p. 7.
17. *Disciples of Christ Year Book, 1945*, p. 43.
18. *Ibid.*, p. 46.
19. *Disciples of Christ Year Book, 1946*, p. 76.
20. *Disciples of Christ Year Book, 1951*, p. 53.
21. David Sageser, *What is a Christian College*. National Council of Churches, 1958, pp. 3-53. George Williams, *The Theological Idea of the University*. National Council of Churches, 1958, pp. 1-22.

22. *Disciples of Christ Year Books, 1950-1960.*
23. "Arise, Ye Silent Class of -57!". *Life*, June 17, 1957; reprinted in Joseph Satin, *The 1950-s: America-s Placid Decade.* Houghton Mifflin, 1960, pp. 165-167.
24. Philip Jacob, *Changing Values in College.* Harper & Brothers, 1957, p. 4.
25. *Disciples of Christ Year Book, 1963,* p. 92.
26. *The Mission of the Christian College in the Modern World.* Council of Protestant Colleges and Universities, 1962, p. 12.
27. *Ibid.*, pp. 44-45.
28. *Ibid., et. passim.*
29. Manning Pattillo and Donald Mackenzie, *Church-Sponsored Higher Education in the United States.* American Council on Education, 1966, p. 21.
30. *Ibid.*, p. 199.
31. George Lee, *Culver-Stockton College.* 1984.
32. Lisa Cooper, *The Drury Story.* 1982, p. 324.
33. Clarice Campbell and Oscar Rogers, *Mississippi: The View From Tougaloo.* University of Mississippi Press, 1979, pp. 198-217.
34. Cummins, "Preachers & Promoters," p. 7.
35. *Ibid.*
36. *Higher Education Evaluation Task Force Report.* Christian Church (Disciples of Christ), June 1976, p. 1.
37. *Ibid.*, p. 10.
38. Appendix B.
39. *Task Force Report*, p. 13.
40. *Ibid.* p. 14.
41. Robert Bellah, et. al., *Habits of the Heart.* University of California Press, 1985, p. 285.
42. Daniel Bell, *The Cultural Contradictions of Capitalism.* Basic Books, 1978, p. 89.
43. John Naisbitt, *Megatrends.* Warner Books, 1982, p. 131.
44. Marilyn Ferguson, *The Aquarian Conspiracy.* St. Martin's Press, p. 29.
45. Christopher Lasch, *The Minimal Self.* Norton & Co., 1984, pp. 16-17.
    Christopher Lasch, *The Culture of Narcissism.* Norton & Company, 1979, p. 9.
46. Bellah, et. al., p. 142.
47. *Ibid.*, pp. 55, 227.
48. Arthur M. Schlesinger, Jr., *Cycles of American History.* Houghton-Mifflin, 1986, pp. 40-42.
49. Bellah, et. al., p. 286.
50. Daniel Bell, pp. 146-171.
    Robert Bellah, pp. 219-249.
    George Beazley, *The Christian Church (Disciples of Christ) An Interpretative Examination in the Cultural Context.* Bethany Press, 1973, pp. 49-58.
51. Loren Lair, *The Christian Church (Disciples of Christ) and its Future.* Bethany Press, 1971, p. 232.
52. Ann Updegraff-Spleth, "Who We Are." *The Disciple*, October 1986, pp. 17-18.
53. Appendix D.
54. Cummins Institutional Survey, August 1985.
55. Cummins Survey, August 1985.
56. *Ibid.*
57. Appendix E and F.
58. Under the careful guidance of a statistical-measurements professor at St. Louis University, Patrice Rosner and D. Duane Cummins prepared a survey instrument which was distributed to 809 congregations in thirty-five regions.
59. Rosner-Cummins Survey, Fall 1985.
60. William Nelson, "LECNA and Lutheran Higher Education: A Partnership for Proclamation." Presidential Address, January 19, 1986.
61. *Year Book and Directory of the Christian Church (Disciples of Christ, 1968.* Office of General Minister and President, p. 163.
62. Rosner-Cummins Survey, Fall 1985.
63. Arthur Levine, *When Dreams and Heroes Died.* Jossey-Bass Publishers, 1980, pp. 21-26.
64. *Wall Street Journal*, August 22, 1985.
    The Chronicle of Higher Education, August 7, 1985.

65. Lofton-Cummins Study, Summer 1986. (This study was compiled from Disciples college and university catalogues by Deanna Lofton and D. Duane Cummins.)
66. Lofton-Cummins Survey, Summer 1986.
67. Schroeder-Cummins Study, Spring 1986. (This study was compiled from the Disciples colleges and university catalogues by Leslie Schroeder and D. Duane Cummins.)
68. *Schroeder-Cummins Study*, Spring 1986.
69. Alexander Astin, *Four Critical Years*. Jossey-Bass Publishers, 1977, pp. 69, 230-231.
70. Ronald E. Osborn, "Divinity's need of the Humanities." *Encounter*, Volume 46, No. 3 (Summer 1985), pp. 200, 211.

APPENDIX

COMITY PRINCIPLES REFINED

Comity relationships between the institutions of higher education and the geographic regions of the Christian Church (Disciples of Christ) have been in existence for 63 years. During 1983 the Comity Committee devoted its full effort to updating the language of the document below which defines the meaning, principles and purpose of comity. The refined text is reproduced here in its entirety with the hope that congregations, regions and institutions will be assisted in the mutual resourcing of their common work.

PRINCIPLES: The Comity Relationship is designed to provide an effective means of communication and interpretation between the Christian Church (Disciples of Christ) and its affiliated higher education institutions; to provide concrete and specific geographic and institutional relationships; and define the geographic promotion of capital from congregational sources.

Each region shall be related in an effective way to at least one affiliated seminary or foundation house and one college or university affiliated with the Christian Church (Disciples of Christ). Each of the fifteen colleges and universities in covenant and each of the seven seminaries and foundation houses shall be related to at least one region.

The regional manifestation of the Christian Church (Disciples of Christ) desiring to affirm its commitment to the role of higher education in the fulfillment of its total mission, and the institutions of higher education related to the Christian Church (Disciples of Christ) desiring to affirm their role within the total mission of the Church therefore join together in appropriate comity relationships.

RESPONSIBILITIES: **The Region**—The region and its congregations will promote and interpret those institutions, with which it has joined in a comity relationship, to develop a sense of identification and pride.

The region shall make provision for those institutions, with which it holds a comity relationship, to participate in its capital campaigns and/or capital programs.

Regional ministers shall be available to serve as members of the boards of trustees and/or in other advisory capacities to those institutions with which they are joined in comity.

The region, where geographically feasible, will assist in the identification and encouragement of field education and internship opportunities for seminary students attending a theological education institution with which it is joined in comity.

The regional commission on ministry shall function in close concert with the seminary or foundation house with which it is joined in comity.

The Institution—The institution shall serve as a resource center to the regions with which it is joined in comity, especially in the process of implementing the priorities of the Church.

The institution shall be encouraged to serve as a center of continuing education and life-long learning for the intellectual growth of those regions with which it is joined in comity.

Institutional personnel shall be available to serve as members of the regional board of directors and/or in other capacities in the region with which they are joined in comity.

Seminaries, foundation houses and colleges will assist the regions wherever possible in providing ministerial leadership for congregations.

Seminaries and foundation houses will function in close concert with those regional commissions on ministry where they are joined in comity.

144

Recruitment and Individual Solicitation—The comity relationship does not apply to the recruitment of students by institutions.

The comity relationship does not apply to the solicitation of financial resources from individuals.

PROCESS: **STEP A**—Recommendations regarding comity relationships are formulated by the Comity Committee of the Division of Higher Education on its own initiative or at the request of:

- a region,
- an affiliated institution;
- the Commission on Finance or a plenary body of the Church.

STEP B—The Comity Committee shares any proposed recommendations for review, advice and counsel of the Commission on Finance.

STEP C—Following the receipt of counsel from the Commission on Finance, the Comity Committee will forward any recommendations to the board of directors of the Division of Higher Education.

STEP D—The Division of Higher Education will forward its recommendations to the boards of directors of the regions and institutions.

STEP E—In the spirit of covenant, the final decision requires mutual consent of the Division of Higher Education, the region and the institution.

INSTITUTIONAL COMITY RELATIONSHIPS
COLLEGES AND UNIVERSITIES

ATLANTIC CHRISTIAN COLLEGE—North Carolina, Georgia and South Carolina

BETHANY COLLEGE—West Virginia, Ohio (one-half only), New York, Northeast and Pennsylvania

CHAPMAN COLLEGE—Pacific Southwest, Arizona and California North-Nevada

COLUMBIA COLLEGE—Mid-America

CULVER-STOCKTON COLLEGE—Mid-America and Upper Midwest

DRURY COLLEGE—Mid-America and Arkansas (northern two tier counties)

EUREKA COLLEGE—Illinois-Wisconsin and Indiana

HIRAM COLLEGE—Ohio (except east counties) and Michigan

JARVIS CHRISTIAN COLLEGE—Southwest, Arkansas, Louisiana and Oklahoma

LYNCHBURG COLLEGE—Virginia, Capital Area and Florida

MIDWAY COLLEGE—Kentucky

NORTHWEST CHRISTIAN COLLEGE—Oregon, Idaho-South, Montana, Northwest and Utah

PHILLIPS UNIVERSITY—Oklahoma, Arkansas (except northern two tier counties), Central Rocky Mountain, Kansas and Nebraska

TEXAS CHRISTIAN UNIVERSITY—Southwest and Louisiana

TRANSYLVANIA UNIVERSITY—Kentucky, Alabama, Mississippi and Tennessee

WILLIAM WOODS COLLEGE—Mid-America

SEMINARIES AND FOUNDATION HOUSES

BRITE DIVINITY SCHOOL, TCU—Southwest and Louisiana

CHRISTIAN THEOLOGICAL SEMINARY—Indiana, Michigan, Northeast, Ohio (one-half only), Pennsylvania and Upper Midwest

LEXINGTON THEOLOGICAL SEMINARY—Kentucky, Alabama, Capital Area, Florida, Georgia, Mississippi, North Carolina, Ohio (one-half only), South Carolina, Virginia and West Virginia

THE GRADUATE SEMINARY, PHILLIPS—Oklahoma, Arkansas, Central Rocky Mountain, Kansas, Nebraska and Mid-America

DISCIPLES DIVINITY HOUSE, CHICAGO—Illinois-Wisconsin

DISCIPLES DIVINITY HOUSE, VANDERBILT—Tennessee

DISCIPLES SEMINARY FOUNDATION, CLAREMONT—Pacific Southwest, Arizona, Montana, Oregon, South Idaho, Northwest, California North-Nevada and Utah

COLLEGE/UNIVERSITY MINORITY ENROLLMENTS
Data Compiled from Fall 1982
(As reported in *The Chronicle* - December 5, 1984)

Institution	Amer. Indian	Asian	Black	Hispanic	White	Foreign Students	Total
Atlantic Christian College	0.3	0.3	12.2	0.1	85.7	1.4	1,537
Bethany College	0.0	0.3	1.7	0.9	94.2	3.0	778
Chapman College	0.1	1.4	1.0	1.2	93.0	3.3	5,585
Columbia College	0.8	1.6	16.2	2.4	76.1	2.9	2,358
Culver-Stockton College	0.2	0.0	6.6	0.2	93.1	0.0	619
Drury College	0.4	0.7	3.0	0.6	94.3	1.1	2,532
Eureka College	0.0	0.0	8.2	0.2	89.9	1.7	537
Hiram College	0.1	0.4	4.7	0.2	93.9	0.6	1,223
Jarvis Christian College	0.2	0.0	99.3	0.2	0.0	0.4	547
Lynchburg College	0.0	0.5	2.9	0.3	95.2	1.0	2,357
Midway College	0.0	0.0	0.6	0.0	95.0	1.4	701
Northwest Christian College	0.0	0.0	0.9	0.4	93.8	4.8	227
Phillips University	0.2	0.2	4.5	0.2	84.8	10.2	1,132
Texas Christian University	0.2	0.5	4.1	2.9	92.3	0.0	6,881
Tougaloo College	0.0	0.0	100.0	0.0	0.0	0.0	775
Transylvania University	0.0	1.6	1.7	0.3	95.0	1.4	701
William Woods College	0.3	0.1	2.8	0.8	95.8	0.3	793

12/19/84

GRADUATES MATRICULATING INTO SEMINARY

Institution	1978	1979	1980	1981	1982	1983	1984	1985	1986	Nine Year Total
Atlantic Christian College	6	5	5	2	3	4	6	11	14	51
Bethany College	5	4	0	2	1	1	4	1	1	19
Chapman College	1	0	8	7	1	2	4	0	0	23
Columbia College	0	1	2	0	0	0	0	0	0	3
Culver-Stockton College	1	1	4	0	1	2	2	1	1	13
Drury College	0	0	1	1	0	1	0	0	1	4
Eureka College	1	0	3	0	0	2	2	1	2	11
Hiram College	4	4	8	2	0	2	1	1	3	25
Jarvis Christian College	3	4	4	3	1	2	3	0	1	22
Lynchburg College	3	1	2	0	0	2	0	1	2	9
Midway College	0	0	0	0	0	0	0	0	2	0
Phillips University	22	12	12	13	10	6	9	7	4	94
Texas Christian University	20	5	5	12	6	9	14	9	5	85
Transylvania University	3	2	6	2	2	2	1	2	0	20
William Woods College	0	1	0	1	0	0	0	0	0	2
Totals	69	40	60	45	27	34	46	34	33	381

1/86

UNDERGRADUATE DISCIPLES FTE

Institution	1978-79	1979-80	1980-81	1981-82	1982-83	1983-84	1984-85	1985-86	1986-87
Atlantic Christian College	117	137	131	132	129	126	112	99	99
Bethany College	79	77	78	76	65	59	70	83	88
Chapman College	95	100	80	65	58	56	63	75	72
Columbia College	37	42	44	35	29	29	35	37	19
Culver-Stockton College	72	73	73	95	100	101	88	107	100
Drury College	90	100	100	100	95	98	100	110	120 est.
Eureka College	72	68	67	79	70	78	71	67	66
Hiram College	60	60	64	85	72	60	55	41	59
Jarvis Christian College	52	113	133	118	107	89	78	79	59
Lynchburg College	118	117	125	116	87	67	60	53	59
Midway College	48	42	45	47	16	36	46	28	15
Phillips University	455	433	259	289	277	275	252	234	247
Texas Christian University	452	476	568	592	555	514	498	469	467
Transylvania University	124	128	113	120	101	99	109	157	189
William Woods College	71	65	68	52	47	52	55	50	44
Totals	1,942	2,031	1,948	2,001	1,808	1,739	1,692	1,689	1,703

1/86

TUITION AND STUDENT FEES FROM 1980-81 to 1985-86
DISCIPLES RELATED INSTITUTIONS

Institutions	1980-81	1981-82	1982-83	1983-84	1984-85	1985-86
Atlantic Christian College	$2,215	$2,516	$2,994	$3,260	$3,680	$3,930
Bethany College	*	*	5,800	5,910	6,570	7,185
Chapman College	3,790	4,970	5,570	6,220	7,200	8,200
Columbia College	3,000	3,795	4,045	4,495	4,695	4,875
Culver-Stockton College	3,060	3,350	3,700	4,040	4,380	4,600
Drake University	4,060	4,590	5,230	5,750	6,200	6,630
Drury College	2,955	3,150	3,650	4,020	4,250	4,855
Eureka College	*	3,750	3,750	3,350	3,775	4,875
Hiram College	4,197	5,237	5,865	6,659	7,481	8,000
Jarvis Christian College	*	*	*	2,520	3,300	3,500
Lynchburg College	3,450	4,200	4,900	5,350	5,950	6,250
Midway College	2,100	2,400	2,730	3,030	3,300	3,500
Northwest Christian College	1,700	3,000	3,340	3,606	3,805	3,985
Phillips University	*	*	*	3,144	3,846	3,994
Texas Christian University	*	3,300	4,110	4,630	5,010	5,410
Tougaloo College	1,925	2,200	2,450	2,800	2,960	3,160
Transylvania University	4,000	4,800	5,320	5,700	5,925	6,255
William Woods College	3,865	4,160	4,540	5,050	5,050	5,800

*Institutions not reporting tuition and fees to *The Chronicle.*
(Data taken from the August 14, 1985 *Chronicle of Higher Education*.)

AVERAGE FACULTY SALARIES, BY RANK AND SEX, FOR 1982-83

Institution		Assoc. Prof.	Asst. Prof.	Prof.	Inst.
Atlantic Christian College	Men:	23.4	19.5	16.9	—
Wilson, North Carolina	Women:	—	18.6	17.2	14.8
Bethany College	Men:	26.1	21.1	17.8	16.3
Bethany, West Virginia	Women:	—	21.4	16.5	—
Chapman College	Men:	32.3	26.4	21.9	—
Orange, California	Women:	—	25.4	19.7	—
Columbia College	Men:	21.9	17.7	17.1	—
Columbia, Missouri	Women:	20.9	18.1	13.8	—
Culver-Stockton College	Men:	26.5	20.6	18.6	—
Canton, Missouri	Women:	—	—	16.9	—
Drury College	Men:	25.5	21.0	17.4	—
Springfield, Missouri	Women:	—	20.0	16.1	12.8
Eureka College	Men:	21.3	16.3	14.2	—
Eureka, Illinois	Women:	19.8	16.8	15.8	—
Hiran College	Men:	27.8	22.7	19.3	—
Hiram, Ohio	Women:	—	20.7	17.2	14.3
Jarvis Christian College	Men:	21.8	19.2	16.6	14.3
Hawkins, Texas	Women:	24.4	19.8	—	15.6
Lynchburg College	Men:	27.7	22.6	20.2	—
Lynchburg, Virginia	Women:	27.5	21.1	17.9	—
Northwest Christian College	Men:	13.3	14.6	—	—
Eugene, Oregon	Women:	—	—	—	—
Phillips University	Men:	25.1	21.5	19.8	—
Enid, Oklahoma	Women:	—	20.5	18.3	—
Texas Christian University	Men:	35.9	26.8	22.9	—
Fort Worth, Texas	Women:	32.6	23.8	21.2	18.8
Transylvania University	Men:	25.6	23.8	19.3	17.9
Lexington, Kentucky	Women:	—	19.6	19.2	—
William Woods College	Men:	—	20.9	17.9	12.1
Fulton, Missouri	Women:	25.4	22.0	18.4	14.3
Butler University	Men:	29.6	24.5	20.2	—
Indianapolis, Indiana	Women:	29.3	22.2	18.2	16.6
Drake University	Men:	28.1	23.8	20.2	17.9
Des Moines, Iowa	Women:	24.6	23.0	19.3	17.7

STATEWIDE AVERAGES FOR FACULTY SALARIES, 1982-83

	Professor		Associate Professor		Assistant Professor		Instructor	
	Men	Women	Men	Women	Men	Women	Men	Women
California	$38,351	$35,024	$28,347	$27,354	$23,572	$22,480	$21,148	$19,773
Illinois	35,654	30,572	26,666	25,335	22,715	21,221	18,800	17,721
Indiana	33,566	29,646	26,197	23,917	21,590	19,643	17,627	14,775
Iowa	33,024	28,913	25,831	24,675	21,615	20,048	18,316	16,772
Kentucky	31,061	28,012	24,645	23,028	20,843	19,422	16,939	16,186
Mississippi	29,660	26,434	24,331	22,969	20,002	18,699	16,021	15,512
Missouri	32,388	29,564	25,627	23,898	21,068	19,636	16,981	16,337
North Carolina	32,859	27,709	25,458	23,691	20,997	20,049	17,957	16,272
Ohio	35,042	30,513	27,255	25,399	22,163	20,838	18,239	17,256
Oklahoma	34,507	30,355	28,272	26,884	24,678	22,938	20,953	19,325
Oregon	31,116	28,823	24,589	23,708	20,981	19,436	17,129	16,392
Texas	36,442	31,611	28,403	26,228	23,671	22,070	19,041	18,444
Virginia	34,292	28,925	26,147	24,084	21,623	20,049	17,211	16,296
West Virginia	27,927	25,259	23,259	21,357	19,618	18,383	16,158	15,196

BIBLIOGRAPHY

STATISTICAL SURVEYS AND REPORTS

Cummins Institutional Survey, Summer 1985.

Division of Higher Education Congregational Survey, January 1986.

Division of Higher Education Statistical Research and Institutional Reports, 1978 through 1986.

Lofton-Cummins College Curriculum Survey, Summer 1986.

Rosner-Cummins Student and Pastor Survey, Fall 1985.

Schroeder-Cummins Faculty degrees Survey, Spring 1986.

Spencer, Claude. Unpublished list of colleges, Disciples of Christ Historical Society, 1964.

Cummins, D. Duane, et. al., *Higher Education Evaluation Task Force Report.* Christian Church (Disciples of Christ), June 1976.

UNPUBLISHED DISSERTATIONS

Bennett, Rolla J., "History of the Founding of Educational Institutions by the Disciples of Christ in Virginia and West Virginia." Unpublished Doctoral dissertation, University of Pittsburgh, 1932.

Edwards, Arthur B., "Alexander Campbell's Philosophy of Education." Unpublished Master's thesis, East Tennessee State College, 1960.

Ferre, Gustave., "A Concept of Higher Education and its Relation to the Christian Faith as Evidence in the Writings of Alexander Campbell." Unpublished Doctoral dissertation, Vanderbilt University, 1958.

Flowers, Ronald B., "The Bible Chair Movement in the Disciples of Christ Tradition: Attempts To Teach Religion in State Universities." Unpublished Doctoral dissertation, University of Iowa, 1967.

Hamlin, Griffith, "The Origin and Development of the Board of Higher Education of the Christian Church (Disciples of Christ)." Unpublished Master's thesis, Southern Illinois University, 1968.

Lewis, Elmer Clifford, "A History of Secondary and Higher Education in Negro Related to the Disciples of Christ." Unpublished Doctoral dissertation, University of Pittsburgh, 1957.

Morrison, John, "Alexander Campbell and Moral Education." Unpublished Doctoral dissertation, Stanford University, 1967.

Shaw, Henry K., "Alexander Campbell - Educator." Unpublished Master's thesis, University of Akron, 1942.

INSTITUTIONAL HISTORIES

Atlantic Christian College

Ware, C. C., *A History of Atlantic Christian College.* Atlantic Christian College, 1956.

Bacon College

Stevenson, Dwight E., "The Bacon College Story 1836-1865," *The College of The Bible Quarterly*, Vol. XXXIX, No. 4, October 1962.

Lexington Theological Seminary, Bethany Press, 1964.

Bethany College

Carty, James W., Jr., *The Gresham Years*. Bethany College, 1970.
Woolery, W. K., *Bethany Years*. Standard Publishing, 1941.

Butler University

Burns, Lee, "The Beginnings of Butler College," *Butler Alumnal Quarterly*, Vol. XV, No. 1, April 1926.
Shaw, Henry K., "The Founding of Butler University 1847-1855," *Indiana Magazine of History*, Vol. LVIII, No. 3, September 1962.
Charter and By-laws of the North-Western Christian University, 1857.

Chapman College

Chapman, Charles C., *C. C. Chapman: The Career of a Creative Californian*. Anderson, Ritchie & Simon, 1976.

Columbia College

Hale, Allean, *Petticoat Pioneer: Christian College Story 1851-1951*. Columbia College, 1956.

Culver-Stockton College

Lee, George R., *Culver-Stockton College: The First 130 Years*. Culver-Stockton College, 1984.
Peters, George L., *Dreams Come True: The Story of Culver-Stockton College*. Culver-Stockton College, 1941.

Cotner College

Moomaw, Leon A., *History of Cotner University*. Christian Church in Nebraska. 1916.

Drake University

Blanchard, Charles, *History of Drake University*. Drake University, 1931.
Ritchey, Charles, *Drake University Through 75 Years*. Drake University, 1956.

Drury College

Clippinger, Frank W., *The Drury Story*. Drury College, 1982.

Eureka College

Adams, Harold, *The History of Eureka College 1855-1982*. Eureka College, 1982.
Dickinson, Elmira J., *A History of Eureka College*. Eureka College, 1894.

Hiram College

Green, F. M., *History of Hiram College: 1850-1900*. Hubbell Printing, 1901.
Trendley, Mary B., *Prelude to the Future: The First Hundred Years of Hiram College*. Associated Press, 1950.

Jarvis Christian College

Taylor, Clifford, "Jarvis Christian College." Unpublished Bachelor of Divinity Thesis, Texas Christian University, 1948.

Lynchburg College

Wake, Orville, "A History of Lynchburg College 1903-1953." Unpublished Doctoral Dissertation, University of Virginia, 1957.

Midway College

Giovannoli, Harry, *Kentucky Female Orphan School*. Midway College, 1930.
Peterson, Lucy, *Miss Lucy's Story*. Keystone Printery, 1960.

Phillips University

Marshall, Frank and Powell, Martin, *Phillips University's First Fifty Years*, 3 Volumes. Phillips University Press, 1957-1967.
Osborn, Ronald, *Ely Von Zollars*. Christian Board of Publication, 1947.

Texas Christian University

Hall, Colby, *History of Texas Christian University*. Texas Christian Unviersity Press, 1947.
Moore, Jerome A., *Texas Christian University: A Hundred Years of History*. T.C.U. Press, 1974.

Tougaloo College

Campbell, Clarice and Rogers, Oscar, *Mississippi: The View From Tougaloo*. University of Mississippi Press, 1979.

Transylvania University

Jennings, Walter W., *Transylvania: Pioneer University of the West*. Pageant Press, 1955.
Wright, John D., Jr., *Transylvania: Tutor to the West*. Transylvania University Press, 1975.

William Woods College

Hamlin, Griffith A., *In Faith & History: The Story of William Woods College*. Bethany Press, 1965.
Hamlin, Griffith A., *William Woods College: The Cutlip Years: 1960-1980*. William Woods College, 1980.

ANALYTICAL STUDIES OF DISCIPLES COLLEGES

Books

Davis, John, *Light on the Lighthouse* (pamphlet) Board of Higher Education, 1944.
Gresham, Perry E., *Campbell and the Colleges*. Disciples of Christ Historical Society, 1973.
The Sage of Bethany. Bethany Press, 1960.
Reeves, Floyd and Russell, John, *College Organization and Administration*. Board of Higher Education, 1929.
Survey of Service. Christian Board of Publication, 1928.
Yearbook and Directory: Christian Church (Disciples of Christ). Christian Board of Publication, 1896-1986. (90 volumes)

Articles

Carpenter, G. T., "Our Colleges," *Christian Quarterly Review*, Vol. IV, July 1885.

Cummins, D. Duane, "The Preacher and the Promoter," *Discipliana*, Vol. 44, No. 1, 1984.

Eminhizer, Earl E., "Alexander Campbell on Moral and Quality Education - Some New Light," *The Iliff Review*, Vol. XLI, No. 2, 1984.

Forrest, Albertina A., "Status of Education Among Disciples," *The New Christian Quarterly*, Vol. V, No. 4, October 1896.

Gresham, Perry E., "Proud Heritage," *West Virginia History*, Vol. 15, 1954.

Osborn, Ronald, "Divinity's Need of the Humanities," *Encounter*, Vol. 46, No. 3, Summer 1985.

REGIONAL HISTORIES: CHRISTIAN CHURCH (DISCIPLES OF CHRIST)

Burlingame, Merrill G. and Hartling, Harvey C., *Big Sky Disciples*. Christian Church (Disciples of Christ) in Montana, 1984.

Butchart, Reuben, *The Disciples of Christ in Canada Since 1830*. Canadian Headquarters Publication, 1949.

Cauble, Commodore W., *Disciples of Christ in Indiana*. Meigs Publishing Company, 1930.

Cole, Clifford A., *The Christian Churches of Southern California*. Christian Board of Publication, 1959.

Cramblet, Wilbur H., *The Christian Church (Disciples of Christ) in West Virginia*. Bethany Press, 1971.

England, Stephen J., *Oklahoma Christians*. Bethany Press, 1975.

Forster, Ada L., *The Christian Church and Church of Christ in Minnesota*. Christian Board of Publication, 1953.

Fortune, Alonzo W., *The Disciples in Kentucky*. Christian Churches in Kentucky, 1932.

Hall, Colby D., *Texas Disciples*. T.C.U. Press, 1953.

Hamlin, Griffith A., *Remember, Renew, Rejoice: Disciples in Mid-America 1837-1987*. Christian Church in Mid-America, 1986.

Harmon, M. F., *History of the Christian Churches in Mississippi*. Christian Churches in Mississippi, 1929.

Haynes, Nathaniel S., *History of the Disciples of Christ in Illinois 1819-1914*. Standard Publishers, 1915.

Hayden, A. S., *Early History of The Disciples in the Western Reserve, Ohio*. Chase & Hall Publishers, 1875.

Hodge, Frederick A., *The Plea and the Pioneers in Virginia*. Everett Waddy Co., 1905.

Lair, Loren E., *From Restoration to Reformation: The Christian Church (Disciples of Christ) in Iowa*. Christian Church in Iowa, 1970.

McAllister, Lester G., *Arkansas Disciples*. Christian Church (Disciples of Christ) in Arkansas, 1984.

Moseley, J. Edward, *Disciples of Christ in Georgia*. Bethany Press, 1954.

Norton, Herman A., *Tennessee Christians*. Reed and Company, 1971.

Peters, George L., *Disciples of Christ in Missouri*. Missouri Convention, Disciples of Christ, 1937.

Peterson, Orval, *Washington-Northern Idaho Disciples*. Christian Board of Publication, 1953.

Shaw, Henry K., *Buckeye Disciples*. Christian Board of Publication, 1952.

Hossier Disciples. Bethany Press, 1966.

Stanger, Allen B., *The Virginia Christian Missionary Society*. Christian Church in Virginia, 1975.

Swander, C. F., *Making Disciples in Oregon*. Oregon Christian Missionary Society, 1928.

Updegraff, John C., *The Christian Church (Disciples of Christ) in Florida*. Anna Publishing Co., 1981.

Ware, Charles C., *North Carolina Disciples of Christ*. Christian Board of Publication, 1927.
> *South Carolina Disciples of Christ: A History*. Christian Churches of South Carolina, 1967.

Ware, E. B., *History of the Disciples of Christ in California*. Christian Churches in California, 1916.

Watson, George H. and Mildred B., *History of the Christian Churches in the Alabama Area*. Bethany Press, 1965.

GENERAL SOURCES: CHRISTIAN CHURCH (DISCIPLES OF CHRIST)

Ahlstrom, Syndey E., *A Religious History of the American People*. Yale University Press, 1972.

Beazley, George Jr., *The Christian Church (Disciples of Christ): An Interpretative Examination*. Bethany Press, 1973.

Blakemore, W. B., *The Renewal of the Church*. Bethany Press, 1963.

Crain, James A., *The Development of Social Ideas Among the Disciples of Christ*.

Cummins, D. Duane., *A Handbook for Today's Disciples*. Christian Board of Publication, 1981.

DeGroot, Alfred T., *The Restoration Principle*. Bethany Press, 1960.

Garrison, Winfred E., *Christian Unity and Disciples of Christ*. Bethany Press, 1955.
> *Religion Follows The Frontier*. Harper Brothers, 1931.
> "Characteristics of American Organized Religion," *Annals of the American Academy of Political and Social Science*, Vol. CCLVI, March 1948.

Garrison, Winfred E. and DeGroot, Alfred T., *The Disciples of Christ: A History*. Bethany Press, 1948.

Harrell, David E., Jr., *Quest for a Christian America: The Disciples of Christ and American Society to 1866*. Disciples of Christ Historical Society, 1966.
> *The Social Sources of Division in the Disciples of Christ 1865-1900*. Publishing Systems, 1973.

Lair, Loren E., *The Christian Church (Disciples of Christ) and its Future*. Bethany Press, 1971.
> *The Christian Churches and Their Work*. Bethany Press, 1963.

Lawrence, Kenneth, *Classic Themes of Disciples Theology*. Christian University Press, 1986.

Lyda, Hap, "Black Disciples in the Nineteenth Century," *The Untold Story: A Short History of Black Disciples*. Christian Board of Publication, 1976.

Mead, Sidney, "American Protestantism During the Revolutionary Epoch," *Church History*, Volume XXII, No. 4, December 1953.
> "From Coercion to Persuasion: Another Look at the Rise of Religious Liberty and the Emergence of Denominationalism," *Church History*, Volume XXV, No. L, December 1956.

Moore, R., *Religious Outsiders: The Making of Americans*. Oxford University Press, 1986.

Moore, William T., *A Comprehensive History of the Disciples of Christ*. Fleming H. Revell Company, 1909.

Morrow, Ralph, "The Great Revival, The West and The Crisis of the Church," in *The Frontier Re-Examined*. University of Illinois Press, 1967.

Neibuhr, H. Richard, *The Social Sources of Denominationalism*. Henry Holt and Company, 1919.

Osborn, Ronald E., *Experiment in Liberty: The Ideal of Freedom in the Experience of the Disciples of Christ*. Bethany Press, 1978.

The Reformation of Tradition, Bethany Press, 1960.

Teegarden, Kenneth L., *We Call Ourselves Disciples*. Bethany Press, 1975.

Tucker, William E. and McAllister, Lester G., *Journey in Faith*. Bethany Press, 1975.

West, Robert Frederick, *Alexander Campbell on Natural Religion*. Yale University Press, 1948.

Whitley, Oliver Read, *Trumpet Call of Reformation*. Bethany Press, 1959.

Wilburn, Ralph G., *The Reconstruction of Theology*. Bethany Press, 1963.

PERIODICAL LITERATURE: CHRISTIAN CHURCH (DISCIPLES OF CHRIST)

Christian Baptist 1823-1829
Christian Messenger 1826-1844
Christian Quarterly Review 1885
Church/Campus 1980-1986
Discipliana 1984
Lard's Quarterly 1865
Millennial Harbinger 1830-1870 (Forty volumes)
The Christian 1837
The College of The Bible Quarterly 1946, 1962
The Evangelist 1832-1842
The Disciple October, 1986
The New Christian Quarterly 1896

CONTEMPORARY LITERATURE ON CHURCH-RELATED HIGHER EDUCATION

Ash, James L., Jr., *Protestantism and the American University*. Southern Methodist University Press, 1982.

Bender, Richard, *The Church-Related College Today: Anachronism or Opportunity*. Board of Higher Education United Methodist Church, 1971.

Carlson, Edgar M., *The Future of Church-Related Higher Education*. Augsburg Publishing House, 1977.

Doescher, Waldemar O., *The Church College in Today's Culture*. Augsburg Publishing House, 1963.

Fisher, Ben C., *New Pathways: A Dialogue in Christian Higher Education*. Mercer University Press, 1980.

Geier, Woodrow, *Church Colleges Today*. Board of Higher Education, United Methodist Church, 1974.

Hassel, David J., *City of Wisdom*. Loyola University Press, 1983.

Hesburgh, Theodore M., *The Hesburgh Papers: Higher Values in Higher Education*. Andrews and McMeel, 1979.

Jacobs, Philip, *Changing Values in College*. Harper & Row, 1957.

Martin, Warren B., *A College of Character*. Jossey-Bass, 1984.

Moots, Philip and Gaffney Edward M. Jr., *Church and Campus: Legal Issues in Religiously Affiliated Higher Education*. University of Notre Dame, 1979.

Newman, John Henry, *The Idea of a University*. Doubleday, 1959, 1852.

Palmer, Parker, *To Know as We are Known: A Spirituality of Education*. Harper and Row, 1983.

Parsonage, Robert R., *Church-Related Higher Education*. Judson Press, 1978.

Pattillo, Manning and MacKenzie, Donald, *Church-Sponsored Higher Education in the United States*. American Council on Education, 1966.

Ringenberg, William C., *The Christian College*. Christian University Press, 1984.

Sageser, David, *What is A Christian College*. National Council of Churches, 1958.

Solberg, Richard W., *Lutheran Higher Education in North America*. Augsburg Publishing House, 1985.

Tewksbury, Donald, *The Founding of American Colleges and Universities Before the Civil War*. Columbia University Press, 1932.

Welch, Claude, *Religion in the Undergraduate Curriculum*. Association of American Colleges, 1972.

Williams, *The Theological Idea of the University*. National Council of Churches, 1958.

Wynn, Daniel, *The Protestant Church-Related College*. Philosophical Library, 1975.

A College-Related Church. National Commission on United Methodist Higher Education, 1976.

Church and College: A Vital Partnership. Vol. I, *Affirmation*. Vol. II, Accountability. Vol. III, *Exchange*. Vol. IV, *Mission*, National Congress on Church-Related Higher Education, 1980.

New Strategies for the Mission of the Church through Higher Education. Presbyterian Task Force on Higher Education, 1982.

Report of the Blue Ribbon Committee on the Future of Church-Related Higher Education. Division of Higher Education, United Church Board for Homeland Ministries, The United Church of Christ, 1984.

United Methodist Related-Colleges and Universities. Division of Higher Education, General Board of Higher Education and Ministry of the United Methodist Church, 1985.

The Mission of the Christian College in the Modern World. Council of Protestant Colleges and Universities, 1962.

CONTEMPORARY STUDIES IN HIGHER EDUCATION

Books

Astin, Alexander W., *Achieving Educational Excellence*. Jossey-Bass, 1985.

Four Critical Years. Jossey-Bass, 1977.

Astin, Alexander W., *Four Critical Years*. Jossey-Bass, 1977.

Bowen, Howard R., *The Costs of Higher Education*. Jossey-Bass, 1980.

The State of the Nation and the Agenda for Higher Education. Jossey-Bass, 1982.

and Schuster, Jack H., *American Professors: A National Resource Imperiled*. Oxford University Press, 1986.

Brubacher, John S., *On The Philosophy of Higher Education*. Jossey-Bas, 1977.

Chapman, John W., *The Western University On Trial*. University of California Press, 1983.

Chickering, Arthur W., *The Modern American College*. Jossey-Bass, 1981.

Fleming, Jacqueline, *Blacks In Collge*. Jossey-Bass, 1984.

Gamson, Zelda F., *Liberating Education*. Jossey-Bass, 1984.

Grant, Gerald and Riesman, David, *The Perpetual Dream: Reform and Experiment in the American College*. University of Chicago Press, 1978.

Hofstadter, Richard and Hardy, C. DeWitt, *The Development and Scope of Higher Education in the United States*. Columbia University Press, 1952.
and Metzer, Walter, *The Development of Academic Freedom in the United States*. Columbia University Press, 1955.
Jencks, Christopher and Riesman, David, *The Academic Revolution*. Doubleday, 1968.
Levine, Arthur, *When Dreams and Heroes Died*. Jossey-Bass, 1983.
Mayhew, Lewis B., *Legacy of the Seventies*. Jossey-Bass, 1977.
Surviving the Eighties. Jossey-Bass, 1980.
Newman, Frank, *Report On Higher Education*. U.S. Department of Health, Education and Welfare, 1971.
Riesman, David, *On Higher Education*. Jossey-Bass, 1980.
Rudolph, Frederick, *The American College and University: A History*. Alfred A. Knopf, 1962.
More Than Survival. Carnegie Foundation. Jossey-Bass, 1975.

National Reports

A Nation At Risk. The National Commission on Excellence in Education, April 1983.
College: The Undergraduate Experience in America. The Carneige Foundation, January 1987.
Integrity in the College Curriculum. Association of American Colleges, February 1985.
Involvement in Learning. National Institute of Education, October 1984.
Opportunity for Excellence. The Ford Foundation, March 1985.
To Reclaim A Legacy. National Endowment for the Humanities, November 1984.

SOCIAL INTERPRETATIONS OF AMERICAN HISTORY

Bartlett, Richard A., *The New Country: A Social History of the American Frontier: 1776-1890*. Oxford University Press, 1974.
Bellah, Robert N. and Associates, *Habits of the Heart*. University of California Press, 1985.
Bell, Daniel, *The Cultural Contradictions of Capitalism*. Basic Books, 1976.
Boorstin, Daniel J., *The Americans: The Colonial Experience. Vintage Books, 1958.
The Americans: The National Experience*. Vintage Books, 1965.
The Americans: The Democratic Experience. Vintage Books, 1973.
Commager, Henry Steele, *Documents of American History*, Ninth Edition, Prentice Hall, 1973.
The American Mind. Yale University Press, 1950.
Ferguson, Marilyn, *The Aquarian Conspiracy: Personal and Social Transformation in the 1980's*. St. Martin's Press, 1980.
Hofstadter, Richard, *Anti-Intellectualism in American Life*. Vintage Books, 1962.
Jones, Landon Y., *Great Expectations: America and the Baby Boom Generation*. Coward, McCann, 1980.
Lerner, Max, *America as a Civilization*, Vol. I & II. Simon and Schuster, 1957.
Lasch, Christopher, *The Culture of Narcissism*. Norton & Co., 1978.
The Minimal Self. Norton & Co., 1984.
Marx, Leo, *The Machine in the Garden: Technology and the Pastoral Ideal in America*. Oxford University Press, 1964.
May, Henry F., *The Enlightenment in America*. Oxford University Press, 1976.
Morison, Samuel Eliot, *The Intellectual Life of Colonial New England*. Cornell University Press, 1936.

Naisbitt, John, *Megatrends*. Warner Books, 1982.

Nash, Roderick, *Wilderness and the American Mind*. Yale University Press, 1967.

Nye, Russell B., *The Cultural Life of the New Nation 1776-1830*. Harper and Row, 1960.

O'Neill, William L., *Coming Apart: An Informal History of America in the 1960's*. Quadrangle Books, 1971.

Satin, Joseph, *The 1950's: America's Placid Decade*. Houghten Mifflin, 1960.

Schlesinger, Arthur M. Jr., *The Cycles of American History*. Houghton Mifflin, 1986.

Silverman, Kenneth, *A Cultural History of the American Revolution*. Thomas Crowell Co., 1976.

Thomas, John L., "Romantic Reform in America, 1815-1865," *American Quarterly*, Vol. XVII, No. 4., Winter 1965, pp. 656-681.

Welter, Rush, *The Mind of America 1820-1860*. Columbia University Press, 1975.

Index